What Do We Believe?

WHAT DO
WE BELIEVE?

The Stance of Religion in America

by

Martin E. Marty, Stuart E. Rosenberg

and

Andrew M. Greeley

Meredith Press / New York

PART THREE:

NIHIL OBSTAT: Lawrence A. Beeson, J.C.D.
Censor deputatus

IMPRIMATUR: L. V. Lyons, Administrator
Diocese of Des Moines
June 25, 1968

The Nihil Obstat and Imprimatur are official declarations that a book or pamphlet is free of doctrinal or moral error. No implication is contained therein that those who have granted the Nihil Obstat and Imprimatur agree with the contents, opinions or statements expressed.

First edition

Library of Congress Catalog Card Number: 68-26326

Manufactured in the United States of America for Meredith Press

CONTENTS

v

PART ONE

by
Martin E. Marty

1. THE PROTESTANT COMMUNITY SURVIVES

No analysis of American Protestantism should begin without some sense of wonder, of surprise, of astonishment over the survival of a faithful community. A Gallup poll confronts readers, and they immediately immerse themselves in the quest for signs of change within the religious families, taking for granted the presence of these families themselves. Should they?

Two hundred years ago, at the time of the birth of the Republic, it would have been legitimate to raise the question whether the Protestant churches themselves would persist into the national period. A forecaster could have found good reasons to predict that the day would come when there would be no warm bodies for the movement, no people to respond to the analysts.

Today the more mournful Protestants and the more nostalgic Americans look back on the days of their founding fathers as the good old days from which all later religious life should be measured. Institutionally, there are few good reasons for doing so. True, Protestants had the field pretty much to themselves. Perhaps 20,000 Roman Catholics cluttered the scene in a population of almost 4,500,000—hardly enough to give anyone a sense of crowding. Jews were present in negligible numbers. Protestants not only were uncrowded; they also had done much to give the nation its shape, so far as spirit and customs were concerned. But institutionally they were in sorry condition.[1]

The serene celebrators of the American Enlightenment looked

---

[1] For a general statistical survey of Colonial religion see Edwin Scott Gaustad, *Historical Atlas of Religion in America*. New York, Harper, 1962, pp. 1–36.

3

with hope to nature and reason. Benjamin Franklin paid the churches decent respect, and Thomas Jefferson showed some regard for certain kinds of Protestant churches. Yet they and their peers consistently give the impression that they could afford to do so because they believed the days of the churches were numbered. Perhaps, in their eyes, there should always be institutions which cultivated morality and attended to the needs of the spirit. But "John Calvin's God" seemed to be living on borrowed time just as much as did that vestige of medieval superstition, the Roman Catholic Mass. Reason would prevail, and the faithful fellowship of Protestant Christians would no longer need to celebrate the mysteries of faith or respond to revelation. Our educated guesses suggest that less than 6 percent of the population was active in the churches, and that number was dwindling.[2] Picture how minute our interest in a Gallup poll would be if it were to concentrate on a dwindling 6 percent of the population! Instead, it can deal with over 60 percent in the churches, the majority of these Protestant, and, because of the survival of these institutions, it can deal with the whole population, which feels the impact of them and responds to their appeals; almost all the people, for instance, say that they believe in God. Such an answer seems unthinkable apart from the ongoing witness of the majority of the population through its participation in worship and the works of the churches.

If the enlightened founding fathers would have had good reason to see the disappearance of the churches, and if the chroniclers of that time could with some accuracy write the annals of their demise, we receive an equally problematic picture if we listen to the preachers of the time. *They* were already looking back on good old days, the days when a more pious breed had come to these Colonies, or the days when (back in the 1730's and 1740's) the Colonies had known a great awakening of Protestant religion. Back then, giants like Jonathan Edwards and George Whitefield and a thousand lesser but no less energetic men had called the people back to their covenant—and a Protestant-sounding covenant it was—for the sake of the Colonies' health.

Edwards and his contemporaries, for all their reputed theological gloom, were capable of speaking optimistically about the fu-

[2] Franklin H. Littell, *From State Church to Pluralism* (New York, Doubleday, 1962), p. 32, places the figure in 1776 at 5 percent.

ture of the Colonies and of God's special regard for them.[3] In America he would no doubt reveal his later glory and set up his millennial kingdom. But this quickening of hearts did not last long, and its permanent effect on the size of the Protestant churches was surprisingly small. Forty years later, at the time of the birth of the nation, most of these effects had passed, and the people had settled back into complacency. In Boston they seemed to be drifting away from distinctive Protestant views of revelation and were signing up for the calls to reasonableness which characterized the Enlightenment itself.[4] In the other cities and in the back country the majority of the people took the churches for granted, but did not seem to care much at all.

Here it is not possible to trace the two centuries of history which led to a reversal of trends and a thwarting of the predictions about the end of the Protestant community. Early in the nineteenth century a new wave of revivalists came upon the scene; they were as gloomy as their fathers had been about the survival of the churches. But they did something about the situation; even as they exaggerated the low estate of their churches, they worked up a fever in order to bring about a higher estate, and America became a churched nation. At every crossroads in the West, God and Satan, good and evil, revivalist preacher and tavernkeeper waged their little battle as part of the war of the ages. Often the battle was fought to a draw, if we take the revivalists' words for it; yet both sides grew stronger during the battle and left institutions behind to prove it.

Prophets and preachers have not been alone in their predictions of problems for the future of Protestantism. Theologians, historians, and many sociologists have also pointed to trends which, if worked out toward their logical conclusions, would lead to the end of the Protestant community. The overall term for the process is secularization. Secularization is ordinarily ill defined, and there seems to be no single unitary process to which it points.[5] But to most people who use the term it suggests a concentration on this

---

[3] See Alan Heimert, *Religion and the American Mind* (Cambridge, Massachusetts, Harvard University Press, 1966) for an accounting of Calvinist optimism.

[4] This development is recounted in Conrad Wright, *The Beginnings of Unitarianism in America.* Boston, Beacon Press, 1955.

[5] See David Martin, "Towards Eliminating the Concept of Secularization" in *Penguin Survey of the Social Sciences,* Julius Gould, ed., Baltimore, Penguin, 1965.

age at the expense of an age to come or on this world at the
expense of otherworldliness; it implies the decline of religious
institutions and, through specialization, the removal of many
functions once held by religious institutions to secular institutions. Secularization ordinarily means the screening out of beliefs
in a transcendent order, a minimizing or final and total expunging
of religious interpretations of man and the world.[6] Certainly it
implies the peoples' preoccupation with matter-of-fact life, their
dealing with their environment without explicit reference to God.

The theologians and many historians have seen secularization as
the great new fact of the modern era, as a relentless and consistent
process which sweeps up all that is before it. America was born in
the secular age. Given its environment, it had good reason for
preoccupation with the material—after all, there has been so much
of the material here. Mastering the environment has demanded
expenditure of energies and the employment of methods which
have rarely allowed for recourse to God as problem solver or as a
useful hypothesis in laboratory or legislature. Americans have
been a preoccupied people; no one should be surprised to see
them crowd out God and the churches.

The reader of this new Gallup poll, if he goes by external appearances only, must wonder where the prophets and annalists of
the secularization gain their vision and get their data. While religion is constantly undergoing transformation and change, it survives. While Protestantism has new company on the scene in the
presence of many millions of Roman Catholics and Jews, it has not
been "done in" by secular man, atheism, agnosticism, or anticlericalism.

So this is the first grand lesson to be drawn from the polls, and
the one most easy to overlook: that in the middle of a secularizing
world—whatever that will come to mean—the faithful community
of Protestants survives. Before the reader gets into the apparently
forbidding and certainly abstract statistics, he does well to visual-
ize something of what the enterprise of the faithful means in concrete terms. We can take a dry run:

Tens of millions of Protestants bring their children to the
churches for baptism or for rites of dedication. Perhaps the majority of them do it because, in part, it is the thing to do in the
culture. Some sort of initiation rites seems to be called forth by the

---

[6] Harvey Cox, *The Secular City*. New York, Doubleday, 1965, p. 2.

simple act of forming families in this environment. But they do it; they do not not do it. They must have some sort of belief in the religious meaning of their act. Actually, they bring them from a bewildering variety of motives, a variety hard to ascertain from polls which seek to grasp the great parts which make up the whole of society.

Almost as many tens of millions send these children later to Sunday school or some other institution for their religious training. As can be seen in this poll, many of them do it with some sense of dissatisfaction over the efficacy of such training and with less than happy recall of their own experience. But, again, they do it, without doubt hoping that some spiritual and more-than-secular set of values will rub off on their children, without doubt thereby making some minimal contribution to the survival of the churches.

When these young establish their own families, they worry about matters of the faith—especially of their spouses' faith—at the time of marriage. They may worry less and less, as the 1965 poll demonstrates, but this change has come about as much through increase of a kind of tolerance as it has through a decrease of interest in the faith itself.

The Gallup people have no way of interviewing the dead or the dying, but thousands of ministers and millions of families can testify to the fact that at the end of life millions recall the mysteries of faith, dwell on the meaning of revelation, invoke the name of Jesus Christ, and depart in hope, a hope nurtured inside their Protestant religious communities.

The life cycle which we have pictured here has many institutional implications. Each year Protestants spend the better part of a billion dollars to house their churches. Most nights of most weeks numbers of them can be seen on the premises of the churches, busy at a variety of projects devoted to education, socializing, or service. Many of the causes seem to make minimal demands upon them and may seem trivial to the outsider; yet, the response must mean something.

Culturally and socially, Protestantism retains many kinds of impact. In many a local community, it determines who shall or shall not be elected to public office. Mass communicators ordinarily take care not to offend the adherents of this or other families of believers. The American South, the Midwest, the suburbs—many such locales by their mere mention conjure for us a sense of on-

going Protestant power, power for politics and for determining
customs and practice in the community. The predictions of our
enlightened founding fathers and our gloomy religious forefathers
have manifestly not come true. The theologizing about secularization has been in part inaccurate. As the Gallup people amply
demonstrate, the churches are alive and kicking. They have survived, and that survival has represented no small feat—one so obvious to us that we easily overlook it.

2. NOT SECULARIZATION, BUT RADICAL RELIGIOUS CHANGE

Survival is one thing, stability is another. If the act of surviving
can be so taken for granted that it is overlooked by poll readers,
the act of remaining stable cannot be taken for granted and cannot
be overlooked. Many Protestants, of course, contend that they do
represent an unchanging force in a changing world. American
Protestantism in particular has spawned scores of "primitivist"
groups which have contended that it is possible to overleap the
centuries and to reproduce in pristine purity the doctrine and life
of the earliest Christian community. Millions of American Protestants are "fundamentalist" in that they reject the idea of development or transformation. They may not minimize change in the
world around them; indeed, for many good reasons they will max-
imize it in order to draw a contrast to their own changelessness.
But, for them, real change and development do not occur inside
the churches.

Now it is quite likely that not all churches reveal the same
degree or pace of change, that some are more static in their doctrine and life than are others. Some churches not only do not resist
change, they cultivate it; they are disinterested in a static portrayal
of their life. Since the people who respond to Gallup polls do not
sign their names or identify which sector of a denomination is
their home or their choice, it is difficult to sort out who is most
successful at resisting change. The polls do permit some overall
generalization, and this generalization does point to consistent
change.

Some readers, recalling the drama of the last dozen years, may look for more in these polls than they will deliver. Often such readers may have "felt in their bones" that epochal change in the world of science and the mass media or education will have induced epochal change in one or another of the sectors of the churches' lives. They will consult the statistics of those sectors and find a relatively undramatic change in percentages from 1952 to 1965. (As a rule of thumb, in order to make up a margin for error, I am reluctant to speak about certifiable change when there has only been a change of one or two percentage points.)

Before one generalizes, it is important to realize how brief a time span the poll covers. If Protestantism is 450 years old now, then the poll covers only about one thirty-third of its life; if Christianity is some 1,900 years old, only about one one hundred-fortieth of its years is involved here. Only a moment of human history is implied, yet some strong trends are obvious.

Two stand out. Stand at some distance from the 1965 poll and contrast its main outlines to that of 1952, and two generalizations come to be clear.

First, there is a steady if apparently undramatic erosion of distinctive theological and ecclesiastical positions. Second, there is a growth of positive regard for the faith of others, of positive inter-relationship of the various religious communities. And from these two trends one can draw a third generalization: that these years have seen a considerable stepping up of the trend toward the development of a civil or societal or folk religion. If there is a "plot" to these two polls, it lies in those three observations.

Take them in order. With very few exceptions, there is a slight decrease of orthodoxy in relation to inherited beliefs, a slight decrease of faithfulness in adherence to inherited practices, a slight wavering in loyalty to group norms. The prophet of secularization, whether within or outside of the churches, will be astonished how slight these changes are. In prophetic and dramatic terms, one would be tempted to speak of the total disappearance or diminution of belief in historic viewpoints. In a time of "the death of God" or the presence of "the secular city" or the time of "the world's coming of age" one is naturally surprised to see that the number of people who believe in God has dropped only from about 99 percent to 97 percent. Unbelievable. Somehow it must be explained away. Similarly, almost as many Americans and almost as many Protestants in 1965 believed in the divinity of

Christ, the authority of the revelation in Scripture, the doctrine of the Trinity as did in 1952.

If the decrease in percentages is not always so dramatic, the consistency of the presence of decreases is. In a secular time we take for granted that there will be such a decline. Still, anyone who ponders the future of the Protestant churches must ask himself what will occur through a century if such trends continue and, indeed, are heightened. If somewhere down the line more people than in the past believed in a certain doctrine, more people were loyal to a certain institutional practice, matters would be different. But these increases are rare and marginal. Yet these thirteen years between the polls are supposedly the years of one of America's greatest religious revivals and one of its greatest moments of renewal. Clearly revival, renewal, and revolution do not represent stability or return to the old ways. Subtle change is occurring constantly.

If the answers to the first thirty poll questions portray this consistent if not always dramatic decline in distinctiveness, the last half of the poll reveals greater toleration between groups.

Without doubt, few years in American history would have revealed such sudden changes in intergroup relations. When the nation was born, of course, there had to be a give-and-take of religious groups, not all of whom (indeed, none of whom) could expect to be established and supported by law as most of them had been in the Colonial era. But these groups were all Protestant, all "in the family," so to speak. In general, American pluralism has forced a kind of toleration on the people. But during these thirteen years there were stronger pressures and appeals than in the past, and this time they encompassed Protestants and Catholics and Jews plus other religious and nonreligious communities.

The activities of various brotherhood groups, the common appeals of mass media of communications, the experience of mass higher education with its implicit pluralism, and the Vatican Council are among the factors which brought about the change. Whatever the sources of change, it is evident that after thirteen years, on almost every issue which poll takers chose to bring up, people were more ready than formerly to place a positive valuation on their "separated brethren's" faiths and to seek creative ways of living with them. Given the four centuries of hostility which predate this period, it is astonishing to see the suddenness of change in Protestant-Catholic relations. Protestant-Jewish relations are more mutually positive and tolerant than they were in the past, though here change has been less sudden or violent.

Looking back to 1952, one could hypothesize that at the moment intergroup relations may have been artificially tense and that, therefore, the early poll reflects an atypical situation. It was taken, after all, at the height of the McCarthy era, when Americans were being trained to be mutually suspicious. The more difficult church-state problems were beginning to confront the courts, and we may expect that there was public reaction to these. However, there are good reasons to believe that 1952 was not an artificial time to take a poll. For one thing, McCarthyism cut across the lines of religious communities, particularly those established by Protestants and Catholics. That is, it was ecumenical: it brought together mistrustful anti-Communist Protestants and Catholics into alliance against others in their own communities who did not come up to their standards. And, so far as church-state issues are concerned, they were as problematic in 1965 as they had been in 1952, nor did 1952 represent the only time when these problems had been acute.

Rather than see too much in the two years of the polls, it seems more advisable to recognize that in their consistency they reveal a positive change in intergroup relations. Or, at the very least (if we wish to keep suspicious and critical guards up), they suggest that the idea of tolerance itself is positively valued, even where we have not yet learned to like the neighbor of a different faith.

These two Gallup polls are by no means alone in their reinforcement of the conclusion that Americans are growing more tolerant or placing a higher valuation on tolerance. Charles Herbert Stember and others[1] believe that the long trend of polls in the past third of a century suggests a consistent, if unspectacular, drop in anti-Semitism. Their study is typical of the many surveys which show how Americans seek internal concord.

We are as a nation less decisive in our attention to particular faiths and more decisive in our devotion to regard for each others' faith. Most analysts concur that these two trends are part of the process which is producing a "blanket" religion, an overall value system to which the vast majority of Americans are committed

---

[1] See *Jews in the Mind of America.* New York, Basic Books, 1966.

before they make specific faith commitments, or in addition to such commitments. While most Americans reveal remarkable denominational loyalties, there seems to be little of cognitive value in the symbols of those denominations. Membership in specific Protestant denominations does not tell us as much as we would like to know about peoples' ultimate hopes.

The relationship of erosive Protestantism to this emergent national religion has been the outstanding preoccupation of analysts during the past decade; support for this preoccupation comes from these two Gallup polls; tracing some of its implications will be the main plot of my chapter. All in all, these polls suggest support for the generalization that America is not seeing the emergence of any sociologically "neat" secularization; instead, it is experiencing radical religious change, even when the symbols (Trinity, Bible, etc.) do not radically change.[2]

3. YEARS OF REVIVAL, YEARS OF REVOLUTION

To make sense of these polls, both for their more startling indications of change and their more puzzling indications of nonchange, the reader does well to recall that in the conventional picture of the years between 1952 and 1965 America underwent, first, a revival of religion and, second, a revolution in religion. The revival began to be noticed around 1952, about the time of the earlier poll; it seemed to crest somewhere around 1956 or 1958 and began to dwindle and decline by 1960, when a radical change in America's religious interests was evident. There are signs today that that change, often spoken of as a "revolution," itself has been supplanted in the late 1960's, beyond the scope of the era of these two polls. Now it is more important to notice the interplay of revival and revolution.

After the preoccupations of "the jazz age" of the twenties, the Depression (and religious depression) of the thirties, the distractions of war in the forties, there were good reasons to believe that the age of America's religious revivals had passed by the fifties.

[2] See J. Milton Yinger, *Sociology Looks at Religion*. New York, Macmillan, 1963, pp. 67ff.

Billy Sunday had been the last rough-and-tumble mass evangelist, and he was long forgotten. Harry Emerson Fosdick had been the last of the great fashionable preachers. People foresaw no resurgence of interest in mass religion. Then, in the 1950's, such a resurgence came.

Some scholars, noting how minimal were the institutional and ethical effects of religion in the 1950's, have questioned whether or not a revival ever really existed.[1] Comment on that question depends largely on one's definition of religion and revival. If by it we mean that there was a certifiable gain in authentic religious response, it would be difficult to answer. If by it we mean an increase in public attention to or interest in religion, the signs are more obvious. Almost all the news media and particularly mass-circulation magazines and newspapers called attention to the revival. Perhaps they were celebrating a pseudoevent or a nonevent, were manufacturing news where there had been no "hard" news. But in a media-oriented America these "pseudoevents" serve as well as hard news to fashion people's attitudes.

At any rate, soon they were talking about the subjects to which they give attention in these polls. Without embarrassment, but usually with considerable vagueness, they talked about the social values of belief in God (often over against atheistic Communism). Church attendance rose, church building became a contagious fever, cover stories of *Life* magazine worried about Sunday school, a new President who typified the revival and the decade's spiritual values spoke in terms of leading a crusade and practiced what he preached even to the point of joining a church and getting baptized himself.[2]

Religious books became best sellers. Collegians, often reputedly resistant to religious appeals, flocked to a pervasive but short-lived event called Religious Emphasis Week. New personalities came on the scene: Bishop Fulton Sheen, Rabbi Joshua Loth Liebman, and —most important of all—evangelist Billy Graham. Mass evangelism under the tutelage of Graham experienced a new birth. The Gal-

[1] *See* Charles Y. Glock, "The Religious Revival in America?" in *Religion and the Face of America,* Jane C. Zahn, ed. Berkeley, University of California. 1959, pp. 25ff.

[2] For a chronicle of this era, *see* William Lee Miller, *Piety Along the Potomac: Notes on Politics and Morals in the Fifties.* Boston, Houghton Mifflin, 1964.

lup poll of 1952 reflected a sampling of opinion in the early years
of that revival. Civic or societal religion received a great impetus
from that revival, as it was generalized, inoffensive, nationalist,
noncontroversial religion that was being preached. Even Billy
Graham, a would-be particularist who preached the offense of
the cross of Jesus Christ, was inoffensive. "Everybody" liked him—
secularists, Jews, Catholics, Protestants. Only a few crabby Protestant theologians raised questions.

Looking back, it is hard to recall any ethical achievement growing out of that revival. World and domestic poverty were not
being attacked. The great racial crisis was largely overlooked by
the revival-minded. The American Business Creed was not called
into question. The President assured the people that America was
the greatest instrument that God had ever placed on his footstool.
When a sour prophet from New York's Union Theological Seminary reminded the nation that the Psalmist says that "he who
sitteth in the heavens shall laugh," few listened. Positive thinking,
peace with God, peace of soul, peace of mind, brotherhood, success, Americanism—these are the values we recall from the religion
of the 1950's.

Not that the revival was without effect. In fact, had it not produced people for the churches, and churches for the people, it is
questionable whether there would have been people for the
prophets of the 1960's to lead, cajole, harangue, bug, mourn over,
or sway. If one takes seriously the cultural impact of the prophets
and theologians of the 1960's one is ready for *more* change than
will be found in the 1965 poll. Perhaps the preaching of the revival, which helped people insulate themselves against change,
served to keep them from being either lifted too high or dropped
too low by the revolutionaries of the 1960's.

If the 1950's saw an enhancement of civic and societal religion,
the 1960's experienced an attack on it. At the turn between the
revival and the revolution there appeared a great number of books
by Protestantism's social analysts. Best known of these were Peter
Berger's *The Noise of Solemn Assemblies* and Gibson Winter's
The Suburban Captivity of the Church. They demonstrated the
degree to which Protestants had joined their compatriots in celebrating the American Way of Life and giving it the ultimate regard they professedly gave only to God. These prophets either had
recourse to historic revelation and tradition or to humanist values

in today's revolutionary world in order to gain an angle of vision for judgment or a place of leverage for change.

The "in" people of the 1950's had been the celebrity clerics, the experts at personal pastoral care, the pacifiers of an anxious nation, the sanctioners of a complacent nation. The "in" people of the 1960's, in the field of religion, were social activists, civil-rights leaders, radical experimenters with the liturgies and forms of the church, revolutionary theologians. The collegian who might have his eye on a seminary in the 1950's might very well claim a Peale or Sheen or Graham as a hero. In the 1960's he would more likely have cited a Martin Luther King, a John F. Kennedy, a Pope John as his religious hero. The mass of people, to whom the calls for commitment are less intense, respond less enthusiastically to both types.

The evidences that the 1960's brought about a revolutionary change in public attitudes to religion are on all hands. NBC could title its report on the clergy, "The Quiet Revolution." *Fortune* could ask, "What on Earth Is Happening to Protestantism?" *The New Yorker* sent Ved Mehta in quest of *The New Theologian.* *Time* asked on its Easter cover, "Is God Dead?" *Newsweek* used a Christmas cover in the same liturgical season (1965–66) to feature the unsettlers in Protestantism. *The New York Times* added a religion editorialist to its staff in order to keep up with the change. One journalist put it this way: "In the 1950's we responded to the revival by enlarging the religion section of Saturday metropolitan newspapers. It was full of sermon titles and advertisements for ground-breakings and smorgasbords. In the 1960's we responded to the revolution by decreasing the religion section and by putting religion on the front page of the newspapers."

In education, particularly in higher education, the change from 1952 to 1965 was obvious. The Supreme Court had ruled out school prayer and devotional exercises but had given a new charter for instruction about religion in two decisions designed to spell out "wholesome neutrality" on the part of the state toward religion. The result: During the 1960's there has been a great increase of religious inquiry in colleges and universities even at a time when many a chaplain noted that his chapel was emptying. Clearly, a new style of religious response seemed to be appearing by the time of the poll in 1965.

4. THE TURN TOWARD RELIGIOUS REVOLUTION

Now that some "backlash" seems to have occurred in reaction to the revolution, it is possible to begin to play the historians' game and to try to determine when, how, and under what circumstances Americans began to relocate the place of religion in personal and national life somewhere halfway between these two Gallup polls. My list is not inclusive, but its parts do illumine the whole change.

The election of John F. Kennedy was one of the symbolic events that represented a turn in American religion. As far as Protestants were concerned, here was the first non-Protestant President. Since the President plays a sort of priestly role in national religion, this change symbolized the displacement of Protestantism from its imperial position. Opposition to Mr. Kennedy's candidacy and election represented the last occasion which brought together old-line Protestant liberals who depended on a kind of nationally taken-for-granted theism with old-line Fundamentalists who were merely anti-Catholic. But Mr. Kennedy's Catholicism, never obtrusive in policy matters, was less significant than was that elusive quality called "style" which he imparted to a new generation. In place of Mr. Eisenhower's revivalist oratory and late-stage idealism, here was a cultivatedly tough and youthful pragmatism, tempered by its own kind of idealism which seemed to endorse a new elite in religion: civil-rights- and activist-oriented, if less pious.

With the Kennedy style, one must cite a hard-news event which more markedly inaugurated change in American religion. This was the racial revolution, which began to gather momentum after the Supreme Court decision of 1954 and the bus boycott in Alabama of 1956 but which reached public consciousness in the long, hot summers of the 1960's and probably crested, so far as Protestant clergy participation is concerned, with the Alabama marches of the spring of 1965. After two hundred years of church-endorsed slavery and one hundred years of church-tolerated segregation, no event did more to embarrass or quicken the conscience of churches. No other event served so readily to rally young activists in quest of a cause. Perhaps the church needed "the movement" more than the movement needed the church; at any rate, after the summer of 1966, the alliance between Negro civil-rights leaders and white churchmen seemed to be threatened. But the race problem remains as the urgent cause, the test of the ethical seriousness of the churches. For Protestantism, all the churchly talk about God and Trinity and Jesus sounded hollow so long as it was not matched by worldly talk about this social problem. Meanwhile, America's societal religion dictated just how much the clergy could become involved in this "secular social issue," and some lay reaction seems evident in the Gallup poll, where people display continued reluctance at seeing the clergy involved in issues of this type.

The discovery of urbanization and metropolis was another factor which brought about change. When the industrial city was first perceived on the American landscape, Protestants began to try to adapt their institutions to serve it. The result was the Social Gospel, Christian Socialism, and Social Christianity on the left and various kinds of institutional churches and the Salvation Army on the right, as it were. But the Protestant forms, the denominations, and the localistic parish church did not easily adapt, and Protestants continued to minister to the city with forms basically accommodated to town and country life.[1]

In the 1960's it was no longer possible to avoid the meaning of the city. The seminaries prepared a new kind of leadership. The churches continued fleeing to the suburbs but making token payments in support of inner-city outpost experiments. While little institutional change came about in white Protestant circles, there was at least much talk about ministering to people who live in slums or the isolation of urban high-rise apartments. Inevitably, tension grew between those who wanted Protestantism to represent village values and those who celebrated secularity, pluralism, and the politics of the city. Reaction to this kind of involvement of the city also is no doubt a factor in ongoing resistance to clerical involvement in social issues, as revealed in the poll.

Talk of a new personal morality characterized religious life in the 1960's. It is clear from the poll that most Americans, including

---

[1] An account of earlier experiment appears in Aaron Ignatius Abell, *The Urban Impact on American Protestantism, 1865–1900*. Hamden, Connecticut, Shoe String Press, 1943, and Henry F. May, *Protestant Churches and Industrial America*, New York, Harper, 1949.

younger ones, feel that religion plays a smaller part in determining moral choice than it did in the past. Most regard the old days
as times of greater honesty and integrity. This finding would not
be significant if we had only the poll of 1952, or only of 1965; it
seems almost to be a part of human nature to feel that in earlier
times moral integrity was easier to come by, that in the golden
days of the past the fathers had it easier in their attempt to apply
religion to life. But we have the two polls for contrast, and here
is one of the more spectacular changes in all the findings: Clearly,
Americans feel that a fundamental change in assessing moral values is coming into being.

The religious leaders have taken part in this revolution. Protestant Episcopal churchman Joseph Fletcher's *Situation Ethics* was
only the best known of countless essays at defining what some
called "the new morality." The impulses for Protestant advocacy
of ethical change were complex and varied. Ordinarily they began
with a critique of current and comfortable ethics, a tired legalism
which inconvenienced no one but which—within the ceremonies
of the religious revival of the 1950's—could be made to look Protestant and godly. The new ethics was to be an inconveniencing
one, the removal of the legalist crutch. This critique then moved
to the point of an attempted recovery of what these Protestants
claimed was at the heart of biblical and Reformation ethical impulses. So advocacy of "situation ethics" grew as much out of the
century's theological revival as it did out of assessment of the current moral situation and its possibilities.

Whether the public faulted the religious leadership for their
assault on the comfortable if obsolete ethic or for their failure to
come up with a satisfactory new ethic, or whether it was being
merely nostalgic, it is clear that by the time of the 1965 poll a
wider section of the public than in 1952 felt that religious controls
over action were weaker. Unfortunately, these polls do not go into
detail on complex specific ethical questions, such as the wars (first,
in Korea; then, in Vietnam) which have troubled the Protestant
conscience. The division within the clergy and between clergy and
laity on the military-nationalist issue is itself another factor in the
revolution in religion in the 1960's.

Not all the occasions for change came from the outside and
goaded the church into action. Some of the revolutionary elements

were chosen by the church; in such instances it was an agent and
not merely a victim of change. Two of these should be cited at this
point as we chronicle the turn from revival toward revolution.

The first is the ecumenical movement. Certainly, external forces
here played their part in occasioning the change in the church.
The shrinking globe, the jostling of people with competitive
Christian value systems, the scandal of division made manifest in
an age of mass media, the new sociological opportunities for Christian interaction—all these helped bring Protestants (and later
Eastern Orthodox) together in their half of the ecumenical movement beginning around 1910 and climaxing institutionally near
the time of the first poll with the formation of the World Council
of Churches and the National Council of Churches. Similarly,
Pope John, in convoking the Catholic ecumenical council named
Vatican II, made clear that he was being sociologically responsive
to change. At the same time it was patent that these religious
leaders were acting upon theological impetuses gained from a re-
reading of the Scripture and a revisiting of the tradition of the
churches.

The ecumenical spirit is reflected positively in these polls. The
second half of the questionnaire was given over to interfaith issues.
Here the degree of acceptance between Protestants and Catholics
of their separated brothers' beliefs, values, clergy, practices, and
attitudes cannot be explained without recall of the impact of
Pope John and the similar spirit of countless leaders on both
sides of the historic wall of Christian separation.

At the same time the poll reveals the durability of denomina-
tionalism, which Sidney E. Mead has called *"the shape of Protestantism in America."*[2] For all the talk about ecumenism, most
Americans are either members of denominations or think of themselves as such. There is surprisingly little apostasy, surprisingly
little change from denominational pool to denominational pool.
Between 1952 and 1965, the housing boom in the suburbs and the
boom in higher education purportedly exposed people to new
denominations and supposedly led to a great measure of casual
identification with churches. Not according to Gallup, who finds a
considerable degree of faithfulness to inherited denominational

[2] In *The Lively Experiment*. New York, Harper, 1963, pp. 103ff.

loyalties even if the lines between denominations were regarded as largely irrelevant by both the partisans of religious revival and of religious revolution!

The second revolutionary change which came chiefly under the agency of churches acting in a voluntary way was a radical theological revolution. This occurred, so far as the public was concerned, *after* the religious revival. The revival leaders, knowing well the American instinct for nominal orthodoxy (where is the "modern man" of the theologians' hypothesis?) catered to it. The liberal theologians criticized Norman Vincent Peale for perverting the Gospel of Jesus Christ. Peale would regularly respond by writing an article for his denominational paper in defense of the Virgin Birth or other symbols; one of his disciples actually combed Peale's sermons and came up with a word count which suggested his orthodox obsession.[3] And few questioned Billy Graham's adherence to the orthodoxy of nineteenth-century Protestant evangelicalism, just as they found no reason, in Catholicism, to see theological experiment in Sheen. During the revival it was assumed that the theological message inherited from the fathers could be preserved intact, put into new packages for communication and for reasons of persuasion.

The churchly revolution of the 1960's began with a theological critique of that approach. It insisted that the orthodoxy was merely nominal, that it disguised radical religious change. The two Gallup polls substantiate this charge. Most Americans believe that the Bible is the authoritative revealed word of God, but few read it or express curiosity about its contents. It has a symbolic, not a cognitive import for them. They regret inadequacies in their own religious education, wish for something better for their children, but manifest no enthusiasm for developing institutions or methods which might correct the inadequacies. Having the child in Sunday school, no matter how pale and weak an instrument of education it may be, has a symbolic value which is determinative.

Nowhere is the merely nominal character of American orthodoxy more evident than in the response to the questions about heaven and hell. Sophisticated theologians may find ways of reinterpreting the biblical message to minimize its concern, particu-

---

[3] Allan R. Broadhurst, *He Speaks the Word of God.* Englewood Cliffs, Prentice-Hall, 1963.

larly in the New Testament, over eternal damnation. Historic Protestantism in Europe down into nineteenth-century America gained considerable momentum from the public response to threats of hell. But preaching of damnation is embarrassing and inconveniencing; the God implied by it does not square with the comfortable Deity of the American Way of Life. So American free enterprise takes over to adapt the teaching of that Bible which has been overwhelmingly accepted as the authoritative revelation of the will of God: Almost no Americans, including American Protestants, seem to regard the threat of hell as a threat to them.

The theological revival of the time was not devoted merely to the illusory character of Protestant orthodoxy, or to mere exposure of its sham. It had a positive intent. Seeing the quiet adaptation and steady erosion of distinctive Christian teachings, it wanted to arrest the process of accommodation to the public mind and to ascertain anew what was true in the tradition. Sometimes it did this naïvely through its own simple adaptation to its own simple construct called "the modern mind" or "modern man." But more was involved than the task of meeting this mind. A half century's enterprise had gone into a fresh exploration of the word of God and the witness of the reformers in a movement often called neo-orthodoxy. Karl Barth's impetus was soon transformed into Rudolf Bultmann's attempt to demythologize the New Testament and into Paul Tillich's desire to correlate theology and philosophy through an understanding of symbolic forms. Meanwhile, Dietrich Bonhoeffer wanted to work out a religionless Christianity, one in which people would be free to follow Jesus Christ without becoming committed in advance to specific philosophies or pieties or otherworld views. These endeavors occurred in Europe, with a safe separation of salt water intervening. Or it occurred in seminaries, mythically ivory towers remote from church life and public life.

In the 1960's this changed; halfway between these two Gallup polls, American theology became public in a way that no living people could remember. A number of popular books of theology reached best-seller status: the imported *Honest to God* of Bishop John A. T. Robinson or *The Secular City* of Harvey Cox and eventually the *Radical Theology and the Death of God* by William Hamilton and Thomas J. J. Altizer were the most publicized examples. Less widely distributed but no less influential were

works like Paul van Buren's *The Secular Meaning of the Gospel*
and Gabriel Vahanian's *The Death of God*. These books and the
public appearances of their authors occasioned the front-page
stories on theology on the basis of which the public made up its
mind concerning stirrings in Protestantism.

To many the change represented a "going over the hill" into
treason on the part of theologians. To others the talk was merely
attention-getting and determinedly outrageous. To have theologians, whose vocational name implies talking about God, com-
plaining about the meaninglessness of God-talk; to have Protestant
church leaders do an about-face after centuries of decrying the
secular; to have professors of religion proclaiming "the death of
God"—these apparent incongruities led people who never before
had paid attention to theology to show some sort of interest.
Whether or not this theological change had an impact on the
people sampled in this poll would be hard to determine. We would
need a similar poll from around 1958 to learn more. Did the
change in theology lead to confusion and loss of faith on the part
of the few who are represented by a statistic as having less faith,
less loyalty than did their symbolic representatives of 1952? Or
did the antics (as they see it) of theologians lead people to react
with compensatory vigor and to suggest that they are more faithful, more loyal than we would find them to be? Or does even the
most widely celebrated theological movement in decades reach
only so small an elite that it is not reflected in the polls? We cannot answer; it would be good of Mr. Gallup to follow through on
questions that would illumine this point.

5. THE RESPONSE TO REVOLUTION

We have suggested that American Protestants are undergoing not
secularization so much as radical religious change under continuity of unchanged symbols, and that their clerical and lay elites
have been trying to inaugurate a kind of religious revolution in
reaction to that change, especially as it was incarnate in a revival
of interest in religion in the 1950's, and that the Gallup polls
taken before the latter-mentioned event and after the first phase of
"the revolution" reflect some elements of public response but frus-

trate our curiosity on others. How has revolution been perceived in the culture?

The overall evidence of the polls suggests that the public's religious change is independent of and uncontrolled by the theological and ecclesiastical elites. The majority of the Protestant public is apparently content with nominal orthodoxy even while it is manifestly not curious about the substance of that orthodoxy. The theological elite (not isolable in these polls, but demonstrably so outside them) is apparently less orthodox, but it is manifestly curious about theological substance. But other parts of the revolution have reached public consciousness. Martin Luther King leading marchers, priests praying in coffeehouses, jazz masses, clerical participation in housing issues, ecclesiastical lobbying on political matters, denominations speaking out on ethical questions—these are known. What have been the effects of this knowledge? Responses are varied.

The first, mere ignorance, is hard to sustain. The interest of the mass media in reporting on and stirring up controversy is too obvious and their achievements too noteworthy. The man in the pew is being reached both by those who would persuade him to accept a new value system as well as by those who exploit his reluctance to face change. Still, public awareness is selective. The churches' involvements in racial change are much better known, of course, than are details of theological change. So it is possible for many people responding to these polls to be oblivious to many kinds of change being evoked today.

Second, there is enthusiastic participation on the part of a minority. Most cells, parishes, denominations, or other units count a minority of laymen who are themselves pacesetters in the attempt to bring Protestantism into a new age, beyond the confines of its captivity in the American Way of Life. Some of them are better poised than are the clergy to carry on their work and witness, as in the world of business and industry. Others are vocationally less mobile, less free to do so than are the clergy. On the more technical points of theology we would not expect professional commitment on the part of the laity (though here and there are signs of surprising sophistication); but as for the attempt to devise new forms and to carry out the activities, more laymen are involved.

A third response leads to what I have called elsewhere a "hushed-up revolution" which is tending to pull apart the one kind of clergy-laity coalition from the other. The people who join the church in order not to be bothered are bothered when the church bothers them. As Peter Berger observed, during the religious revival the only "offense" or "scandal" to faith was the decision over which congregation of which denomination offered one the least demanding constitution.[1] After I had joined, others would make ethical decisions for me. People who joined the church on that basis have become disturbed now when the props and crutches are pulled out from under them. They are asked to make up their own minds about Vietnam, capital punishment, premarital sex, and even about the existence or life of God!

The faithful who occupy pews but do not want to be disturbed, who pay for the varnish on the Sunday school gym floor, who subsidize missions to Africa, did not necessarily commit themselves, so far as they knew, to identification with revolutionary people of the world or—more embarrassingly—to work for integrated housing in the American city and in their own neighborhood. There are some signs that instinctive reaction to controlled religious change has expressed itself through a decline in support of religious institutions (though few people in this poll actually think of the churches as money-grubbing, fiscally demanding institutions). There are also demonstrable signs that counter-elites have been formed to exploit the confusion and uncertainty accompanying change.

Almost every major Protestant denomination has seen the rise of well-financed lay organizations (which usually do not lack clerical chaplains) to serve as lobbies to counter religious change. Since theological change in the interest of the Christian tradition will normally call into question the American Way of Life, there are ready "angels" to back such opposition to change as can be organized. Since most institutional change is a challenge to the immediate past's forms, there are always at hand plenty of defenders of those forms who are ready to fight back.

Where the growing tension between clergy and laity, between two kinds of clergy-lay coalitions will lead, is anyone's guess. I would not hazard a prediction. The weight of numbers and finan-

[1] See "The Religious Paradox," *The Noise of Solemn Assemblies*. New York: Doubleday, 1961, Chapter II, Part 3.

cial power is in the interest of those who support the civic religion that is enhanced by Christian symbolism. The overwhelming weight of the upcoming clergy is on the other side; perhaps they can easily be starved out and the churches will develop a whole new kind of leadership. Perhaps more will be converted to change. More likely there will be a new form of political relationship between the two elites in the future, and some compromises will be struck. As of the 1965 Gallup poll, it is still clear that the majority of the American Protestant churchgoers does not understand the social involvements of the clergy. I know of no institutional problem which plagues present-day Protestantism more than this one.

Another response to change is a "wait and see" attitude. The American Protestant laity has long ago learned the art of creative foot-dragging. Often in the past it has accepted change, and there is no reason that it cannot do so again. But no complex and adapted social movement can be easily compelled or persuaded to change *en masse* to a more demanding and less comfortable position. Protestants aver that they carry with them a principle of self-criticism and prophetic judgment directed first to their own community. Therefore, there are no *a priori* reasons why they cannot respond to controlled change and cut themselves off from drift. Such change occurred when evangelical Protestantism became missionary and humanitarian in the late eighteenth and early nineteenth century. In the years of these two polls it occurred in the sudden general decline in anti-Catholicism. If compelling threats or inducements can be presented, it is possible that people will accept change.

6. AMERICA'S REAL RELIGIONS

Throughout this comment I have assumed that the revivalists of the 1950's basically devoted themselves to applying and enhancing the inherited symbols of Christianity in support of America's civic religion and that the revolutionaries of the 1960's have devoted themselves to questioning these symbols and applying them selectively in order to bring about controlled, as opposed to uncontrolled, religious change. Since the Gallup polls have no way of

asking people, "What is your *real* religion? What stands behind
your affirmations of traditional belief, accompanied by your disin-
terest in its substance or implications?" it is necessary to suggest
some dimensions of the "real" religion of America. It will be seen
that this approach counters that of those who see America as a
pure-form secular society; we are very, very religious, but this religion has changed (whether for better or for worse it is not necessarily the task of the analyst to judge).

These polls do reveal, in 1952 as well as in 1965, the great
change that has occurred in popular religion since Protestantism
took shape 450 years ago in Europe or 350 years ago in America.
The inherited symbols (God, Trinity, Christ, Bible, heaven, hell)
then were seen against a cosmic screen or backdrop on the "beyond" side of which destinies were being shaped and toward which
religion pointed. The polls show that such belief in a transcendent
order has not disappeared; indeed, to the men of the Enlightenment or the agents of secularization, the persistence of beliefs
in such an otherworldly reality as evidenced by these polls would
be astounding and frustrating. But there is no longer consistency
in response to this transcendent appeal; a smaller percentage holds
to it in 1965 than in 1952 without consequent change in beliefs
in its corollaries.

To those who define secularization as otherworldliness turned to
this-worldliness, modern America is bewildering. The question is
whether such a definition is valid. Zen Buddhism and any number
of Eastern religions have never been otherworldly, yet they have
been religions. How do *they* secularize? And, if otherworldliness
means waiting for deferred benefits, asks British sociologist David
Martin, then what do we make of a Texas Baptist millionaire who
insists on an otherworldly Gospel (and pays well for it) but who
represents to all the world pure this-worldly materialism and desire for immediate benefits?[1]

So where these polls reveal continued belief in otherworldliness
or a transcendent order, they do not demonstrate secularization;
they substantiate our contention that radical religious change is
occurring. Look at the other side: Note the disappearance of re-

---

[1] *See* David Martin, "Towards Eliminating the Concept of Secularization,"
p. 71 in *Penguin Survey of the Social Sciences,* Julius Gould, ed., Baltimore,
Penguin, 1965.

gard for the importance of this transcendent cosmic screen. All but 1 percent of self-named Protestants somehow believe in God; 77 percent think of him as a loving Father (down from 82 percent in 1952); 86 percent are content with the Trinitarian formula; 73 percent think of Jesus as God; 85 percent (same as 1952!) see the Bible as the revealed word of God; 94 percent pray to God. Vague otherworldliness persists in that 78 percent believe their soul will live after death; 71 percent believe in after-life heaven; only 54 percent believe in after-life hell; only 15 percent (up from 12 percent in 1952!) see hell as a real possibility for themselves. Only 60 percent think of what will happen to them after they die. Most significant: When asked, "Which do you think you, yourself, are most serious about—trying to live comfortably; or preparing for a life after death?" 42 percent chose "trying to live comfortably" and 24 percent chose "preparing for life after death." (By the way, comparable figures were 45 percent and 22 percent in 1952; at least Americans have not grown less otherworldly in an affluent society.)

Perhaps there is a bad conscience among some over their choice of comfort over afterlife. At any rate, only 22 percent think they *should* be most serious about trying to live comfortably, and 53 percent feel they should be most serious about preparing for life after death. But when asked, "Which do you think is most important for the church to do—to convert people to a spiritual belief so that they can earn a happy life after death; or to teach people how to live better every day with all other people?" only 20 percent of the Protestants opted for conversion to spiritual belief and 47 percent wanted people taught to live better, while 32 percent answered "both." These figures are virtually unchanged since the 1952 poll. Overall, it would seem that while 99 percent of Protestants claim to believe in God, 75 percent claim to belong to church, less than half have afterlife or otherworld as first concern, and only about one in six could have hell-fire preaching as a potential reminder of threat to them. Belief in a life to come, or "another world" then has not disappeared, but it does not appear to be vivid or to be the central motivation or preoccupation for most Protestants—to say nothing of the public at large.

The real drama goes on, then, here and now, where people have to learn to live "comfortably" and "with each other." Religious threats and promises, demands, and appeals will normally be de-

voted primarily to this realm. Here is where the vivid, motivating,
and preoccupying religious concerns lie.

The first dimension of this "real" religion, enhanced by support
of a continuity of Christian symbols, is civic. The civic realm is
granted its own autonomy. Only 24 percent of American Protestants feel that it is right for clergymen to discuss political candidates *or issues* from the pulpit. (In 1952 this was 23 percent.)
Two thirds of the Protestants are opposed to such discussion. Such
a response would have been unthinkable in most of Colonial
America, which was in many instances formally theocratic.
Nineteenth-century evangelicalism gave support to the individual-
istic idea that the political order should develop autonomously
and that individually converted Christians could then commute
from beneath the pulpit, where they would hear of otherworldly
reconciliation, to the legislature or marketplace, where they would
work for a better world, as citizen individuals now cut off from the
church.

This means that in the evangelical tradition (which American
Catholics have also largely accepted), the church as such is expected not to be involved critically in social-political issues. A
preacher may very well criticize a public official for crawling into
bed with someone else's wife, but in this ethos, he is not to protest
if that official's policies enslave, imprison, brutalize, or even kill
people. It is obvious why this arrangement should be attractive to
social, economic, and political leaders. It permits complete autonomy and uncritical development of their approach so long as they
keep personally morally pure (and do not propose issues which set
churches on edge, like Vatican ambassadorships, taxing of church
property, elimination of devotion from schools, gambling—at
which times preachers, also in the evangelical tradition, can talk
politics and find popular response).

Americans have clearly not reckoned with the modern power
situation, and with the difficulty one has to reach to the root of
social problems. In a highly institutionalized world and in what
amounts to a welfare state, most of the Gospel's injunctions to
justice and charity have to be worked out in a complex political
situation. An occasional lonely Christian commuter between value
systems may sometimes as citizen, though not as Christian, have an
impact. But the churches as such are not expected to speak formally, and the clergy most of all are expected to keep silent. That

was the ethos in 1952 during the revival, and it remains so after the radical upheavals of the 1960's, so far as three fourths of American Protestants and almost four fifths of the American people are concerned, according to the Gallup survey.

This does not mean that the churches and the clergy have no political role to play. When in a political world large social groups refuse to take a stand, they are taking a stand. A church which withstands integration and supports exploitation of the Negro poor through silence over the practice or failure to act positively is not less political than the one which takes the opposite stand. And a minister who supports the Vietnam War in his pulpit and prayers is not less political than the one who opposes it. National custom is on the side of the "nonpolitical" one who lends political support to the *status quo*.

What has developed, and the tolerance-oriented poll answers support it, is a civic religion which is this-worldly, disinterested in doctrinal distinctions, moralistic in outlook. That such a religion has developed in the shadow and under the guise of transnational Christian symbols is unnerving to theologians and wholly anticipated by social thinkers and historians. Complex societies somehow tend to develop common symbols and patterns, some sort of moral consensus. It would probably be intolerable if all the religious groups in America wanted to work out utterly the logic of their private and particular original visions.

When the United States was born, it was seen that each sect would have to yield ground in its claims. The insistent logic of American institutions was toward pluralism and the "wholesome neutrality" on the part of the state of which the Supreme Court now speaks. The jostling and abrasion of these sects against each other served to dull the sharpness of their claims. Others of them had actually begun to adopt the kind of relaxed, reasonable, and latitudinarian positions which characterized Enlightenment religion. This "cool" religion, of Boston Unitarianism and Virginia Anglicanism, seemed to be just what the situation demanded.

Meanwhile, civic leaders held to religious opinions which encouraged tolerant pluralism. Benjamin Franklin was not alone when he observed that what the churches held particularly was of no matter to anyone, so long as this did not get in anyone's way. What mattered was their common support of morality and the common good. On that basis, the American government has tradi-

tionally been relaxed in its sense of "wholesome neutrality," refus-
ing to tax church properties used for church purposes (a position
supported by the majority in these polls).

Civic religion can be minimal in character. That is, people can
withhold consent from it, so far as its ultimate claims are concerned. A man can be a critical nationalist, on Christian grounds.
He can regard the state as an order of creation, a sphere of God's
activity, a realm under Christ's Lordship. He can see the state as a
"minister for good" and can support many of its causes. Yet he
"obeys God rather than man" ultimately.

Or civic religion can be turned into a religious nationalism
which demands utter consent. Carlton J. H. Hayes[2] made extensive
studies of the appeals of modern nationalism and came to the
conclusion that it is the real religion of the modern world; I
would say that it is a most potent factor in that real religion.
Nationalism allows for no heresy, no self-excommunication;
churches today do. Nationalism has its sacred shrines, makes the
demand for ultimate sacrifice, generates hatred for foreign devils,
appeals to the God of battles. Anything done by the churches to
upset the entente between state and church, between powers in
the civil realm and ecclesiastical leadership, meets with criticism.
The religious revival supported this civic religion, and the "revolution of the 1960's," even though it represented the involvement
of the clergy and leadership with the aspiration of many revolutionary people around the world, did almost nothing to jostle the
political religion of America.

A second feature in the "real" religion of America is its societal
dimension, one gained through the experience of Americans with
merchandising, business, and especially industrial ideology. Here
again, certain commonly assented to values are held to durably.
There may be radical change in some features of the value system,
but the symbols remain the same.

Thus, in America, nominal assent is given to hard work, individual enterprise, saving, and refusal to waste, though actually
selective portions of the economy would collapse if people lived on
the basis of these creeds. Why, then, are they commonly held to?
Since this societal religion provides the context of life for the people who respond to these Gallup polls, even though the pollsters

[2] *Nationalism: A Religion.* New York, Macmillan, 1960.

have devised few means as yet to pursue the inquiry, we shall go into some detail.

Ernest Gellner[3] compares the ideology of industrialized affluent nations like the United States to the aspirant nations of the world. Why is America constantly invoking God, why does it promulgate Protestant-type moral values domestically and internationally, why is it not "secularizing" on schedule; why do the majority of the people respond in such orthodox fashion to opinion polls on religion, even as they reveal how noncurious and disinterested they are in the implications of that orthodoxy? Gellner suggests that we have had our revolution, not only politically but through the experience of industrialization, that great event of the modern world.

Societies tend to retain what they can of the ideologies with which they passed "over the hump of transition" into industrialization. When America industrialized, one version of "the Protestant ethic" prevailed, to motivate and to inspire people to productivity and action. It worked. We do not know any other way to do it than the way we did it. We are nervous about a new industrial revolution, with its unforeseeable changes in the way of automation, cybernetics, new leisure. So we retain the dogmas of the earlier time of transition, but we employ them in a different way: to trigger new revolution and to ward off enemies of our mode of industrialization.

So the old doctrines remain the nominal orthodoxy of the new order; the symbols remain, though they no longer carry much of anything cognitively with them. A board chairman of a large firm will doubtless feel threatened by a "death of God" theologian, an advocate of "the secular city" or "radical theology." He will no doubt repair to or support the clergyman who invokes the symbols ("the Blood of the Lamb," "Jesus Saves") which he regards as having been normative a century and a half ago, when those symbols, then bearing cognitive issue, helped carry our society over the hump.

Gellner, in order to help us see this about ourselves, points to the use cool, agnostic young Marxists in the new nations make of Marxism. For them it is less ideology than trigger; it is the force they saw to be successful in other societies which, like theirs, made

---

[3] *Thought and Change.* Chicago, University of Chicago, 1965, pp. 122ff.

the transition without the limitless resources Americans and western Europeans had. Confront such a Marxist with the Hegelian
metaphysical backdrop to the practice which prevailed in the mid-
nineteenth century, and he will tend to be embarrassed, to dismiss
it, to change the subject. He will probably not repudiate it and, if
he is wise, he will not try to demythologize it—modernism gets
dated too fast. But he needs what Marxism can produce.

So with the Christian of the capitalist West, or even more with
the person at the fringes of the Christian community. Remind him
of the metaphysical background Wesleyan evangelicalism had and
he will tend to be embarrassed and hope to move on hurriedly. He
does not read the Bible to learn how to run his business anymore.
But he will not repudiate it or demythologize it; he will probably
subsidize the clergyman who will keep on reassuring him that his
way of doing business is God's way. He needs the ideology which
carried us "over the hump of transition" because he cannot envi-
sion other approaches. So original Marxism and traditional Christianity lie more or less like a glacial moraine on our respective
landscapes. Complete secularization would be unthinkable, but
radical religious change is inevitable. Civic or societal religion is
the result: It lubricates the processes; it glues together the elements
of a complex society. At last, we have what the Greco-Roman
world had developed. And only the prophetic theologian scorns it.
He regrets to see revolutionary ideology (and Wesleyan evangelicalism, for instance, once was revolutionary) now used to support
the antirevolutionary *status quo,* to serve idolatry of the American
Way of Life.

One could speak of other dimensions. An element of "folk religion" would deal with popular beliefs, gained in part from Christian symbols. The Gallup poll does not reveal to us just what
portion of the society adheres specifically to various superstitions,
so we cannot ascertain how often Christian symbols are invoked in
support of superstitious folk religion. But whoever listens to "the
man on the street," watches celebrities on late-night television, or
reads widely, will have great difficulty finding the person described
by the theologians as "secular man," the cool, sunny, happy,
pragmatic-empirical agnostic. Gallup's man believes in God, as
Father or force, but certainly the God of our processes.

Changes from 1952 through 1965 in public response to poll
questions occur within that context, that given framework. It

would take a revolution as dramatic as the American or French
political revolutions, or the industrial revolution, to bring about a
fundamental reorientation within thirteen years—if even then we
could expect a complex society to retool and readjust so exten-
sively. The surprise in reading comparative polls such as these,
assuming that they are relatively accurate, is not that they chronicle so little change, but—given the predestining matrix of American life—that they reveal so much change.

7. ROMAN CATHOLIC ECUMENISM'S IMPACT ON PROTESTANTISM

Beginning with questions 30a, 38a, and 46a in the Gallup poll,
there is a sequence of answers depicting change in intergroup relations. While Protestant-Jewish attitudes have remained fairly consistent or have changed undramatically, in most instances
Protestant-Catholic views of each other represent profound
changes. Throughout the survey there are subtle evidences; for
example, Protestants are in general somewhat more tolerant of
Catholic parochial schools, at least so long as their tax money does
not have to go into their support. And the number of Protestants
who regard Roman Catholicism as their second-favorite communion rose from 5 percent to 7 percent, and the number who saw it as
their least favorite (so far as a possibility for their own belonging
was concerned) dropped from 39 percent down to 34 percent.
These by themselves are not so impressive as are responses to questions which permit people to remain psychically and spiritually in
their own communities. Many percentages indicating past hostility, suspicion, and mistrust have been cut in half in the thirteen-
year period. Respect for each other in some indicators seems virtually to have doubled. Even in controversial areas, in almost no
case is there a higher degree of uneasiness than there was in 1952.
The imagery of the clergyman seems to have changed less than of
the churches at large, perhaps because Catholic clergy have been
equally involved with Protestants during the revolutionary times
of the 1960's. But the church as a whole represents less a problem
than it did in the past.

Many of the reasons for change which were cited earlier could be adduced again: the effect of mass media, higher education, mobility, the move to the suburbs. But the comparison to Protestant-Jewish changes suggests that events inside the Christian churches had a more decisive impact, and we must assume that the personality of Pope John, the new attitude exemplified by Vatican II, and the positive response of Protestants all played their parts. Since this is the first far-reaching opinion poll during the period since the Council (it was taken during the last month of the last session), it seems to be a good time to set this change into context.

When Pope John appeared on the scene, little had occurred to alter the pattern of almost 450 years of hot and cold war between the two major families of Western Christianity. We should not now begin to forget the part brotherhood groups like the National Conference of Christians and Jews had played. But these groups had to confine their activities to the external, civil, and societal realms. They were not permitted to intrude into ecclesiastical and theological areas. There were pioneering quiet study groups, but these seemed hardly licit and rarely had much public impact.

Since the Council, it has become clear that Protestantism and Roman Catholicism do not have separate destinies in the world. It is true that in some areas Catholicism predominates and the Protestant presence is very small: The Mediterranean nations and Latin America would be examples. And in one or two leftover areas like Scandinavia, Roman Catholicism is weak. But in most of the industrialized affluent West and in the other nations where there has been a Christian missionary effort, Catholics and Protestants live side by side, and no longer separately as they did from 1517 until about 1960.

The Vatican Council has made it possible for the separated churches with a common destiny to set themselves into perspective. They had taken their internal problems and possibilities too seriously. Alfred North Whitehead remarked once that from the viewpoint of world history, the Protestant Reformation of the sixteenth century was a family quarrel of Northwest European people.[1] The Eastern Orthodox looked on with serene indifference. Meanwhile the new scientific-technological world view was being born, and Western Christianity in both versions addressed

---

[1] *Science and the Modern World.* New York, Macmillan, 1948, p. 1.

itself to the problems and style of living which antedated the rise of that world.

Not mindful of the new world around them, Christians glared at each other inside the walls, as it were. What do people do about family quarrels? They can bury the hatchet. This is easy to do in the instance of trivial issues, though we all know how in family life it is the trivial issues that can be repeatedly resurrected to haunt people who seek concord. It is a mark of maturity not to bring up the trivial; the Vatican Council helped Protestants come to that point. They no longer hold present-day Catholics responsible for all that their fathers did; they are learning to apply equally rigorous standards of criticism to themselves as they do to Catholics.

Or, elements in a family quarrel can face and solve the issues. That occurred, too, in Vatican II and in the present-day life of Protestantism, probably more so than is reflected in these surveys. Many substantial issues, if not the central doctrinal matters, have been faced. Resolution of complex problems does not "trickle down" rapidly, and the signals have not been passed all along the way. There is a good chance that if the questions of the last half of these polls were distributed only among the clerical leadership of the communions, a much greater degree of new concord might be evident.

Again, in a family quarrel, people can stress what they hold in common against other forces in the world. Vatican II made some of this possible, though American Protestantism and Catholicism have not been able to develop this commonalty. Had present-day Catholicism remained absolutely and totalistically militant toward Communism, one kind of American Protestant could have joined forces with it. Since ecumenical Catholicism seeks dialogue with Marxists and other unbelievers, American Protestants and Catholics alike have been too confused to try to regroup themselves. Similarly, in a world where both are confined to the historically "Christian" nations, this would be a fruitful moment for them to plan joint missions, were either one of them at the height of missionary self-certainty and concern. So far, there has been little "joint force" work.

Finally, in a family quarrel, people can get to work on remaining issues. Catholics and Protestants have begun to do so. These also will not early be reflected in surveys like the Gallup poll. The doctrine of God, of the Trinity, of Jesus Christ have not been seriously at issue between the communions. The authority and character of the Bible have been, but not in such a way that the new survey is illuminating. Protestants held to the view that the Bible is really the revealed word of God, with an 85 percent positive response in both poll years. Catholicism averages out to the same, having dropped from 88 percent to 82 percent in positive response. I would not have the competence even to speculate over the reasons for that figure. The questions of grace, faith, the place of Mary and the saints—none of these show up in the poll, and we would have to go elsewhere to measure change in attitude on them.

One reason we may not be curious enough about answers to those questions to place them in the poll is this: The churches of the twentieth century have a different set of issues in common than were the issues which separated them. In the sixteenth century, they asked, "Is God gracious?" Today, they find people asking rather, "Is God?" But since the God-talk, God-language, God-death matter has been so technical and arcane in theological circles and so disguised in lay circles (where God can come to mean almost anything), the poll throws little light. Eighty-eight percent of Catholics, 85 percent of Protestants are "absolutely certain" there is a God, and 10 percent and 11 percent, respectively, are "fairly sure." (There is a slight drop in all these figures since 1952.) God is "a loving Father" to 76 percent of the Catholics, and to 77 percent of the Protestants; he is "some kind of power" to 19 percent and 17 percent of them, respectively. Clearly, the doctrine of God in these billboard-sized outlines of questioning is not at issue.

Where the ongoing life of Protestants vis-à-vis Catholics will be judged will be in the more terrestrial matters of the kind suggested in the Council's Schema XIII on The Church in the Modern World. Birth control, the bomb, population questions, issues relating to marriage—these can be tested in the family circle and can be reported on in the polls. Most of the replies to such questions are of more interest to Roman Catholics than to Protestants, and I shall not comment on them here.

The emergence of Roman Catholicism as a completely accepted partner in American civil life and Christian life represents many problems for Protestants, however. We have begun to notice a crisis of identity among many. Protestants had always made much of the fact that their communion represented the church "always reformed and always being reformed." In recent times it has been noted that Catholism is experiencing more far-reaching reforms than is Protestantism, that it is more capable of carrying out such reforms, and that in many areas it has begun to look more "Protestant" than many Protestants appear to be.

In the development of radical theology, under the influence of Teilhard de Chardin and others, Catholicism is reexploring the question of human origin and coming up with new answers; it is proclaiming evolutionary views of human destiny. Protestants of liberal stripe no longer hold a monopoly on the ability to relate positively to science. Nor are Protestants any longer monopolists of the Bible. A biblical revival has swept Catholicism, and both in positive regard for the revelation and for sophistication of critical scholarship, Catholicism has become Protestantism's partner and peer.

Many issues which once served to help make Catholicism look retrogressive and Protestantism advanced have been posed in new ways. Questions about birth control and clerical celibacy are openly discussed; nuns adapt their garb, and priests often appear in street clothes. The old mystery concerning the Mass is dissipated, along with the use of Latin for most of the Liturgy, along with changes in practices associated with penance and devotion. As the experience of living-room dialogues expands, as lay people of Protestant and Catholic provenance find more common actions possible, as they are more exposed to each others' clergy, we may expect increased regard, following the trends depicted in the polls from 1952 to 1965. Meanwhile, Protestants will continue to grope for mission and identity if they continue to find separate existence valid (and the poll gives no indication of their desire to merge with Catholics, or vice versa). What is it to be a Protestant in the world of civic, societal, and folk religion, between Catholicism and secularity? This is the urgent question, a question given a new context between 1952 and 1965 by Vatican II and the new ecumenical spirit.

8. THE CONTINUING PROBLEMS
OF CHURCH AND STATE

One area of the poll will carry an element of surprise for many in
the political realm. This has to do with the complex of issues relating to church and state. They have certainly undergone considerable change in recent years, spurred as Americans have been by the
brotherhood movements in the spiritual realm and the need to
find new ways to meet political problems in the social realm. It has
been widely assumed that Americans, in their general acceptance
of "Great Society" legislation (as was manifest in congressional
activities in 1965) were prepared to undergo a fundamental shift
in their attitudes toward how church and state relate.

Much ecclesiastical leadership, in the ecumenical era, seems prepared to bury old hatchets. No longer is Protestant concern over a
line of separation between church and state motivated so clearly as
it was by anti-Catholicism and fear lest Catholics receive a bigger
slice of the pie should there be a change. But more important than
ecumenism was the actual change in practice undertaken by many
kinds of Protestants involved in institutional responsibility.

The new situation came to light in a meeting sponsored by The
National Council of Churches at Columbus, Ohio, in 1964. An
attempt was to be made there to bring new formulations that
would speak meaningfully on the complexity of church-state issues. The conference did not come forth with clear guidelines or
with much of a helpful consensus. Some suggested that the reason
lay in the fact that much leadership was softheadedly ecumenical
and pro-Roman Catholic, unwilling to insist on Protestant positions for fear of alienating Catholics. Not so. What occurred was
something much simpler.

In denomination after denomination there was a split, but not
between pro-Catholic and anti-Catholic forces. Rather, a certain
kind of theologian who defended the "absolute wall of separation
between church and state" was confronted by college presidents,
hospital administrators, and social-welfare executives of his own
tradition. These men and women, whether they would have
chosen the new "welfare" world or not, were living in a world in
which they saw the survival of their institutions dependent, in

part, on their relationship to the government. Thus colleges with a church base, in order to expand and to compete, accepted government loans for science buildings and dormitories. Such a practice conflicts with any idea of "absolute separation" and could prove to be an embarrassment to those who oppose all forms of aid to students in Catholic elementary schools.

Today colleges in most denominational traditions (parts of the Southern Baptist Convention are the major exception) have begun to accept such aid. They know that not a different logic but a different practice is operative here than the one which they want imposed on elementary education so far as parochial schools are involved. They prefer—and this is an honored American tradition —to "muddle through" without ideological neatness.

Many features of Great Society legislation extended this logic, and observers commented regularly that the public seemed to be welcoming more and more governmental support for institutions which included religious elements in their purposes and practices. The sample of the population reached in this Gallup poll hardly indicates that attitudes are changing rapidly. On issue after issue, in subsample after subsample, there was relative consistency of positions from 1952 to 1965.

One great issue remains relatively untouchable. States exempt church property from taxation. Peter Berger[1] once ventured the provocative guess that, given the size of American church properties, this practice represented an indirect subsidy greater than the direct subsidies any established European churches receive. There is no well-worked-out rationale for such a practice. Some churchmen argue that this exemption is an indirect payment for services rendered to the state; such argument sounds strange on Protestant lips, and hardly is consistent with the logic of "absolute separation." But Americans, from their highest courts on down, have agreed to be ideologically messy here; to engage in other practices would be unpopular, if not physically devastating, to the churches. So the Gallup poll finds that only 13 percent of the Protestants in 1965 (11 percent in 1952) think church property used for religious purposes should be taxed. (The total-population sample figures are 14 percent in 1965, 12 percent in 1952.)

---

[1] "The Religious Paradox," *The Noise of Solemn Assemblies.* New York, Doubleday, 1961, Chapter II, Part 3, pp. 61ff.

Resistance is growing to tax exemption for profit-making properties; Protestants and Catholics alike resent injustice, as they see
it, on this issue. The really telling issues come up on the traditional question of parochial education. (The words "Roman
Catholic" were not added to the word "parochial" in the questions, but we may assume that for most Americans the two are
virtually equated.) More Protestants in 1965 felt that Catholic
schools were good for the country (a mark of ecumenism), though
fewer felt that parochial schools gave as good an education (perhaps a sign of the new premium, post-Sputnik, on education). But
when asked whether free bus service or free books should be given
to children in religious schools, only 40 percent of the Protestants
said Yes, down from 41 percent in 1952; the Catholic figure, by
the way, dropped from 79 percent to 73 percent. A similar decline
(from 63 percent to 55 percent for Catholics, and from 34 percent
to 32 percent for Protestants) was shown on the general question
of tax support for parochial elementary education. Nor is released
time growing in favor; Protestants who thought it was a good idea
declined in number from 49 percent to 44 percent (figures for
Catholics and the whole population are comparable in their degree of decline), and only 18 percent of Protestants favored use of
public-school buildings for shared-time-type activities (compared
to 24 percent in 1952).

This response is revelatory of many features of American life.
For one thing, it shows how deep "the great tradition of the American churches," as Winthrop Hudson dubbed the idea of church-
state separation, remains.[2] For another, it might suggest a time lag
between the moment when responsible elites know they must
make some policy change and the time it reaches the rank and file.
Third, it might show how unreflective people have been concerning certain administrative problems—or it shows that they are
much more willing to be personally sacrificial in support of education than this poll anywhere else indicates. For Protestants in general seem to want to have religious education play a bigger part in
their children's lives than it had in their own. They express some
growing discontentment with Sunday school. Yet almost none of
them wish they had gone to parochial school, nor do they support

[2] *The Great Tradition of the American Churches.* New York, Harper,
1953.

the existing proposals for alternative institutions (released time, shared time). Here again, we must surmise that support of the idea of religious education (the nominal symbol) is much higher than is support for intensified religious education. Eighty-nine percent of American Protestants in this sample want their children to receive Sunday-school education; only 13 percent indicate other institutions outside their homes where they would like to have their children's religious education occur. They express faith in the magical, culturally approved, less-than-an-hour Sunday school in a way that the most partisan leaders of the Sunday-school movement themselves would hesitate to express it.

Whether Protestantism can continue to propagate itself as a religious force in a world full of competitive symbols, given the theological illiteracy of the home (where 49 percent want their children to receive some religious instruction), and the brevity and low-keyedness of Sunday school, is a question hardly faced, so far as we can learn from the matter-of-factness and routine character of answers to the questions on education. Does the element of the automatic and the routine, or does devotion to existing views of church and state shape responses here? We cannot tell from the polls; no doubt both factors play a part. So far as the transmission of faith to the younger generation is concerned, Protestantism cannot be in anything but deep trouble.

9. THE PROBLEMS OF PROTESTANTISM

The Protestantism which emerges from the sample in the Gallup portrait looks anything but vital. I hope a catalog will not be wearying; let us remind ourselves:

Protestants feel that people today lead less good lives than they used to and that they have much less sense of right and wrong than they once did; they find religion to be slightly less important in their lives than they did thirteen years earlier. More of them think that children should be raised as church members than before, but they are doing little institutionally to help raise them so. They give little evidence that they know enough or care enough to teach them, and the only institution to which most of them will give any support is the Sunday school—which hardly stands up to the weight of tests. It is part of the problem, not of the solution. They regret their own childhood religious training, but take fewer pains for their children than were taken for them.

Protestants who attend church regularly attend church more regularly than they used to; the semiregulars have grown less faithful. They believe in God, Father, Force, Trinity, Jesus Christ, the Bible with a faithfulness that must astonish the revivalists. (Who is left to convert?) But they do not read the Bible (*see* 12b and 12c). They pray, for a variety of reasons—chiefly to ask God for favors, help, guidance, and strength. There is reasonable assent to the idea of the soul's living on, and to heaven, some assent to hell, very little to the possibility of hell for oneself. They are most religious when the going gets rough, though many find that "it makes no difference" whether matters are rough or smooth. They are as interested in comfort as in their eternal destinies, and want other churches to be more concerned with teaching a good way of life than working for spiritual conversion.

Protestants are still uneasy about interfaith marriages, but are unworried about divorce, birth control, and other controversial practices. They want the role of religion to be larger in peoples' lives, but do not want the clergy to discuss politics. Far more of them claim to be members of church groups than can be found by the church groups. Almost half of them have never tried to get anyone else to join their religious group, though a large percentage of those who ever tried did succeed. They are content with their clergymen's sermons and personal ministrations and do not feel financially harassed by their churches. Not too many drift off from their churches or from the church itself. And they are increasingly the beneficiaries of more tolerance from non-Protestants, even as they express more tolerance themselves.

By now we are on precarious ground, dropping the subtleties of percentage points in order to generalize on the basis of a minuscule portion of the whole Protestant population. But we have confidence in the Gallup profile; it "checks out" with scores of other polls and with conclusions drawn from the thousands of items one reads in the course of a career in church history and religious journalism.

Daniel Boorstin's summary of American expectations fits much of what is revealed concerning Protestantism here. "We expect everybody to believe deeply in his religion, yet not to think less of

others for not believing. . . . We expect . . . to go to a 'church of
our choice' and yet feel its guiding power over us, to revere God
and to be God.''[1]

Whether or not one should view Protestantism's part in the
development of civic and societal religion positively depends on
one's point of view. Sociologist Milton Yinger contends that a
static view of religion is implied in Protestant judgments against
folk religion, that the laity should be given credit for having devised a new religion right under the noses of the clergy.[2] A new
day in a complex, pluralistic, industrial society demanded a new
religion, and this is what the people produced. And, after all: Are
not the radical theologians who do so much of the judging also
busy innovating?

These are issues that must be settled by Protestants, depending
upon their point of view. The Protestant faction which has most
reason for concern is that which denominates itself "evangelical."
It may represent the majority of Protestants so far as nominal
orthodoxy is concerned. It tries to revivify the symbols to which
Americans instinctively gravitate, and professes to despise the attempt to adapt the Gospel to the needs of modern man. In the
process it has revealed some mistrust of the ecumenical movement
and a great deal of mistrust of the social involvement of clergymen and churches.

In doing so, evangelicalism has made itself particularly attractive to those who have the greatest stake in the *status quo*. This is
not to say that there are not self-sacrificial evangelicals in the inner
city, involved in humanitarian and benevolent activities; they may
well outpace some of the liberal theoreticians. Nor can one contend that it is not possible for private evangelicals to lead wholly
private lives, hoping in God and believing in Jesus Christ, apart
from the world. But whenever evangelicalism takes on a partisan
character, whenever it rallies and organizes and mobilizes as a
social force, it is willy-nilly involved in the political realm as a
churchly form and movement. It is particularly exploitable by
nationalist, military, industrialist, and business elites and ordinarily speaks predictably for the point of view associated with civic

---

[1] Daniel J. Boorstin, *The Image, or, What Happened to the American
Dream.* New York, Atheneum, 1962.

[2] J. Milton Yinger, *Sociology Looks at Religion.* New York, Macmillan,
1963, p. 72.

and societal religion. Can it do this and still claim to represent the prophets and Jesus *against* the religion of the pious, against the faithlessness of the people? Can it represent the stable center of gravity in society, the taken-for-granted solid base—and still shatter the powers that be with a thunder of judgment, or redeem the world with a message of healing? Evangelicalism's future contribution to Protestantism, to the church, and to the world will depend on the degree that it can extricate itself from the wholly predictable identification with one kind of political force.

Evangelicals regularly name their counterparts in Protestantism "the ecumenicals." While it is unnecessary to buy this idea of a two-party system in Protestantism, it is true that evangelicals do stand apart from ecumenical organizations, chiefly because they feel that a compromise of the Gospel may be called forth from them there, and because they find leaders of the ecumenical churches too much involved in social issues. The ecumenicals have plenty of difficulties facing them, too. They are less predictable and more divided on social issues, paradoxically, than are the anti-social evangelicals. Theologically there is some latitude, though not much more than there is in evangelicalism. The evangelicals have agreed on a certain set of fundamentals and range widely thereafter. The ecumenical spokesmen tend to operate on the basis of emerging consensuses in theology and to have less interest in enforcing detailed agreement.

The Protestant ecumenical movement early institutionalized and has tended to fail to grasp the imagination. The Protestant-Catholic interaction is much more dramatic. Intra-Protestant divisions no longer excite curiosity; attempts to overcome them seem to belong more to the technical expertise of committees than to the broad mass of laity. Involvement in social issues breeds controversy and tends to separate forces within the ecumenical movement; overcoming separation involves compromise which also dims prophetic luster. The breakup of neo-orthodox theologies has not been followed by a new, commonly accepted, formulation, though there have been some creative gropings in the middle of the chaos.

Attempts to re-form the church in the literal sense, to restructure it institutionally, have been more talked about than enacted. For sixty years denominations have been called in question theologically, yet they persist and survive—as the Gallup poll amply demonstrates. The nineteenth century charter for carrying on missionary work is no longer operative, but the ecumenical churches have neither found forms to supplant it nor been willing to cease promoting missions. The educational forms, like the Sunday school, were born at the beginning of the industrial revolution, and few educators still believe in them, but (as this survey also shows), they remain virtually the only culturally recognized and supported institution for Protestant education of the young.

In the period between these polls, the local parish was the most beset of all Protestant institutions. Its overadaptation to the immediate environment remains a liability. While it serves to minister to certain private and familial dimensions of life, it is notoriously incapable of serving as an instrument of mission in a metropolitan or global sense. And people make too many of their important decisions in areas untouched by most existing local parishes. Between 1952 and 1965 a debate raged between those who argued that new forms of ministry and church life would have to emerge and that parishes, like dying underbrush, would have to be killed off in order for the new forms to survive on the one hand—and, on the other, those who argued that parishes would have to undergo very radical restructuring while new forms emerged.

Not much happened. We can still tick off on the fingers of two hands the memorable "new form" experiments, the East Harlem Protestant parishes, the Urban Training Centers, the occasional coffeehouses or ecumenical ventures or mission-and-service programs which were durable enough to stand up under scrutiny as potential models for others. And many parishes have undergone genuine and well-intentioned renewal. But for the most part, as the expectations of people in the Gallup poll demonstrate (e.g., in their contentment with sermons as they are!), most Protestants are content to follow the routinized patterns determined by the old village culture of nineteenth-century Protestantism.

In national life, Protestantism as a cultural force plays a questionable role. Compare it to modern France: In world affairs it is big enough to be pretentious but not significant enough to do more than get in the way. Negro Protestantism, for a short time at least, has found a churchly leadership role. But white Protestantism is as a force poorly organized and not self-reflective enough to have impact. A WASP elite still exists in the executive world (if

we are to believe E. Digby Baltzell[3]), but in what ways distinctive
Protestantism is operative there is unclear. More likely it represents only the old school tie or mere non-Catholicism, non-Juda-
ism in its clubbiness.

Protestantism has no cultural figures comparable to the Catholic
novelists of the 1930's and 1940's or to the alienated urban Jewish
novelists who form the new literary establishment. As a bloc, Protestants may have political "clout," but few of them operate in
congruence with anything like the clarity to which recent Protestant political theoreticians have aspired. Protestantism suffers
from its long identification with American culture. Rarely cred-
ited for positive contributions (to religious freedom, to modern
education), but regularly remembered for its failures (anti-intel-
lectualism, prohibition, Southern support of slavery, participation
in colonialism), it can be taken for granted in the culture. It has
about it little of the exotic character which somehow seems attractive in Catholic and Jewish cells and spokesmen.

Some Protestants have opted for a kind of aristocratic role,
much like that which Greece occupied in Rome's vital days. They
console themselves by reminding themselves of past contributions:
to human freedom, to democracy, to literacy and education, to
benevolent and humanitarian activities, to theology and the development of churchly forms in the past. In the past. . . .

As a personal force, it lives on. The Gallup poll, as we have
reminded ourselves, demonstrates how much it means to people in
the private sphere. Whether it can survive and retain its distinctiveness if it can neither help people in their overall interpretation of the world or in changing it is another question.

10. CURRENT UNREST AND
THE PROTESTANT FUTURE

Given the context described here, it is no wonder that Protestant
theologians have ventured, trying to inspire a revolution in recent
years. This theological and ecclesiastical revolution has taken

[3] *The Protestant Establishment: Aristocracy and Caste in America.* New
York, Random House, 1964.

forms which must appear bewildering to the outsider, even as it would to most of the Protestants who replied to the Gallup interviewers.

The revolution was based on an attack on religion. From Dietrich Bonhoeffer down through Harvey Cox to the celebrated "death of God" theologians, there has been a consistent attack, in the name of Jesus Christ, on human religion. To the neo-orthodox, human religion was a self-devised construct which served to satisfy people spiritually so that their ears were stopped and they could not hear again the judging and justifying Gospel of Jesus Christ. To the post-neo-orthodox radicals, human religion (including the civic and societal and folk religions of America) is by nature and by definition enslaving. It busies people with self-justification and causes them to celebrate idols of nation and success. So the new Protestant theology has been, in intention if not always in practice, utterly Protestant. It has been iconoclastic, stormy, shattering.

The new theology could not only be negative, however. It had to "pick up the pieces." Along the way, its spokesmen sought new alliances. They found them not in religion but in "the secular." They gave a theological interpretation to a trend of recent centuries. In this trend God was used less and less to explain mysteries in the laboratory or to be hauled out on stage to bail humans out of dramas too complicated for their own devices. The very symbol "God" was questioned. What do you mean by God, when you claim him only for our side in every battle, in every war, in every football game? What do you mean by God when you cannot demonstrate his being or his effects? What do you mean by God when you cannot verify the word or when your affirmations cannot be refuted or falsified with counterproofs?

The secular man was seen then as a clean, cool ally to help people purge themselves of false God-talk. God even "dies." The survivor? Remember, we are on Protestant soil: Jesus Christ survived, as author and finisher of faith, as exemplar and enactor of freedom, as agent of desacralization in nature and of secularization in history, as critic of religion, as first fruit of the new creation, first citizen of "the secular city." How he could be repaired to as man without such activity representing idolatry, or as the wholly unique one without resorting to God-talk is something the newer theologians have not yet well worked out. Some of them are be-

ginning to be self-critical about the secularization they have
bought and are beginning to seek new modes of "God-talk."

What does one "do" with the faith and freedom which are a gift
of Jesus Christ? He does not remain in the sanctuary, say the
revolutionaries. The way we have put the world together we have
systematically built in poverty, hunger, hatred. We have made it
possible consistently to overlook human need, and to sanction this
overlooking by joining a church and conforming to its niceties and
nicenesses. But the law of God and the Gospel of Jesus Christ do
not permit such screening out from vision of the breadth and
depth of human need. They do not permit Protestants to resort to
historic formulations about the individual and private character of
salvation in order to prevent original application of churchly resources to the world of need. Meanwhile the Gospel sets out to
transcend the joyless conformities of sanctuary-suburban life, and
to instill in people a real eucharistic spirit.

So run the program and the scenario of the new theology, form-
seeking, and social-activist Protestant leaders. Most of them would
have ambivalent attitudes to what is revealed by polls like these.
More than ambivalent; I surmise that they would scorn most of it.
They would mistrust that 97 percent figure representing belief in
God; they would not be moved by the nominal orthodoxy of
people who give no indication of curiosity about the meaning of
historic Christian symbols. They would take little comfort from
the expressions against clerical involvement in politics, but they
would not be surprised: The new theology has not been designed
as a crowd pleaser.

On the other hand, something should be said for the astonishing
religiousness of the American people. From the viewpoint of theological justification, it may be scorned. But could it be that the
secular-minded theologians have underestimated certain positive
features in human religion? Even more: Have they underestimated the complexity of resuming theological conversation with
wholly secular man? When secular man appears, and when with
utter logical and psychological resources he sustains a nonreligious
approach to life, how can one bring "a biblical perspective" to
bear on that life? The same religion which is a problem for the
Gospel can be pierced and can become a possibility for it. "Whom
you ignorantly worship, him I declare unto you," has been a possibility in the past.

The Gallup polls seem to tell us that flows in American religion are not as rich, nor the ebbs so far receding as we believed them to be. The revivals are not so profound nor the revolutions so extensive as journalists find them to be, or as many of us regard them to be intuitively. We are not as Christian a people as our Christian apologists claim, nor so secular as our prophets charge or our newer theologians want us to be. As a nation, we grope—out of habit, with ambiguity, without urgency, lacking direction, not easily swayed en masse. Whatever else we find ourselves to be, we are at this point incapable of expressing ourselves wholly nonreligiously.

The Protestants of the future would have to seek power and ingenuity to pierce this religion and rescue the religionists for what they regard to be higher human values and for the love and service of God. If the Gallup polls are accurate, such Protestantism does not lack raw materials, nominal members, and reasonably warm bodies for its movement. It is less sure where it wants to move. But if it moves, it moves by a word, and it has to be both reviving as well as revolutionary. As an early great spokesman for Protestantism, Martin Luther, put it: "The most permanent fate of God's word is that for its sake the world is put into uproar. For the sermon of God comes in order to change and revive the whole earth to the extent that it reaches it."[1]

[1] Paraphrased by Hannah Arendt, *On Revolution*. New York, Viking, 1963, p. 288.

PART TWO

by
Stuart E. Rosenberg

1. THE CATHOLIC DIGEST SURVEY

Some are certain that religion in America is in eclipse, the hapless victim of an overwhelmingly secular environment. Others, defenders of the faith, sensing the threat of such possibilities, rush out to survey the field, and, returning with a sigh of relief, manage to report that "99 percent of you and your neighbors believe in God!"

Meanwhile, at the command posts of American institutional religion, there is a climate of urgency, too; informed, often sophisticated, but agonized, nonetheless. And it runs a wide gamut from ecumenical interest to theological reconstruction, from a new awareness of religious pluralism to a serious concern with a sociological analysis of the American religious communities.

Through all of this, and largely oblivious, the "average American" continues to attend or not to attend church or synagogue, to treat his religious life like almost any other minor concern—family, golf, or the United Appeal—and to worry precious little about the possible discrepancies between what he believes and what he practices. Inevitably, old and new myths, the facile bromides of some, the sincere questing of others, the widespread superficial indifference, are all fused and mixed in the caldron of social anxieties and communal change. The pattern is not clear, which makes it easier for the oversimplifiers to get a good hearing.

If all this is so, what kind of an investigation and with what major objectives may one intelligently undertake to measure the American religion of our time? If our sketch of the representative American mirrors the reality, an "average" study of the "average American" would indeed be hinged to a series of conventional questions intended to elicit conventional, uncomplicated answers.

Moreover, since all investigations are initiated by some special concern and are directed from a specific posture, any research into religious life conducted on behalf of a Catholic institution must, perforce, rely heavily on Catholic definitions and the religious usages of the church.

Beneath its conventionality, America conceals a great variety of social modes and styles. Despite the apparent aspiration for consensus, there are real differences, differences which are the result of particularistic traditions, ethnic styles, conflicting and even antagonistic value systems, and of contending and rival world views.

How does the serious student of religion manage to reflect all of this if his research is essentially geared to statistical analysis? What is more: How are the real differences, hidden under the apparent consensus, given their due significance in this survey of American religion whose assumption often seems to be little more than "The family that prays together stays together!" C. Wright Mills has put it tellingly: "In the cross-section moment . . . there may be so many common denominators of belief, value, institutional form, that no matter how detailed and precise our study, we will not find truly significant differences among the people and institutions at this one moment in this one society. In fact, the one-time and one-locale studies often assume or imply a homogeneity which, if true, very much needs to be taken as a problem. It cannot fruitfully be reduced . . . to a problem of sampling procedure. . . ."[1]

That this particular study compares two different times and deals with several locales does not really help matters. It sets down the November, 1965, results of a very small survey sample of 2,783 persons (we are asked to project, after all, in at least two critical categories, from exceedingly slight numbers—from some 261,602 young people aged 18–24, and from a handful of 75,141 Jews) beside those of an equally anemic 1952 sample, and this, too, can hardly satisfy critical prerequisites for intelligent comparison. Considering the small size of the sample in order for any real pattern to emerge significantly, the respondents would have had to be the same in both of the years studied—in 1952 and 1965. For such questions as "Do you believe in God?" definitive conclusions

[1] *The Sociological Imagination.* New York, Oxford University Press, 1959, p. 147.

become highly problematical. To regard the drop among Jews who answered that they were absolutely certain there is a God (from 70 percent in 1952 to 39 percent in 1965) as reflecting anything other than what was "found" among the Jews of the new sample would be patent exaggeration and folly. Unfortunately, some observers have already seen fit to do just this and have made the bold assertion that "the most dramatic change has occurred among the Jewish people—14 percent of them have ceased to believe in God in thirteen years. This change is simply astounding. We can assign no reasons, but reasons should be sought, because if this process continues in 1980, 17 percent will be atheists and 13 percent will not know, making a third of the Jewish people unbelievers. . . ."[2] But this is wildly extravagant and misleading. I am not here arguing only against the statistical validity of the data; I am questioning inferences and suppositions made by an adaptation of untested and unspecific generalizations of irrelevant statistical data! C. Wright Mills has already described such statistical sleight of hand: "These logical tricks are used to give apparent structural and historical and psychological meaning to studies which by their style of abstraction have eliminated such meanings."[3] The proper use of a statistical survey is vitiated from the start, when such "tricks" are allowed to become identified with "truth."

"The study," we have been informed, "proposes to measure the religious beliefs and practices of American adults . . . to determine, if any, what changes have come about since a comparable study in 1952." But if we are only interested in the "measure," our compulsive need to quantify is bound to produce shallow, misleading, even deceptive results when it tackles the complexities of religious meaning, theological attitudes, and personal religious identity in the context of rapid social change, and when it does so with tools unsuited for the task. We will need a survey instrument (if surveys about religion are what we think we need) which sensitively asks significant questions, leaving alternatives to the respondents. Not: "When are your religious feelings strongest, when everything is going well or when things get rough?" (What are religious feelings anyway?) but rather, "In what ways do you live as a religious

---

[2] *Catholic Digest,* 1966.
[3] Mills, *op. cit.,* p. 71.

person?" Though answers to such a question are not likely to fit
into predetermined tables and convenient punch cards, nevertheless, with such questions, we will come much closer to "surveying"
religious attitudes and the meaningful practice of religion. *We
would have, then, to put the same question to the same person
after a significant time has elapsed.* (A significant time lapse is one
which embraces a crucial period for the individual himself.) For
example, when a student has finished his education, married, and
has young children; the workingman during his productive years
and after his retirement; or any similar time lapse which spans a
pivotal period of change in an individual's life. Only then can we
talk about real change and the relationship between the course of
an individual's life and the shaping of his own religious attitudes.

What is more: We cannot ignore historical and biographical
contexts and hope to understand the implications of changing attitudes in a changing world. The eighteen-year-old of 1965 is not
the eighteen-year-old of 1952 despite the built-in assumptions of
the survey. The only way a real trend could be established would
be to follow through on the original sample of young people. If a
sizable drop in the percentage of those professing positive religious
beliefs were then to emerge, it would be possible, through careful
questioning, to arrive at some idea of what had influenced the
change in attitude. The young people interviewed in 1965, however, represent a new sample, shaped by other sets of experiences
and formed by new social and religious milieus.

To the question, "Do you think that young people today have as
strong a sense of right and wrong as they did, say, fifty years ago?"
those 18–24-year-olds who answered Yes show a sharp decline,
from 55 percent in 1952 to 43 percent in 1965. We are on dangerous ground, however, if, from this, we infer any change or trend
among our youth. After all, youth derives its self-image from the
cues broadcast by society at large. Young people give us what we
seem to expect. If we describe them as rebellious, they will oblige
us and appear as rebels. Furthermore, they have equal access to all
of the public and private adult uncertainties about war, about
peace, about what makes a good life, and certainly they are privy
to the ambivalence and confusion concerning the role of religion
in our lives.

The pollsters should be forewarned: They are working here

with a very blunt instrument on a very delicate and subtle material—the ethical attitudes of diverse groups in the intricate realm of religious values and judgments. Far from revealing truth, conventional questions elicit conventional answers and conventional thoughts which only serve to mask the inner feelings. For we know ultimately very little about the stuff of private attitudes, except what the individual is able to tell us himself. Social scientists are painfully aware of the fact that there is no sure way of evaluating a man's (let alone a group's) self-report of measuring his demonstrable public attitudes against his true, private beliefs. Indeed, there is great intensity and variety of reaction to varying symbols signifying different values for different groups. Nor is there any objective device available which can measure intensity of reaction. All we can do is to ask subjects how strongly they believe a given opinion. Lee J. Crombach says, "Attitude tests have been severely criticized because they have been used without their validity having been established. The failure to demonstrate that attitudes are valid measures of belief is in part due to the difficulty of finding criteria."[4]

It is particularly difficult to establish criteria in a survey dealing with religion. The Catholic definition of religion lays stress on membership in a divine institution, the Church, and the personal acceptance of clearly enumerated dogmas. It would be wrong, of course, to define religion in any terms other than those in which Catholics themselves define it, in a survey directed only to Catholics. Our survey, however, sets out to gauge the religious beliefs, practices, and attitudes of Protestants and Jews, as well. In addition to the Catholic religious heritage, America has also produced many Protestant traditions, and Protestant definitions of religion comprise not one convention, but many. North and South, in the United States, have even produced antagonistic theologies within the same Protestant denomination! What then of the Jewish convention, which is no less complex, varied, and conditioned by more ancient factors? If our survey were so constructed (and it is not!) to explore all these subtleties, it would still only do so in sociological terms. We would still be left with the key question: Have we found out anything significant about religious attitudes and beliefs? Apart from its institutional structures and policies,

[4] *Essentials of Psychological Testing.* New York, Harper & Row, 1960, p. 21.

the religious life is based primarily upon the inner thought of man—and it is thus primarily a psychological rather than a sociological phenomenon.

Ultimately, one is led back to the question of meaning: What do the questions mean and what do the people's answers mean? To illustrate (Question 12a): "Do you believe the Bible is really the revealed word of God; or do you think it is only a great piece of literature?" Words such as "really," "revealed," and "only" are weighted with subtle bias and with either-or implication. In this statement, as the question is worded, "a great piece of literature" is clearly on a less exalted level than "the revealed word of God." It also leaves no room for subtle variations that conform to more liberal biblical theologies. Of the total of twenty-four words in the question, five are words of value judgment—"really," "revealed," "only," "great," "piece." Indeed, they are the most pivotal words in the question. Basically this is a dead-end kind of question, forcing an answer in terms that may be religiously irrelevant to many.

Similarly: "Do you think your soul will live on after death?" What does the questioner mean by the word "soul," and what do the different respondents understand? What specific and what varied resonances does the concept have for Protestants, Catholics, and Jews?

Still more, the 2 percent of Jews in 1965 and the 8 percent in 1952 who said they believed in the Holy Trinity either misunderstood the question, had no idea of what the Trinity is, or weren't Jews!

What can one say about this question (16b): "Which do you think you should be most serious about—trying to live comfortably, or preparing for a life after death?" Again, this question leads directly to a dead end because of its black-and-white alternatives. "To live comfortably" has distinctly materialistic implications. The question offers no subtle possibilities, no recognition of lives devoted to the pursuit of wisdom, to the betterment of society, to the arts, to the sciences. A young person living in squalor in Africa or South America on a Peace Corps assignment is hardly devoting his life to living comfortably. But he may also not be preparing for his life after death!

In this context, it is interesting to note that no Jews felt that they could be serious about preparing for life after death despite the fact that 17 percent expressed the belief that their souls would live on after them. In this light, what can it mean when 86 percent of the Jewish respondents feel that one should be most serious about trying to live comfortably? Are Jews hedonists? Are they unmindful of spiritual values and concerned only with their standard of living? Or did they respond to this question out of a background that stems from another system of values? And is this not one of the obvious difficulties in trying to ask Catholics, Protestants, and Jews questions that "sound" differently when heard against the rhythm of other civilizations?

In our eagerness to find consensus we tend to lump together the diverse strands of Western culture under a facile rubric we call the "Judeo-Christian ethic." This is a convenient canopy phrase and often enough adequately describes what we are talking about. But there are many occasions when the differences shaped by the specific history of a given group are the most salient and crucial facts. "Social science deals with problems of biography, of history, and of their intersections within social structures . . . The problems of our time—which now include the problem of man's very nature—cannot be stated adequately without consistent practice of the view that history is the shank of social study, and recognition of the need to develop further a psychology of man that is sociologically grounded and historically relevant. Without use of history and without a historical sense of psychological matters, the social scientist cannot adequately state the kinds of problems that ought now to be the orienting points of his studies."[5] Only in this spirit can one understand the reasons behind the Jewish response to the question of living in comfort now rather than getting prepared for life after death. An adequate awareness of Jewish history and religious traditions and the ways in which these differ from those of the Catholics and the Protestants are a prior need to an understanding in depth, of what the so-called this-worldly orientation of the Jews implies. We will turn to some of this now. If to embrace this world, here and now, as a congenial abode for man and society, is to be a secularist, then Jews have been secularists since the time of Abraham, and the Hebrew Bible remains a faithful record of ancient "Jewish secularity."

[5] Mills, *op. cit.*, p. 143.

2. RELIGIOUS TRENDS AMONG JEWS

The semantic problem presented by the concept *religion* is not completely overcome by breaking it down into questions about belief in God, in afterlife, heaven, hell, and the like. To some, religion means church or synagogue membership, to others, a firm belief in an anthropomorphic God, to still others, a vague belief in an undefined deity; there are those for whom religion consists of a clear set of dogmas and those for whom it implies a certain way of life. There is an old Hasidic tale about a Jew who came to his rabbi in great despair because he claimed to have lost his faith. The rabbi counseled him to go home and continue to live as if he had not lost his faith, to carry out all the commandments, and that, in good time, his faith would return. Some months later the Jew came back. He had followed the rabbi's advice and still his faith had not returned. The rabbi gave him the same counsel again. Months later the Jew returned in despair, once more. The rabbi repeated his prescription. "But what," asked the Jew, "if my faith never returns?" "Never mind," answered the rabbi. "At least you will have lived a good life and be sure to go to heaven."

The story illustrates the inherent difficulties in quantifying theological matters, or using statistical methodology to reflect the nature of religious commitment. There are surely many who, like the Jew in the tale, live religiously oriented lives without orthodox beliefs of any kind, and others who fully believe in a living God yet shy away from any ecclesiastical institutional commitment. Moreover, in between these extremes, there are surely many and varied nuances of religious meaning.

Nevertheless, despite these and other limitations, some of the survey's findings may be regarded as interesting and even significant.

To begin with, we should examine some of the changes that took place from 1952 to 1965. Regarding those questions that deal with religious beliefs, we find modest changes among Protestants and Catholics, more decisive ones among Jews, and, in many cases, important changes among young people. The overall percentage of those professing an absolute belief in God has declined from 87 percent in 1952 to 81 percent in 1965. The drop is most marked among Jews and youth; the former moving from 70 percent to 39

percent and the latter from 87 percent to 71 percent. A similar
drift is evident in the response to the concept of God "as a loving
Father." A drop of 6 percent in the overall total is reflected in all
the groups, again most markedly among Jews and youth. The responses to questions about heaven and hell appear to indicate the
same kind of diminution of the "conventional" expressions of belief as do the statistics dealing with attitudes to divorce as sin.

The statistics for all three religions seemingly indicate a moving
away from literal notions of traditional theological concepts. We
are living in an age of rapid change—social, political, technologi-
cal. The last five decades have seen an explosion of knowledge
greater than has occurred in the two thousand years before. The
pace, if anything, is accelerating even more today. Perhaps half of
the subjects studied in school today are likely to be outdated by
the time the students are ready to take their place in the world.

The jet age has nevertheless produced serious dislocations.
Winston Churchill once described the problem when asked about
his jet flight across the Atlantic: "My body is here," he said, "but
the rest of me is still sailing across the ocean on a steamship."
The extraordinary rate of change of our world presents challenges
to every area of life, and we are not always ready with answers that
reflect our considered opinion or our thoughtful responses. We
just have not had enough time to think them through. A world
which has experienced the systematic destruction wrought by
Nazism as the nadir of man's humanity now reaches toward a
zenith—the conquest of outer space for peaceful purposes. In such
a world as this, values handed down to us from past ages are inevitably being reexamined. It is no accident that in these very years
we have witnessed apposite and conflicting things: the Ecumenical
Council of the Catholics, the emergence of the "Death of God"
theology, the rewriting of Sunday-school texts, and the recasting of
large bodies of traditional theological ideas which had once been
facilely accepted at face value.

Any discussion of theological change must be seen in this context. Movement away from traditional concepts such as heaven
and hell cannot be studied in a social vacuum. Perhaps one is
correct in saying that considering our unstable world, with its
numbing changes, it is nothing less than remarkable that so many
of the old beliefs and religious values still hold up at all!

Nowhere else is the trend away from a supernatural religious belief as marked as among Jews. In the 1965 survey

it is as starkly apparent as it was already characteristic of those Jews studied in 1952. There are those who will surely find the statistics astounding—only 39 percent of the Jews studied believe with absolute certainty in God; only 17 percent believe the Bible is the revealed word of God; a similar small percentage believes that their souls will live on after death; 6 percent do believe there is a heaven, while a resounding 83 percent do not believe in an afterlife, and 97 percent do not believe in the existence of hell. Further, 86 percent of the Jews questioned feel that they should be most serious about living comfortably. None sees any meaning in devoting himself to preparations for life after death.

If reasons should be sought to explain the apparent trend of such "unbelief" among contemporary American Jews, they will not be found within the theological frame of reference or the general religious categories set out by the *Catholic Digest* survey. Indeed, had we posed similar questions, in this way, to pious Jews living a hundred years ago in Europe, or to Maimonides and his rabbi-philosopher colleagues many centuries ago in Spain, we would likely have run into the same Jewish heterodoxy, the same degree of skepticism, the earthbound religious convictions that one's life is with people on this earth, here and now.

Let us try (Question 14b): "Do you think there is a heaven, where people who have led good lives are eternally rewarded?" Answer: "If I love God, what need have I of the reward of the world to come?"[1]

(Question 13a): "Do you pray to God? How many times . . . ?" Answer: "God said to Moses: My children are in trouble, the sea shuts them off on one side, the enemy pursues them on the other, and you stand and make long prayers. And God said, There is a time to lengthen prayer and a time to shorten it."[2]

(Question 10c): "How do you think of God—as a loving Father who looks after us . . . ?" Answer: "He is not a magnitude that any quality resulting from quantity as such could be possessed by Him. He is not an animate being that he should have a certain disposition of the soul or . . . certain properties as meekness, modesty etc."[3] Or as a latter-day Hasid, a descendant of generations of

---

[1] Israel ben Eliezer (Baal Shem-Tob, c. 1700–1760), the founder of Hasidism in Poland.

[2] Rabbi Eliezer ben Jacob, 1st century C.E. (A.D.)

[3] Maimonides, 1135–1204.

Hasidic rabbis, has put it: "The surest way of misunderstanding revelation is to take it literally, to image that God spoke to the prophet on a long-distance telephone. Yet most of us succumb to such fancy, forgetting that the cardinal sin in thinking about ultimate issues is *literalmindedness*. . . . God is called Father, but he who takes this name physiologically distorts the meaning of God."[4]

Enough, then, for us to be reminded that for Jews, unlike Christians, questions of dogma were never ultimate. What mattered most for Jews, where religious practice was taken for granted and where forms underwent continuing adaptation to new intellectual circumstances and social situations, was a man's personal commitment to a God who demanded private response and communal action in the ethical realms of human achievement. Synagogue membership shows an upward trend of from 50 percent to 62 percent in 1965.[5] Additionally, in all questions dealing with intermarriage, Jews are the only group increasingly opposed (Questions 17, 32c, 40c, 48c). How are we to interpret these statistics, especially when viewed alongside those which, in the terms set out by the makers of the survey, seem to indicate an alarming lack of religious belief among Jews? Can we make the facile assumption that Jews are joining synagogues in order to "belong," to be like everybody else? But if, as some believe, Jews join synagogues largely as an expression of conformity to the American norm, why then do they stand apart from the others and so clearly? In any case, we may conclude American Jews are, increasingly, determined to retain their Jewish identity, not merely to join Jewish institutions in the American way. What Jews understand by "Jewish identity" is, unfortunately, not to be determined by the results of this survey.

To find out something about what motivates Jews to join syna-

[4] Abraham Joshua Heschel, *God in Search of Man: A Philosophy of Judaism*. New York, Farrar, Straus, 1955, pp. 178–179.

[5] On the fallibility of poll-taking techniques it is worth noting that George Gallup's American Institute of Public Opinion showed in 1965 a new low of 44 percent in overall church and synagogue attendance. This contradicts the *Catholic Digest* survey, which finds the following increases: Catholics from 82 percent to 87 percent, Protestants from 58 percent to 67 percent, and Jews from 44 percent to 61 percent. When the discrepancies were brought to Dr. Gallup's attention, he conceded that while his audit showed a decline in overall church attendance during the past ten years, synagogue attendance during this period did, in fact, increase!

gogues, to plumb their ardent need—whatever it may mean "to remain Jewish"—to analyze their changing commitments to Jewish values and to Judaism as a way of life and as a religion would require an altogether different survey.

In such a survey, synagogue membership or attendance in itself would be given much less importance than those questions which would attempt to explore critically what is the content and the nature of faith, of Jewish ethical values, and the existential dimensions of Jewish identity and belonging. The practice of Judaism never was, and is not even today, contained within the synagogue. The most fundamental acting out of Jewish tradition is in the home—the Sabbath is first welcomed at home; the Passover Seder is celebrated in the home; the Purim seudah is enjoyed at home; the Sukkah hut is built onto the home. Indeed much of the Jewish religion revolves, not around the synagogue, but around the family axis, in its domestic setting. Thus, we would have different questions to ask. Our query would not be: "Do you think children should be raised as church members, or do you think they should be free of formal religion until they are old enough to make up their own minds?"

Rather, we would ask questions such as these: "What Jewish values do you hope to transmit to your children?" "To what extent are life choices, your sense of right and wrong, your value judgments, shaped by your Jewishness?" "Are there conflicts between the values of your Judaism and those of society at large?" "Will your children find any conflict in the Jewish values you transmit to them and the values of society at large?" "How will you handle the conflict?" "How will you teach them to handle it?"

In another survey of our choosing, Jews would not be asked: "Do you ever pray to God?" but rather, "Which of the Jewish holidays do you celebrate?" "How do you celebrate them—at home and in the synagogue?" "Which holidays have the most meaning for you and your family, and why?" "How would you describe yourself—regarding Jewish religious practice—totally observant, partly observant, selectively observant, completely and totally unobservant?" "Do you feel that your observance, as it is, is a result of (a) a belief that a good Jew must obey all the commandments of religious law, or (b) a belief that the commandments are binding but only in varying degrees, or (c) a belief that some observances are worthwhile and others not, or (d) a conviction that the observance of religious law is not central to your Jewishness, or (e) a belief that the Jewish traditions are no longer valid and meaningful?"

Questions such as these are more salient and certainly more interesting an attempt to get at a broader range and wider dimensions of Jewish identity and Jewish self-understanding. To arrive at a wiser knowledge of the American Jew, and to deal with him in greater depth, it would be essential to try to determine how Jewishness is related to the daily habit of the respondents. It would be most important to determine how one's Jewishness is integrated into a total life style—interpersonal relations, conduct in business or profession, choice of recreation and entertainment, child rearing, marriage, response to political and international affairs, and so on.

In a most sensitive area, this survey leaves much that is unanswered. The overwhelming majority of Jews come out decidedly against intermarriage. The figures themselves are interesting, but they do not answer important questions. Why do American Jews take a stand against intermarriage? Are their reasons religious, cultural, or primarily ethnic, or some combination of all three? Is the American Jew's position on intermarriage based on the desire to see Judaism survive? If so, in what way does he want to see it survive? Is his position on intermarriage in any way informed by what happened in Germany in the 1930's and 1940's? Or by an unconscious, inchoate, amorphous fear of the gentile as a potential anti-Semite? Only questions along these lines could begin to make meaningful what is, at this point, an interesting statistic, but little more. Alas, when we finally alight upon something most significant, the survey itself sheds little light.

3. THE AGE OF REASON IN JEWISH HISTORY

"The American Jew," writes Martin E. Marty, "is better off in ripely pluralistic America than he was in Protestant, or would be Protestant-Catholic, America. In many instances he will ally with the avowedly secular, for good reasons."[1] This is clearly borne out in the survey, and the "good reasons" of which Martin E.

[1] *Religion and Social Conflict*, p. 188.

Marty speaks are to be found embedded in Jewish history. The Age of Reason which dawned in Europe in the eighteenth century brought in its wake a host of political and social changes which affected the whole texture of life. The scientific empiricism then set into motion has led, in a direct line, to nuclear fission and space rockets to the moon. For the Jews of western Europe the Age of Reason at last opened the door to the wider world. The enlightenment of the new age helped break down the barriers of medieval authoritarianism, and challenged the church-state-divine-right-of-kings axis which had consigned Jews to the ghettos to live as barely tolerated outsiders.

The hallmark of the Age of Reason was the secularization of learning. Revelation and Scriptures were no longer the key to understanding the universe. Over against tradition as authority, reason was exalted as the new revelation. The rationalists were firmly convinced that progress would inevitably follow the fullest development of reason. They were incurable optimists. By subjecting all human institutions to the laws of reason, they were sure they could ultimately achieve the perfect world. "Within the context of the intellectual traditions and social structure of the modern West, the Age of Reason represented a movement for a more open society—the pursuit of individual happiness, the security of individual liberties, constitutionalism, tolerance, cosmopolitanism, the unfettering of thought and a society of free individuals based on law."[2] The eighteenth century saw the privileges of the nobility and the clergy fall before the rising authority of the nation-state with its strong central government. The closed, self-contained Jewish community in the West also crumbled and finally disappeared in its medieval form on September 28, 1791, when the French General Assembly extended equal citizenship to the Jews of France.

Is it any wonder, then, that the Jews of western Europe eagerly embraced the new world and enthroned its principal deity, rationalism, as God? It seemed to them to be an eminently fair exchange: They traded exclusiveness, and the ethnic-national components of Judaism, for keys offering them entry to the modern world, as men among men. Soon, they set about modernizing and

[2] Louis Snyder, *The Age of Reason,* Anvil ed. Princeton, New Jersey, D. Van Nostrand, Inc., 1955, p. 14.

westernizing their ancient traditions, to bring them into line with the spirit of the times. Their watchwords were reason and rationalism. Above all, these early reformers were anxious to prove that to be a Jew was no hindrance to being a good, loyal, and devoted citizen.

In western Europe, by the middle of the nineteenth century, many Jews were already located in the rising middle class, and like all other members of that group, they were much at home in the bourgeois manner and style of life. They not only spoke the same language as their middle-class neighbors, but they also adopted their mentality and cultural outlook. The business interests of the rising middle class were linked to a political attitude that identified the whole nation with the one state. Historically, in western Europe, the economic nationalism of the middle class served as a mighty engine in feeding power to the new states forming under the flag of a single political nationalism.

These changed economic and political conditions were reflected in the new attitudes of many western rabbis toward the scientific and rationalistic philosophies of the day. Instead of maintaining a posture of defensiveness, they were willing to erect intellectual bridges to span Jewish religious thought and the new knowledge. This rabbinical openness not only permitted the spirit of modernism to be absorbed into the religious life of some of these communities, but it also had a most significant result: Since rationalism was acceptable to these religious leaders, it could not easily be used as an antireligious weapon. Instead, the mid-nineteenth century in western Europe saw the beginning of efforts to reform Judaism in terms of the new philosophies, rather than attempts to attack it on atheistic, irreligious grounds.

In eastern Europe, however, the situation was entirely different. Far from becoming an ally of religion, there the Enlightenment forged Jewish movements new to their historical experience—nationalist movements indifferent to religious sanctions, and even radical, antireligious, movements. There were several basic reasons for this interesting development, and, ironically, virtually all were in some way related to the iron grip held by traditional religion over all of Jewish life. For almost a thousand years in eastern Europe, the authority of rabbinical interpretation went unchallenged in a fenced-in environment made even stronger by its social and cultural isolation.

In contrast to the new, open society in the West, eastern Europe still remained in the grip of the older medieval universalism. Jews in those countries lived in authoritarian, closed societies, with wide uniformity of faith, and close identification of church and state. When glimmers of Enlightenment began to reach into the darkness of eastern Europe in the last years of the nineteenth century, the Jews of those lands turned as eagerly to welcome it as had their brothers in the West. By the end of the nineteenth century, a new Yiddish and Hebrew secular literature had begun to flower, various Socialist and Zionist ideologies had spread through the Jewish towns and villages of eastern Europe, and the masses of Jews yearned to be liberated from czarist thralldom.

In America, both the Jews from the West, who had come earlier, and the Jews from the East, who came in overwhelming numbers between 1881 and 1925, found the kind of open society which the Enlightenment had promised—one built on the precepts of reason, natural law, rational and humanitarian regard for fellow man. For the United States, in many ways, is the child of the Age of Reason. Of the many millions of immigrants who came to these shores, none, with the possible exception of the Irish, came quite as much on the run as the Jews of eastern Europe. For no other group was the decision to come to the New World as much a matter of life and death as for the Jews escaping from pogroms, from crushing poverty, from the kind of precarious existence which could bring blood-libel accusations one day and laws designed to confiscate their meager fortunes the next, with wholesale violence to their communities following that.

It is well to remember this history. Any analysis dealing with Jewish attitudes to religion today must take into account the profound stake of Jews in a rationalist, demythologized world, a world of law, order, and reasonable structures, a world where the medieval power of the church has been stripped by the humanist, democratic power of the modern state. In recent years this has been abundantly evident by the degree of activity generated by Jewish groups to uphold the constitutional separation of church and state, and by the heavy Jewish involvement in the civil-rights movement.

America is a pluralistic society. In the early days of mass immigration, its pluralism inevitably took the shape of ethnic diversity. Those were the days when the theorists of the Melting Pot were

solidly ranged against the proponents of "cultural pluralism."
Today, however, it is evident that neither of these positions are
adequate to explain the real dimensions of the American social
experience. In a sense, there are no winners or losers; something
very new has emerged which could not have been foreseen. In a
phrase popularized by Will Herberg, what we now have can be
more aptly denominated as a Triple Melting Pot containing the
three religious communities—Protestant, Catholic, and Jewish.
Within this Triple Pot the older idea of Cultural Pluralism survives in the new guise of Religious Pluralism. But what is frequently forgotten is that there is yet a fourth "pot," one that turns
out to be the catalyst for the other three—and this is the American
democratic, humanist, secularist tradition. In a fundamental sense,
the three religious groups can be seen as constituting either
coequal minorities or coequal majorities, each operating on the
stage set by the fourth "religion"—American democracy. "The
spokesmen of the 'Religion of Democracy' school are reaching for
and appropriating an authentic parcel of the American past. They
are more accurate in their reading of the founding fathers than are
the unthinking Christians who try to make Protestants out of
them and who try to theologize all the basic documents of our
national history on Christian lines. They are taking aspects of a
consensus which the 'three great faiths' support and elevating
them to ultimacy."[3]

Group conflict in American life today takes the shape of religious rather than ethnic tensions. The religious nature of American pluralism, Herberg has suggested, "helps define the underly-
ing pattern of American life, within which emerge the so-called
'intergroup' problems that confront us today in such a variety of
shapes and forms."

However, neither the shape nor the quality of these tensions
emerges from the data of the survey before us. Rather, they leave
us with the feeling that all's rather well in America between Protestants, Catholics, and Jews—and surely as between Protestants and
Catholics. Between the two Christian groups a general easing of
tensions and suspicions appears to emerge. There is no doubt, for
example, that the election of John Kennedy, the first non-Protes-

[3] Martin E. Marty, *The New Shape of American Religion*. New York,
Harper, 1959, pp. 84–85.

tant President of the United States, was a significant breakthrough. This is resoundingly reflected in the 23 percent increase
among Protestants who would just as soon vote for a Catholic for
President as for a Protestant. The symbolic shattering of the image
of a Protestant monolithic power structure in 1960 is echoed in
the responses to a whole series of questions. True, not all the
changes in attitude are dramatic, but a definite trend emerges of a
growing entente between the two Christian groups. For example,
in 1965, only 28 percent (compared with 40 percent in 1952) of
the Protestants felt that Catholics "stick together too much." Similarly, there has been an 11 percent decrease in the number of
Protestants who believe that Catholics are trying to gain too much
power in the United States. There has been a 5 percent increase,
to 37 percent, in the number of Protestants who would
be willing to see a member of their family marry a Catholic. Protestants, the statistical evidence indicates, are more accepting than
ever before of Catholics. In such areas as influence on the press,
misusing positions of prominence to their own advantage, proselytizing, fairness in business, the evidence points to a growing
sense of Protestant ease with their Catholic compatriots.

In 1952, the Jews, according to the statistics in the survey, generally followed the pattern of the Protestant majority in their attitudes toward Catholics. This is not unexpected, for, as a minority
group, Jews would naturally take their cues from the dominant
culture. However, Catholics and Jews, in sharing the same kind of
immigrant experience, often in close proximity, could not help
but develop a mutual tolerance and sympathy, not infrequently
seeing themselves ranged together against the powerful Protestant
establishment.

In all, the 1952 survey indicated that, where there was a diver-
gence by Jews from Protestants in their attitudes to Catholics, it
was on the side of greater tolerance and acceptance.[4] One would
have expected to find the same pattern repeated in 1956. It is not,

[4] In 1952, a much lower percentage of Jews than Protestants felt that
members of their group had ill feeling toward Catholics; 80 percent of the
Jews, as compared to 70 percent of the Protestants, saw Catholics as being
equally honest in holding public office as themselves; 17 percent more Jews
than Protestants were willing to vote for a Catholic as President, and
5 percent less Jews than Protestants thought that Catholics were trying to
get too much power.

and here we come upon an important change. Even a cursory glance through the statistical material on intergroup relations recorded in the survey draws our attention to a startling reversal in some areas. The percentage of Jews who feel that members of their religious group harbor ill feeling toward Catholics has doubled in the intervening thirteen years—from 15 percent to 30 percent. There is a 14 percent increase in the number of Jews who feel that Catholics look down on them; in 1965, 10 percent more Jews believed that Catholics did not respect the religious beliefs of others; 6 percent more than in 1952 thought that Catholics would discriminate against them in employment; and 8 percent more Jews than before see Catholics as trying too hard to get people to join their church. Similarly, there has been an increase of 7 percent in the number of Jews who think that Catholics are "trying to influence the press"; 12 percent more Jews now feel Catholic magazines and newspapers are not fair to their religious beliefs.

In the entire run of such questions, Protestants responded more positively, in the direction of greater openness and accommodation, than did the Jews. What has happened? It would be quick and dangerous to assume that the Jews of America have, in the years between 1952 and 1965, suddenly become biased, and intolerant of Catholics. A closer look at the data reveals that only in certain areas has there been a change for the worse. In others, the Jew is as much a leader in displaying a positive stance toward Catholics as he was in 1952. For example, 98 percent of the Jews see Catholics as being as loyal to their country as themselves. This is a rise of 8 percent from 1952 and compares with 80 percent of Protestants who express this view (no change from 1952). Five percent more Jews in 1965 feel that Catholics are fair in business, the total being 15 percent above that of Protestants. There is no change in the number (80 percent) who say that Catholics are as honest as they in public office, but this total is also 8 percent higher than the Protestant number (72 percent) who hold this view. More Jews than Protestants are prepared to vote for a Catholic as President: 27 percent more than in 1952—still more than the Protestant increase of 23 percent over 1952, and considerably higher in total (86 percent to 65 percent). The vast majority of Jews still would be quite happy to have Catholics for neighbors (89 percent).

The apparent inconsistency between these two groups of statis-

tics needs explaining. Clearly, in the fundamental areas relating to
social, political, economic, and democratic values Jews continue to
be on the liberal side—progressive, open-minded, and unanxious.
They see Catholics as good citizens, loyal Americans, fair busi-
nessmen, honest public servants, and desirable neighbors. In contrast to all of this, they feel that Catholics look down upon them,
try too hard to convert them, discriminate against them, do not
respect their religious beliefs, and have too much influence on the
press. What has changed, then, is not the Jews' acceptance of
Catholics but their own self-assurance vis-à-vis the Catholic group.
The survey clearly indicates a growing tension, insecurity, anxiety,
even fearfulness, on the part of Jews about the way in which Catholics see and understand them.

Nothing of this is reflected in the attitudes toward Jews expressed by Catholics in this survey. On the contrary, as a group,
Catholics appear to be participating in the overall expansiveness
and opening up of American society. In many cases their attitudes
to Jews is far more liberal than that of the Protestants: 12 percent
more Catholics in 1965 than in 1952 say that Jews are honest politicians, an increase 6 percent higher than the Protestant increase,
with the 1965 total being 19 percent higher than the Protestant
total. Eighty-three percent of the Catholics (an increase of 26 percent over 1952) would vote for a Jew as President, as compared
with 51 percent of the Protestants. Catholics do not see themselves as hostile to Jews as Jews seem to think they are, nor do
they reciprocate the anxieties that Jews feel toward them. (See
Questions 30b, 38b, 46b.) Whatever has happened appears to be
a unilateral development manifesting itself as a Jewish reaction
to Catholics, and not as a reciprocal phenomenon.

To understand this development, we must seek clues in the
events of the thirteen years between 1952 and 1965. Something,
in this span of time, must have occurred to disturb so dramatically
the Jewish sense of security in relation to Catholics. Paradoxically,
the very event which has worked toward greater unity and trust
between Catholics and Protestants, Vatican II and its ecumenical
outreach, may very likely be responsible, in large measure, for new
Jewish anxiety, even suspicion. For decades, Jews and Catholics
have lived side by side in the United States. In the early years of
the century, Irish- and Italian-Catholic immigrants shared the
teeming neighborhoods in the large cities with newly arrived Jews

from eastern Europe. They understood each other as people. Rarely did Catholic theological contentions or their logical extension into a whole body of folklore disturb day-to-day relationships between Jews and Catholics. Both, after all, were insecure minorities. Very far from the American Jewish experience was the real terror of the eastern European Jew who hid for his life behind locked doors when his Catholic neighbors were coming home from a Holy Week Mass which vividly described the Jews clamoring for the execution of Jesus. Frequently enough, the blood bath of a progrom was the outcome of such a service which had stressed that "not only the Jews of Christ's time but Jews of all time were guilty of having killed Christ, the God-man; theologically speaking, they were deicides. . . . The sufferings of the Jews were to be understood as part of their punishment for the crime of having rejected Christ and their original destiny. . . . Judaism was a useless thing, an invalid ethic, an invalid way of life, an invalid method of worship, which had been rendered pointless by the advent of Christ. . . . The Jews were allied with the devil, they were always entering into conspiracies—with Freemasons, with Communists, with atheists, with secularists—for the sole purpose of destroying the Church and wiping Christianity off the face of the earth."[5]

A good many American Jews were never aware that Catholic belief entertained these notions about Jews, and even those who knew intellectually how the Church viewed the Jew, even those who were familiar with the long history of Church-associated Jew-hatred, often regarded these facts as no longer operative, as part of a world past.

But with Vatican II and the Schema on the Jews, all of this largely submerged material became dramatically available on the front pages of America's newspapers. Jews, with varying degrees of sophistication, were often shocked to realize that in 1965, five hundred years after the Spanish Inquisition, three hundred years after the Chmielnicki slaughters in the Ukraine, twenty years after the Nazi genocide had destroyed one third of their people, Catholic prelates were sitting down in Rome to discuss whether or not

---

[5] F. E. Curtus (a pseudonym of a Roman Catholic observer at the Vatican Ecumenical Council), in "Vatican II and the Jews," *Commentary*, January, 1965.

the Jews of today, or yesterday, were guilty of murder. Was it possible?

It *is* possible that, had the original Schema passed the Council unopposed, there would have been little, if any, significant negative reaction on the part of Jews. As it turned out, however, the reactionary efforts of conservative prelates to block the original Schema, the constant bickering, manipulation, and political infighting by the conservative Curia working to produce a statement that would say nothing to alter the past, became a painful, traumatic experience for virtually all Jews—especially those who, in America, had come to view Catholics as good friends and neighbors.

Despite its flaws, I believe that the Vatican statement on the Jews, as finally passed, was indeed a historic one and that it opens the way for a new era of cooperation between Catholics and Jews. But there is also little doubt that the long and tortuous debates at Rome, so widely and continuously publicized in the American press, has caused new scars, particularly in the hearts of American Jews, who, just because they counted on the American bishops to win the day, feel especially betrayed. John Cogley, himself a Catholic and the Religion Editor of *The New York Times,* summed up the problem: "The never-ending controversy over the Jewish statement in the Council has already blunted its intended effect. It was meant to be a word of love and friendship. It has already been the source of bitterness and disappointment, a reason for shame and anguish on the part of many Catholics, and of suspicion and rancor on the part of many Jews."

If the Council's statement is not to become a permanent boomerang, a great deal of new activity is now needed on the part of the American Roman Catholic Church that will be visibly geared to implementing the Council's positive declarations. Now, more than ever before, prolonged hesitation, and a lack of decisive programs, may frustrate Jewish hopes even more and add further to Catholic-Jewish suspicion.

Hopefully, progress can and will be made.

4. A CULTURE WITHIN A CULTURE

We have so far spoken of a Jewishness which is only in very small measure susceptible to survey making. We have noted briefly some of the prehistory relevant to an understanding of the American Jew, located some of the recent events which loom large in shaping some of his attitudes, and posed some questions geared to amplifying our understanding of Judaism as a way of life that stresses acts, rituals, and home and community rather than dogmas and doctrines. As inadequate an instrument as the survey proves to be for exploring such matters as these, it is even less so in presenting us with a vital measure of the changes that have occurred on both the institutional and theological levels of American religious life. On the basis of the survey, one would never suspect that there have been real challenges and real changes—the introduction of the vernacular into the Mass, the new definitions and visions of the role of the Church expressed by a whole new generation of theologians, the entry of the churches into the field of civil rights and community action, a wide range of exciting and radical theological speculation. It is hardly conceivable that all this ferment has completely bypassed Americans to the degree indicated in the survey. Indeed, in these years, greater change was to be noted among Jews than the other two groups, yet, as already has been pointed out, the direction of the questions makes it difficult to gain insight into the intellectual trends.

Change, after all, has been woven into the texture of Jewish life from the very beginnings of its historical experience. The survival of the Jewish people through the centuries has been variously seen as a miracle, an anomaly, a historical aberration. It may, indeed, be all of these things; but one must still plumb the unique nature of Jewish survival. The main threads running through the fabric of Jewish experience are change and adaptability. As a cohesive collectivity—a nation, if you will, even in the prehistory of nations —the Jewish people was forged in the great move out of Egypt and slavery into the nomadic life of the desert and toward freedom. To be sure, that very first exodus was to supply the leitmotiv for much of the Jewish history to follow, across time and space. After coping with geographical and situational strangeness, for forty years, the

Israelites approached the land of Canaan with a self-awareness as a national, not merely a tribal, conscience, with laws and judges to administer them, and a well-developed ethical code. Nor did these spring up fully blown: The laws were an adaptation and refinement of ancient legal codes; the ethics grew out of their very original synthesis of Canaanite, Egyptian, and Babylonian views, transcended and illuminated by their unique Hebrew world view—monotheism. The earliest history of the Hebrew tribes is not fully available to us, but from the glimpses we get in the Bible it is evident that they constituted a group on the periphery of the established centers of Middle Eastern civilization. Their marginality, from the beginning, gave them a unique vantage point from which to view, sift, reject, and refine the life styles and values of those with whom they came in contact. This offside position—within, yet not completely of, a society—has ever since characterized the Jewish people and shaped the patterns of its response to its changing environments.

The Babylonian exile followed a long period of settled existence and creative development in the Jews' own land. The conquerors destroyed the Temple in Jerusalem and carried off the artisans, teachers, princes, priests—the chief resource people of the nation—in order to ensure that there would be no rebellion, no rejuvenation. This was the formula which had spelled extinction to so many peoples who had fallen under the expanding empire of Nebuchadnezzar. The Jews, however, dislocated and without the structure of the Temple service, soon found themselves involved in the creation of another kind of institution, one that far exceeded the Temple's purpose—a house of study, a house of meeting, a house of prayer—in short, a synagogue. This synthesis presented a portable and viable solution to the loss of the Temple and the exile from their homeland.

What is more: Now removed from the land, a minority in a great, foreign urban container, the Jews were learning to respond with communal forms that would one day replace the lost national institutions. This did not mean that Jews remained isolated from the mainstream of culture in the land in which they found themselves. It is enough to remember that Nehemiah, who was the organizing genius of the return to Jerusalem, was at the same time a highly placed adviser to the King of Persia—to realize with what success the exiled Jews adapted themselves to their new surroundings. The Jews in Babylonia demonstrated a high degree of flexibility; they met the secular challenges of a sophisticated urban civilization by adapting their religious traditions to the new environment.

Thus, by the time the Second Temple was destroyed and the great dispersion took place, the Jews had learned how to survive in exile. Franz Rosenzweig has explained how: "To the eternal people, home never is home in the sense of land, as it is to the peoples of the world who plow the land and live and thrive on it, until they have all but forgotten that being a people means something besides being rooted in a land . . . the will to be a people dares not cling to any mechanical means; the will can realize its end only through the people itself."[1]

The work of updating laws, reinterpreting traditions, revising practices, became an ongoing process. The "biblical canon" never really closed; it fed a new literature—the oral commentaries and interpretations by the scholar-rabbis which was to be finally edited around 550, the Christian era, and which became known as the Talmud.

The Talmud, not a book but a vast literature, the collective work of many generations of rabbis, serves as the essential testament of Rabbinic Judaism. It comprises more than six thousand pages, the contents of which were formed over a period of almost a thousand years—from almost two hundred years before to about five hundred years after the beginning of the Christian era. There are references in the Talmud to more than two thousand scholar-teachers who participated in its deliberations—rabbis who lived in Palestine or Babylonia.

Someone has said that if religion is anything, it is everything. For the rabbis, the Bible was everything—the source of life and understanding—since it was God's word to man. They took the Bible seriously as divine revelation and sought to find in its every word nuances that would apply to the evolving human situation in its day-to-day experience. While they did not regard themselves as prophets, they did align themselves with the humane prophetic views over against the ritualistic disciplines and literalistic interpretations of the priests.

[1] Nahum N. Glatzer, compiler, *Franz Rosenzweig: His Life and Thought.* New York, Schocken Books, 1962.

The prophets had spoken of immorality in high places, of the need to love the oppressed and to build the just society. The rabbis incorporated this warm and living feeling for humanity into the daily habit of every Jew by means of the halakah, which literally means "walking." Halakah is the walking in the "way of the Lord." Its critics, from the outside, often described rabbinic halakah as arid legalism, the pouring of religious content into the small bottles of petty, ritualistic concern. But everyone who is conversant with the religious revolution wrought by the rabbis knows how far from the truth such a description is. The Pharisee-rabbis were ranged against the Sadducee-priests. What the priests had made into the cold and impersonal commands of Scripture, rabbinic halakah clothed with the warmth of a new zeal: to build God's kingdom on earth by learning to do his will within the human situation. This meant that all 613 commandments of Scripture had to be carefully and lovingly restudied, from the point of view of human need. In the priestly tradition the commandments were regarded as means of sanctifying God. Halakah made more of the commandments: They now were required to yield opportunities for the sanctification of human life. The halakah of the rabbis reshaped prophetism and gave its lofty, humane concerns a concrete order and structure. Every commonplace, daily human habit could become sacred if it were seen—as the rabbis insisted it should be seen—as an act of worship. The loving deed became more important than the cult of the Temple.

The rabbis proceeded apace to build new rituals, "rituals of interpersonal behavior." The commandments of the written Torah—the Pentateuch—had been very specific and detailed when it came to rules relating to the sacrificial laws and priestly regulations. But what precisely did it mean when it said, "Honor thy father and thy mother"; or, "Love thy neighbor as thyself"; or, "Remember that you were once slaves in the land of Egypt"? The rabbis deliberately concerned themselves with such questions, and the answers they gave made their oral Torah into much more than a commentary or tradition. They deepened, humanized, and universalized it. As the priests had been concerned with codifying the rituals of the cult, the rabbis sought to codify love, loyalty, and human compassion, to transform these into inescapable religious duties of every Jew. How must one love one's neighbor? What are the ways in which one must honor one's parents? What must a man actually do to demonstrate to himself and others that he will not go back to slavery, but seek to remain free?

They answered such questions as these by giving the Pentateuchal commandments new meanings. What had been stated before as general propositions, they now spelled out as specific religious duties, incumbent upon all. In effect, they rebuilt the Jewish religion by translating what had been prophetic sentiment into a personal religion built on "propositions in action." Hospitality to wayfarers, visiting the sick, dowering the indigent bride, giving charity anonymously, attending the dead to the grave, and helping to bring peace to those who lack it: These duties, for example, were never actually adumbrated in the Bible, although they are generally felt in spirit. The rabbis made them, and many like them, into new commandments, or mitzvoth, and thus made communion with God an act that could and should be experienced everywhere and any time, with or without the Temple, the priests, or the sacrificial altar.

Modern Judaism, the religious life of Jews in the contemporary age, has roots in Rabbinic Judaism, and both go back to Biblical Judaism. But it is more directly the product of the modern temper that began to descend upon the Jewish community at the beginning of the nineteenth century. In the Western world, Modern Judaism is expressed in the three religious movements—Orthodox, Conservative, and Reform—which have emerged over the past century or so.

As we have seen, the Talmudic rabbis in the Diaspora of Babylonia had established patterns of living that encompassed the entire life situation of the Jews, and these operated in ways that would make possible the survival of this people as a culture within a culture. In the seventh century, many Jews left Babylonia for North Africa and Spain. Jewish life continued to flourish under Islam, and the Near Eastern and Mediterranean Jewish communities, together with their fellow Sephardi Jews in Spain (*Sepharad* means "Spain" in Hebrew), produced a unique intellectual culture in which scientific investigation—spurred by their intimacy with Muslim culture—grew at the side of mysticism, theology, philosophy, and poetry. In that relatively open society, it was possible for Jews to experience a "golden age" of creative cultural growth, until the days of the Inquisition in Christian Spain, and their expulsion in 1492.

The Ashkenazi Jews (*Ashkenaz* means "Germany" in Hebrew)

had been living, meanwhile, in middle Europe under Christian rule, and their life was one of relative isolation from their neighbors. While the Sephardi Jews were basking in the sun of Moorish culture for almost six hundred years, the Ashkenazim were living in Europe's Dark Ages. Their development took a different turn. Cast out from the world of Christianity, they made their domain the world of the Torah and the Talmud. Their law, science, art, and philosophy were all part of one fabric: the word of God as revealed to their ancestors at Sinai. The scholars, of course, wrote in Hebrew, the Holy Tongue. But some time during the Middle Ages the mass of Ashkenazi Jews absorbed the medieval German language and made it their own, with liberal additions of Hebrew words. This Judeo-German language came to be known as Yiddish, and from those years until only very recent decades, this was the universal language spoken all over the world by Ashkenazi Jews.

Medieval Jewry was subjected to one terror after another. Forced to move about from land to land, the one stable factor of its life was the halakah, which bound Jew to Jew, and all together, wherever they might go, to God. As a nation within nations—Jews had no civil rights, no permission to own land or join guilds—the synagogue served as the national center of their own "welfare state." Education, religion, charity, social welfare, indeed all their human needs found their base in the synagogue. The law that governed their community life was the same law that was sovereign in their private habit: the oral and written Torah, which together constituted rabbinic halakah, was their total way of life.

In response to the increasing terror inaugurated by the Crusades, the Ashkenazi Jews of middle Europe began searching for new exiles. They traveled eastward, and by the fifteenth century had already established communities in Poland, and still later throughout most of eastern Europe. In Russia, they came upon old Jewish communities they knew nothing about, whose settlement went back to Byzantine days: brothers and sisters of those who had gone westward to North Africa and then Spain a thousand years earlier. In Kiev, "mother of Russia cities," a community of Jews from the Middle East had settled even before the eighth century, thus antedating even the Russians. Ironically, eastern Europe, in the late Middle Ages, became the meeting ground of two separate streams of the Disapora community: one which harked back to those who had come directly from the Near East through the Black Sea; the other the newer refugees from western Europe, who now fled eastward. There, in eastern Europe, they were set apart from the Christian communities by the edict of one ruler after the other. In time, they established their own cohesive cultural structure which institutionalized Rabbinic Judaism as a force for Jewish unity throughout Europe.

5. OCCUPATIONAL PATTERNS OF AMERICAN JEWS

The unique relationship of the land of Israel to the religion of Israel is a constant element in Jewish history. The Promised Land was more than a national goal, more than a vehicle of God's covenant with Israel. The Holy Land became the very stage for a system of biblical laws—agricultural and labor legislation—that gave meaning and focus to the ethical character of Judaism. Rooted in the very soil of the land of Israel are biblical laws dealing with social justice, the prevention of poverty, and the public concern due the orphan, the widow, and the dispossessed. Long after the Jews were exiled and forcibly separated from Palestine, and to this very day, the prayers of the synagogue continue to echo the people's nostalgia for the soil and the skies, the rain and the dew, the fruit and the trees of their ancestral homeland—the land of Israel.

Zionism borrowed its political theories from the modern world, but its attachment to Palestine as a national homeland stemmed from these older and deeper sources which flowed out of the religious teachings of Biblical and Rabbinic Judaism. Long years before the dawn of the modern political concept of nationality, pious Jews from various parts of the world continued to return to the Holy Land. There, at the end of their days, they would have the privilege of burial in the sacred earth of the Holy Land, in anticipation of their resurrection, which, they believed, would follow the arrival of messianic days.

The emergence of political Zionism in the late nineteenth century is, in many ways, the most telling example of Jewish flexi-

bility in adapting prevailing historical movements to its own survivalist needs. This was the period when nationalism reached its
final clarification. Many ethnic groups which had been submerged
in larger states or empires began to agitate for self-determination.
The last vestiges of a Europe divided along religious lines were
crumbling in favor of a Europe organized in terms of national
boundaries. Political Zionism reanalyzed "the Jewish problem" in
terms of nationalism: Anti-Semitism was the inevitable outcome of
a people without a homeland, a people living within the borders
of other nations but not completely of them. Give the Jews a
homeland, and they would become like everybody else, no longer
"a nation within a nation." Despite its nineteenth-century trap-
pings of nationalism, Zionism was still the centuries'-old Jewish
religious dream of the Promised Land.

The ethnic ties of American Jews to their people all over the
world were still strong, even if they seemed somewhat attenuated,
by the late 1930's. But the awful facts of contemporary European
Jewish history, which were only more fully revealed at the close of
World War II, had a profound effect on American Jewish life.
The Hitler-Nazi holocaust, the near-fruitless search for refugee
havens in the West, Britain's refusal to open wide Palestine's gates
to Jews, the spectacle of the relentless hunting down of Jewish
refugees by mighty navies on the high seas, the sight of their creak-
ing, sinking boats making their perilous way to Palestine, and
finally, in 1949, the victory of the little David of Israel over the
mighty Goliath of Araby—all these desperate but adventurous
moments helped to invigorate and to unify Jewish life in America.
In those historic years, a sweeping tidal wave of ethnic empathy
erupted in every sector of the American Jewish community—often
an ethnic empathy with religious and personal overtones. Hardly a
Jew in America could avoid the feeling of "There, but for the
grace of God, go I!"

In a sense, then, the major premises of political Zionism had to
wait to be proved right, by the testing of its theories in a most
horrible and horrifying reality. For, despite its growing acceptance
in America, Zionism did not achieve mass Jewish approval here
until World War II, when the revelations of Jewish persecution
and wandering rallied broad sentiment to its cause. When this
occurred, there was no American Jewish movement, organization,
institution, or agency that was not vitally influenced by the spirit

of Zionism. Synagogues, Jewish community centers, religious schools, and virtually all the organizations and societies that comprised the American Jewish community came to espouse the Zionist cause. By the combined efforts of Jews throughout the free world, over one million of their people had been brought to the ancient homeland, from the time the state of Israel was established. And in the pursuit of these goals of the physical redemption and rehabilitation of their fellow Jews, these American Jewish organizations alone had raised more funds than had ever been subscribed for such purposes by any nongovernmental, private group in the history of civilized man!

In a very real sense, the rescue and rehabilitation by American Jewry of these hundreds of thousands of Jews has done more to keep alive the Jews of America than they could ever have planned or hoped for. Because of the events that wiped out the Jewish communities of eastern Europe, American Jews have had to face the challenge of their identity in this land, as a new kind of Jewish community, far sooner than they expected. In a sense, American Jewry is an orphaned community. During the years of the great migration of Jews to these shores, between 1881 and 1925, and in the decades that have followed, American Jews were busy devoting themselves primarily to integrating into the new environment. They did not worry too much about Jewish culture, about producing great Jewish learning, about the survival of Judaism—eastern European Jewry was still alive and very active.

After the Second World War, American Jewry was faced with immediate and pressing problems: It was catapulted into the position of leadership as the largest and wealthiest Jewish community in the world. It had to be responsible for the tragic remnants left in the camps of Europe, their resettlement, and, above all, the international political struggle for a Jewish state. American Jewry has, I believe, acquitted itself nobly, responding dramatically and energetically to these tasks: pouring out vast sums of money, providing inspired leadership, deploying wise political tactics in support of the emerging Jewish state in Palestine, and even mounting significant efforts to send arms and men to fight for Israel. For American Jews this period served as a creative pause—there was a moratorium on the need to think profoundly and ultimately about the direction of their private and communal lives as Jews, about the startling meaning for their own Jewish condition that

the loss of the great centers of learning and culture abroad now
held for them. Zionism, overseas rescue—these now were equated
with the Jewish identity in America, and their lives were informed
with the vicarious values of enlivening others to live. But how
long could they subsist with such fare alone? What of their spiritual concerns?

With the establishment of Israel as an independent nation, the
emptying of the refugee centers in Europe, American Jews have
been left, in a sense, with themselves. Israel needs financial support for a long time to come, but it neither needs nor wants political interference from foreign Jews. Nor, for that matter, do most
American Jews wish to become involved in the internal workings
of a sovereign state to which they have a spiritual allegiance but
certainly not a political one. In fact, it is little more than a single
decade that American Jews have begun to take very seriously the
essential meaning of their spiritual community. In the earliest
years, they were concerned with practical matters of adjustment to
the new land, learning the ways of America, educating their children, earning a living, and fighting off prejudice. Since the end of
the Second World War, American Jews have emerged as a well-
established, entrenched, increasingly secure, largely native-born
community. The problems of immigrant days are virtually over,
save for the usual cultural lags. There are few Americanized Jews
learning to accommodate to a new home. They are not "Americanized"—they are Americans.

It is only very recently that a serious social research of American
Jewry has been emerging. Sociologist Seymour Lipset has noted
that "the phenomenon of Jewish scholars ignoring the Jews as a
field of study is not unique to sociology, although the gap is more
glaring there, since the study of immigrant and ethnic groups has
been so important in the field." Jewish anthropologists were chas-
ing all over the world and ignoring the rich field for study in their
own backyard. And Jewish sociologists had long avoided their own
group as proper and necessary for intensive study. In the last
dozen years, however, the picture has begun to change. A large
literature in the social sciences is emerging dealing with a wide
range of subjects—alcohol and the Jews; delinquency among Jewish children; political behavior of American Jews; Jewish ethnicity; intermarriage; demographic data. This is a growing sign of
the authenticity of the Jew as a proper American, as well as an

index of the interest in the Jew as a barometer of American culture.

Today, one may more easily begin to put together a composite picture of the American Jew based on a review of the sociological and social-psychological data which have recently been gathered. To be sure, we are only at the beginning of this new development, and many researches remain to be undertaken, and many contradictory, tenuous theses await more study. (For example, in the area of intermarriage statistical study alone, depending on which research you read, the figures in the Jewish community of America range from 3 percent to 12 percent and on up to 18 percent.)

Additionally, there are two other important problems that stand in the way of achieving a more scientific national Jewish portrait. First, there are no exact or even reliable figures available on the number of Jews in the United States because the United States Census may not enter the realm of the religious community. As a result, social scientists spend a great deal of time and energy pyramiding, projecting, and devising "scientifically unscientific" ways of arriving at a guesstimate. Second, New York City, where virtually half of America's Jews live, rarely comes under the microscope of social survey and study. Obviously, any national study which excludes the Jews of New York can be hardly reliable or representative.

The Jews of the United States are overwhelmingly urban, and even more—they are metropolitan. The thirteen largest Jewish communities (with populations of fifty thousand and over) make up over 75 percent of the total Jewish population: Baltimore, Boston, Chicago, Cleveland, Detroit, Los Angeles, Miami, Newark, New York City, Philadelphia, Pittsburgh, St. Louis, San Francisco. The predominantly urban distribution is borne out in a number of studies not directly related to demography, and where attitudinal materials reflect the essential cosmopolitan views of the American Jew.

Of the 180 Jewish freshmen who studied at the University of Maryland in 1956, only four came from rural areas, and of these, not a single one had come from a farm. Studies dealing with Jews in small towns reflect a poor outlook for Jewish survival in these nonurban centers. The tendency here is for young Jews in small towns to move to the big city, thus putting further strain on the struggling, diminishing Jews in the small communities, who are already experiencing the highest intermarriage rates of all. Jews, along with increasing numbers of the general population, are becoming a surburban community, with all of the attendant strengths and weaknesses of these mobile people.

The urban-suburban American Jew is, by and large, middle class—socially, economically, and psychologically. In general, Americans are largely middle class everywhere, but from most studies, Jews lead here too. Nathan Glazer has noted that "the rise in the social and economic position of the Jews has been extremely rapid, far surpassing that which can be shown for any other immigrant group, and indeed surpassing . . . changes in the socioeconomic position of long-settled groups."[1] Clearly, such rapid mobility is directly related to the Jewish emphasis on educational attainment. In the generation preceding, about two thirds of Jewish males were high-school graduates, compared to about one quarter who had been graduated from college. Most studies suggest that today two thirds of Jewish youth aged 18–21 are enrolled at college, compared to a little more than one fourth for non-Jewish youth. A few years ago, the President of Notre Dame asked a conference of Catholic educators, "Where are *our* Einsteins, Oppenheimers, and Salks?"

Now, as there emerges a general increase in higher education, the "Jewish lead" is likely to disappear. Studies dealing with the Jewish occupational structure used to stress the "abnormal" nature of the Jewish patterns. Today, most agree that the Jewish occupational structure should not be understood as "abnormal," but rather one that anticipates the future pattern of American society at large. Both in education and in education's outcome— the socioeconomic patterns of America—the Jews seem to be something of a barometer indicating the direction in which all of American society is going. As has often been said: "The Jew is like everybody else, only more so." Perhaps one should add: more so sooner and oftener. All of this notwithstanding, the traditional Jewish commitment to education as a religious value has been noted by many social scientists.

An analysis of the occupational patterns of Jewish youth affords,

[1] Nathan Glazer and Daniel P. Moynihan, *Beyond the Melting Pot: The Negroes, Puerto Ricans, Jews, Italians, and Irish of New York City.* Cambridge, Massachusetts, M.I.T. Press, 1963.

possibly, an even better insight into the subtle ways in which Jews as a group differ from other Americans. While the drive for education can be directly related to traditional values which have been held almost from the time of the Talmudic rabbis, the choice of occupation is conditioned by environmental influences as much as a system of tradition-directed options. A number of studies undertaken in this area show that Jews in America prefer self-employed professional or proprietary occupations.[2] It is true that Jewish immigrants to the United States were primarily town people in Europe, and it is widely known that those ethnic groups which have been urban for the longest period of time tend toward the professional, proprietary, and clerical occupations. On the other hand, a study of Jews of Detroit suggests that significant voluntaristic factors, such as educational choices, will outweigh the historically and socially deterministic ones. The Detroit study finds "extreme differences exist between Jewish and non-Jewish youth," and establishes one major reason for these differences: The number of Jewish youth who have completed college is six times as great as non-Jewish youth. Jewish youth with college degrees who are in semiskilled work number about half the non-Jewish youth with college education. A similar pattern is indicated with regard to Jewish and non-Jewish youth who have only completed high school. Also, at the lower educational level, Jewish youth are about half as numerous as the non-Jewish in the unskilled labor force of Detroit.

What produces such differences between Jews and the people in whose midst they live? Social scientists have begun to see that history, even more than statistical field studies, will have to be called into mind. Joseph Fauman, the author of the Detroit study, suggests that "Jews would behave differently than non-Jews, even if the sociological position of both groups were, in fact, the same." Not only do Jewish values which emerge from the inner life play a role, but a long history in which Jewish occupations were sharply limited by the laws of oppressive societies must not be overlooked.

[2] *See,* for example: Bernard Lazerwitz, "Jews In and Out of New York City," *The Jewish Journal of Sociology,* Vol. III, No. 2, December, 1961; or B. C. Rosen, "Race, Ethnicity and Achievement Syndrome," *American Sociological Review,* 1959, p. 24. J. Veroff, Sheila Field, and G. Gurin, "Achievement, Motivation and Religious Background," *American Sociological Review,* 1962, p. 27. N. Hurvitz, "Sources, Motivation and Achievement of American Jews," *Jewish Social Studies,* 1961, p. 23.

As a persecuted minority, Jews learned to value self-employment
as a defensive measure. They tended to fit into work which could
be portable to allow for their own mobility; they developed a
preference for skills which could be taken easily from place to
place. Most important, the ever-present anti-Jewish discrimination
led Jews to seek those occupational opportunities which would not
make them dependent on the "hiring-firing" policies of others.

There is no doubt that discrimination against Jews in employment has decreased considerably in the last number of years, but it
is equally true that Jews in the United States are still wary, and
still expect to find that, all things being equal, a non-Jew will be
given job preference. (See Questions 33a, 41a, 49a.)[3] It is also
true that there are certain occupational areas where there are virtually no Jews to be found—the large banks, insurance companies,
public utilities, railroads, and the top-level corporate groups. We
cannot be altogether certain how much of this may be due to
current discrimination and how much to a past experience of exclusion which encourages Jews to avoid these fields. Nathan Glazer
points out that "the organization man has status. An observer reports that in the bridge groups on the train to Larchmont, a Jew,
when asked what he does, will say he is 'in textiles' or 'plastics' or
is an 'accountant'; the non-Jew will say he is 'with' General Elec-
tric or Union Carbide, and there is no question who outranks
whom."[4]

In studying Jewish occupational patterns in America, we learn a
good deal about the undying, long-lived characteristics that set
them apart as what cultural anthropologists have called a "folk
community." A folk community may only differ from other
groups in degree, but as compared to these others it will possess a
greater consciousness of its identity and individuality; its members
are more nearly aware of a shared historical experience; it is conscious of its collective destiny, is more endogamous, and keeps
alive a special value system. Jews surely, the occupational studies

---

[3] The question: "Do you think most (Catholic, Protestant) employers
would discriminate against you because of religion or not?" In 1952, 31
percent of the Jews said Yes regarding Catholics and 27 percent regarding
Protestants. In 1965, 37 percent of the Jews said Yes regarding Catholics and
26 percent regarding Protestants. It goes without saying that these Jewish
responses are exceedingly higher than fears of job discrimination on the
part of Catholics or Protestants.

[4] Glazer and Moynihan, *op. cit.*, p. 149.

seem to say, are members of a "folk community," and thus perpetuate their own subculture in America. In the area of occupational choice, the Jewish group is still motivated *as a group* by a different value system from the one operating in the general population. How much traditional culture the American Jews positively possess and to what degree they constitute a community based not only on values derived from negative historical and economic experiences, cannot, of course, be assessed by studies dealing with occupational choices alone. For this material we must look beyond.

6. THE SYNAGOGUE IN THE MODERN COMMUNITY

Before dealing with the question of the nature of Jewish culture and the ways in which Judaism affects the lives of American Jews, it is well to consider still other quantitative material more susceptible of measurement. As with the material on occupations, it is possible to derive insights from some data, which, while not measuring attitudes, help to reveal them.

One fact anyone can substantiate for himself simply by living for a period of time in an American city is that Jews tend to live together. The Jewish neighborhood is easily located by the familiar Jewish stores—delicatessens, bakeries, meat markets—and by synagogues, centers, and a variety of other unmistaken Jewish institutions. From the 1880's on, coinciding with the large influx of eastern European Jews, exclusion began to be practiced. Better neighborhoods, social clubs, resorts went to great lengths to keep Jews out. The peak of exclusionist practice was reached in the 1920's and 1930's, but after World War II the trend was reversed. With the growing introduction of Fair Accommodations laws, restrictions on Jews remain in effect only in exclusive social and golf clubs. Clearly, however, integration has not followed the breakdown of systematic exclusion.

Indeed, the trend seems to be in the direction of increased separatism in self-contained Jewish areas. In New York City, there are communities that are between two fifths and nine tenths Jewish. The building boom after the war brought huge "apartment-cities"

to the Borough of Queens in New York. It was assumed that the
new neighborhoods would surely be integrated, but, as it turned
out, developments which started out mixed became, strongly, and
in some cases, almost exclusively, Jewish. In one suburban city,
where only 15 percent of the population is Jewish, a survey revealed that half of these would like to be in a neighborhood which
is 50 percent Jewish, one quarter in a neighborhood that is 75
percent Jewish.[1]

During the period of large-scale immigration and among first-
generation Jews, such grouping together was natural; the new-
comer to these shores was poor, he spoke another language, and, in
many cases, was an observant Jew who needed a synagogue within
walking distance, and stores nearby which sold Jewish foods and
Kosher meat. Understandably, he would choose to live among
people who spoke his language and observed the same customs and
rituals. But the ghettoization of today is the voluntary choice of
third-generation Jews, most of whom are not ritually observant
and who are members of the middle and upper middle class. And
not only do Jews prefer to live with other Jews—but a great majority send their children to all-Jewish summer camps, the same children who during the year belong to Jewish youth groups at centers, synagogues, or YMHA's. There is little doubt that, if the
educational and occupational patterns exhibited by Jews establish
them as a subculture, the tendency to group together in neighborhoods helps even more to underscore the existence of a separate,
definable, Jewish folk community, in America.

If the American city became the new frontier of the mid-nineteenth century and the European immigrants its builders, then,
a century later, a still newer frontier was being pioneered by the
great-grandchildren—suburban America. About fifty million
"exurbanite immigrants" have already made their way to the
cities' proximate hinterland of towns and villages, and there is no
prospect of a curtailment of this modern exodus yet in sight. By
1975, it is believed that an additional 35 million Americans will
leave the black pavements behind and put themselves down somewhere nearby, where they are sure that the grass grows greener
and their children will grow taller.

[1] Nathan Glazer and Daniel P. Moynihan, *Beyond the Melting Pot.* Cambridge, Massachusetts, M.I.T. Press, 1963, p. 161.

The Jews of America share abundantly in this new nomadic experience. Of their total number of some 5½ million, close to 4 million live in or near ten of the largest cities: New York City, Los Angeles, Chicago, Philadelphia, Boston, Washington, D.C., St. Louis, Cleveland, Baltimore, and Newark. And there, and in the other metropolitan centers they populate, there was every indication that they bulked even larger in the migratory flight to the suburbs than the other members of the general population.

If the general impact of American opinion was a major positive factor in fostering a new approach to this emancipation, then the increasing suburbanization of the Jew has been of even greater influence in forcing him to rediscover the sources of his significance as a Jew. "In moving from the city to suburb," wrote one perceptive Jewish suburbanite of the fifties, "we had, if only subconsciously, a vision of a less 'Jewish' existence . . . a running away from the ghetto, however plush-lined. . . . Still, in seeking a less 'Jewish existence,' no matter how subtly expressed, we find in Suburbia a more 'Jewish existence.' " In the city, he explains, "we had found it unnecessary to think seriously of ourselves as Jews." But the new environment of the suburbs created a new Jewish need: They were now required to revise their old concept of themselves as Jews.

"It is the village neighborliness," he went on, "the same neighborliness that permits a good-morning to any man seen at the station more than twice, and most of the women; an occasional beer with the man next door; a joint effort with the man across the street in clearing the leads and the gutters—that builds the first pressures toward membership in the synagogue. The man next door may go to Immaculate Conception, the man across the street to St. Luke's, and the man on the other side may spend his Sundays at Lee Hills Country Club, but this man is a Jew. He knows it, his neighbors know it, and the other Jews in the community know it. Some positive action seems indicated."[2]

That positive action became symbolized in the new American Jewish phenomenon: the active participation in synagogue life *by all the members of the young Jewish family*. For the youthful matron, the boyish father, and in the synagogue religious school

[2] Harry Gersh, "The New Suburbanites of the '50's," *Commentary*, March, 1954, pp. 218–219.

and clubs for the growing children, there were welcome places waiting.

A new role thus opened for the synagogue in America, as the social, cultural, and religious center of the Jewish community. In the course of its long history, the synagogue, of course, had been all these things before. But then, in the past, it was set into a framework in which each of these significances—the social, cultural, and religious—meant things vastly different from the suburban, or for that matter the urban, American community of the mid-twentieth century.

The move out of the city is motivated by a variety of reasons. Status, which once played the major role in sending people to the suburbs, now vies with other motives—better schools, living space, clean air, less crime and delinquency. Many young Jewish families were led to make the trek to the suburbs because they were anxious to avoid the segregated neighborhoods of the city. Paradoxically, they often found themselves, in short order, surrounded by other Jews and, sooner than they thought, often because of the expectations of Christian neighbors, they were building synagogues. The Jew in the suburbs has lost his anonymity. He quickly becomes known by the people among whom he lives, his neighbors, the storekeepers, the local politicians and, unless he is determined to "pass" (which very few American Jews try to do), he is known as a Jew. Christians build their churches as soon as enough members of their denomination allow for the possibility. They expect that Jews will do the same. Thus, many Jewish suburbanites reported that one of the major reasons they decided to build a synagogue was because it was expected of them.[3]

Another motivation for building and joining a synagogue in the suburbs is the desire to give children a Jewish education. In many cases schoolrooms are constructed before the rest of the synagogue; but also, many families drop out from the synagogue after their children no longer attend the religious school. Not only is the move to the suburbs motivated by the desire to give one's children a better life, but the house of Jewish worship itself becomes child-oriented, child-obsessed.

The "religious revival" of the fifties was predicated on church and synagogue membership enrollments and on the number of

[3] Albert I. Gordon, *Jews in Suburbia*. Boston, Beacon Press, 1959, p. 16.

new houses of worship built, rather than on any hard evidence of inner religiousness or piety. It was an American social phenomenon which paralleled, in time, the great American move to the suburbs. This leads to the conjecture whether the two phenomena are, in very fundamental ways, integrally related. For both Jews and Christians, the move from the inner city and its cover of anonymity had given them a new communal identity in the openness of the suburban life style.

Paradoxically, however, the age is increasingly secular, the basic tenets of religion are being seriously questioned, and increasing numbers of people are rejecting institutionalized faith altogether, particularly among the intellectuals. It is precisely in such a time that Jews are discovering, in America, that there is no other way to identify themselves as Jews than as synagogue-affiliated persons. Indeed, one sees this turning up in young Jews, who are increasingly seeing their "Jewishness" as a matter of religion. In the Riverton Study made by Marshall Sklare and Mark Vosk in 1957[4] (of a northeastern city with a community of ten thousand Jews) eight out of ten parents defined a Jew as one who professed the Jewish religion. Among the adolescents, however, 97 percent said that a Jew was one who identified himself with the Jewish faith. In larger cities with larger Jewish communities it is likely that a greater percentage of first- and second-generation Jews would interpret Jewishness in other than religious terms, but today young American Jews can offer no such interpretations. In the same study, responses to the question, "Why do you go to the synagogue?" varied from "It gives me a good, peaceful feeling"—26 percent; through "I like to follow the services"—17 percent; to "I go to meet other people"—12 percent. Curiously, however, none of the answers included prayer and worship as reasons for attending the synagogue.

Affiliation with synagogues continues to increase at a much faster rate than the Jewish population in the suburbs. But how can we explain their need for a synagogue, considering how few Jews express a genuine religious orientation in terms of piety or religious practice? Albert Gordon suggests that "only one motive— ethnic interest in the Jews as a people—really explains the sub-

[4] "The Riverton Study," New York, American Jewish Committee, 1957, p. 22.

urban Jews' affiliation with the one institution which is openly labeled 'religious'."[5] Apparently, the fundamental theme that characterizes Jewish life is the trend toward survivalism, the continuity of the Jewish community. In Riverton, "people wished not to merge with the general population." Ninety-three percent of the parents interviewed and 95 percent of their adolescent children want Jews to remain a distinct group. Asked what religion they would choose if they were to be reborn ("If you could be reborn, would you prefer to be born as a Jew or non-Jew?"), 82 percent of the parents and 88 percent of the children chose to be reborn Jews.

Here, then, the Jewish communal "will to survive" can be seen as a religious force perhaps equal in fervor to the ecstasy of divine communion. The younger respondents in Riverton do not believe that anti-Semitism has been the chief conserving power in Jewish history. Adults are more likely to see themselves to be living in a potentially, though not always overtly, hostile world. It appears, and this is borne out by the Gallup survey, that the older generation may indeed see more anti-Semitism around than actually exists. The non-Jew seems to have changed more rapidly than the older Jew believes he has indeed changed, and the younger Jews, lacking an earlier experience, may be more aware of this than their parents can possibly be. Indeed, a sense of greater security in the world, coupled to a sense of group identity on the part of Jewish adolescents, has been one of the surprising findings in some recent research. Strong survivalist tendencies have been revealed among Jewish youth.

The synagogue has emerged as the strongest central institution in Jewish life in America, and Jews increasingly identify themselves by their religion. Nevertheless it is evident from numerous studies that the overwhelming majority of Jews are not "religious," at least in ways traditional to Judaism. In "Southville," the fictitious name of a major metropolis with a population of 500,000 and a Jewish population of 8,000, a sample of 285 Jewish families showed 94 percent who claimed affiliation with a synagogue or temple.[6]

---

[5] Gordon, *op. cit.*, p. 153.
[6] An unpublished study of American Jewish Committee.

Observance of Jewish customs, however, was low. Asked to rank which practices or beliefs they considered "essential to being a good Jew," the following list emerged:

To believe in God	95%
To lead an ethical and moral life	93%
To accept being a Jew and not hide it	88%
To gain respect of Christian neighbors	74%
To support humanitarian causes	72%
To belong to a synagogue or temple	71%
To know the fundamentals of Judaism	66%
To promote civic betterment and improvement	59%
To attend services on High Holidays	57%
To marry within the Jewish group	53%
To work for equality for all minority groups	48%
To contribute to Jewish philanthropies	38%
To support Israel	28%
To attend weekly services	19%
To observe dietary laws	13%

The Gallup survey claims that 16 percent of the Jews queried either "do not believe in God or don't know." "Southville's" 95 percent who consider it essential to believe in God provide a diametrically opposite view. This reopens the whole question of "meaning" in surveys. But even more interestingly, the need to "lead an ethical and moral life" as a precondition "to being a good Jew" opens up the problem of what religion itself may really mean to the American Jew of today—who belongs to a synagogue but does not attend it often, and when he does, it is often not prayer at all that brings him to *his House of Prayer!*

It is not clear from this study whether the respondents actually believe in God themselves or think that in order to be a good Jew one should believe. It *is* clear from numerous studies, however, that the belief in God is quite different today from that of an earlier generation. Indeed, "it has been demonstrated by sociologists that there is a relationship between the socioeconomic background of a church's congregation and the eschatological, or otherworldly, emphasis. . . . As the socioeconomic status of a congregation increases, eschatology decreases, and the emphasis moves from an emotional religious experience to an intellectual interpretation."[7] Thus, one can almost predict answers to a questionnaire surveying the reasons for joining synagogues: ranking high in a list of motivations will be education for children and a desire to belong with people of one's faith, *although the content of that faith is not well known or understood.*

Attendance at weekly services is low, and adherence to certain ritual practices, even among the members of Orthodox congregations, is declining. A study conducted among Orthodox Jews in Milwaukee discloses a dramatic falling away from the traditional norms of observance in each succeeding generation, although affiliation with the Orthodox synagogue remains constant. Attendance at Orthodox synagogue worship is hardly different from the general pattern reported for all other Jews: 7 percent attend daily, including those who are in mourning; 11.5 percent attend weekly at Sabbath services; the largest number, 39.9 percent attend mostly on major festivals, alone. Of the commandments observed, the highest number ranks fasting on Yom Kippur as first—81.6 percent, but only 33.7 percent adhere to the dietary laws outside of their own homes.[8]

It appears, then, that throughout the Jewish community, "the precepts of Judaism affecting daily living are being abandoned, and ceremonies which are annual, more or less festive, and more or less convenient are being retained or expanded."[9]

The culture of American Jewry is shaped by that of the society around with its strong Christian component. The process of acculturation has occurred within the life of the individual, the group, and in the changes that have taken place within the synagogue. A whole series of customs are completely unknown among the third-, and even many of second-generation, Jews. Jewish holidays remain important often only because of their proximity or connection to Christian holidays: Hanukkah in relation to Christmas, and Passover has gained in popularity because it corresponds

[7] Raymond A. Mulligan, "Social Change and the Jewish Community," *Journal of Jewish Communal Service,* Vol. XXXVII, No. 4, Summer, 1961.

[8] Howard W. Polsky, "A Study of Orthodoxy in Milwaukee: Social Characteristics, Beliefs, and Observances," in Marshall Sklare, *The Jews: Social Patterns of an American Group.* Glencoe, Illinois, The Fress Press, 1958, pp. 325–335.

[9] Manheim S. Shapiro, "Changing Jewish Attitudes," *Journal of Jewish Communal Service,* Vol. XXXVII, No. 4, Summer, 1961.

to and complements Easter. In short, cultural assimilation has occurred to a very high degree, but not structural assimilation. The Jew joins synagogues and builds them because that is the prevailing pattern of American life. Nevertheless, he is still anxious to maintain his separate identity and has loaded down the synagogue-center with a whole variety of new tasks to fulfill, in order to give himself and, more importantly, his children, a social milieu and a viable vehicle for Jewish survival.

7. THE STORY OF "THE VANISHING JEW"

The high rate of cultural assimilation is accompanied by a low rate of accommodation. Accommodation denotes the amount of social distance that exists between individuals or groups. Jews have moved into the mainstream of American society and exhibit an upward mobility unmatched by any other immigrant group, yet they are not as well accommodated as other racial or ethnic groups. "The socioeconomic status of Jews has improved greatly in comparison with most of these groups, but their intergroup relationships with the larger social system have not."[1] It is evident that American Jewry has voluntarily decided in favor of this pattern. There is little evidence that their complete assimilation would be blocked by prejudice, no more than they would be debarred from moving into "non-Jewish neighborhoods." Jews are practicing a form of "group enclavement" because they want to. "An enclaved group is one that cuts itself off . . . the group that enclaves itself uses social distance or social farness in order to maintain its customs and traditions and to protect itself from what it considers to be undesirable and dangerous invasion from outside. . . ."[2]

What really frightens American Jews most is the prospect of intermarriage. Even those Jewish parents who are anxious that their young children mix with non-Jews, and send them to integrated nurseries and camps, are equally anxious to keep them within the Jewish group when they become teen-agers. Thus,

[1] Raymond A. Mulligan, "Social Change and the Jewish Community," *Journal of Jewish Communal Service*, Vol. XXXVII, No. 4, Summer, 1961, p. 416.
[2] *Ibid.*

youth programs assume major importance at synagogues and Jewish centers. In "A Report on the Findings of a Study of Jewish
Young Adults and the Jewish Community Center," Harry Sprecht
finds that the greatest interest "lies in the social institutions . . . on
the development and maintenance of social ties with other Jews."[3]
This does not mean that they do not anticipate other kinds of ties
to Jewish life later on, when they are married and become parents,
but during their youth the emphasis is on association *with other
young Jews.* They are interested above all in programs which offer
opportunities for courtship, reflecting, in short, their parents' attitudes to intermarriage.

A minority group can lose its identity in a number of ways:
through not reproducing itself, through complete assimilation of
the group as a whole, through a growing rate of intermarriage.
Jews, clearly, are not losing their identity through assimilation or
by merging with the general population. Until recently, studies
have shown that Jews in the United States have been successful in
maintaining their group identity. Intermarriage has always occurred and has always been a matter for concern, but the general
feeling had been that very little was lost through marrying out of
the group, and that, at least in terms of identifiable numbers,
Judaism was flourishing and assured of a future in the United
States.

In May, 1964, however, a sensational article appeared in *Look*
magazine under the title "The Vanishing Jew," by T. B. Morgan.
The burden of the message was that in the not-too-distant future,
American Jews will disappear through a low rate of fertility and a
growing, indeed, alarming, rate of intermarriage. Morgan's conclusions were based on data gathered by Erich Rosenthal, who
claimed that the rate of intermarriage for third-generation American Jews is 17.9 percent, and that 70 percent of the children of
these marriages are lost to the Jewish community.[4] It should be
noted, however, that most of Rosenthal's material and most of
the studies mentioned in the *Look* article are based on data gathered from small towns or cities where Jews are a small minority.
The statistics for New York and its suburban areas are not availa-

[3] From *Journal of Jewish Communal Service,* Vol. XII, No. 2, Winter,
1964, pp. 177–178.
[4] "Studies of Jewish Intermarriage in the United States," *American Jewish
Yearbook,* 1963, pp. 34–51.

ble, despite the important fact that close to half of the entire Jewish population is concentrated in this area. Rosenthal's researches are misleading because they deal with Iowa and its outlying communities, where the intermarriage rate is as high as 28 percent, and Washington, D.C., where it is said to reach 17.9 percent. Washington is probably the least typical of American cities because of its highly mobile population largely concentrated in government jobs. The statistics for synagogue membership in Washington, D.C., are far below the national average, and it does not seem reasonable to generalize from data representing these two unique settings.

It is impossible to find any set of statistics on the rate of Jewish intermarriage which agrees with any other set. Thus, for example, Nathan Glazer, generalizing from the 1957 Current Population Survey conducted by the Bureau of Census finds a national intermarriage rate of 3.5 percent and feels that it is probably lower for New York.[5] Using the same data, Goldstein and Goldscheider[6] come up with the figure 7.2 percent for marriages in which one spouse was Jewish and one non-Jewish.[7] Possibly Glazer, using the figures on conversion to Judaism in intermarriage, on which a number of studies have been done, corrected the uninterpreted statistics to arrive at the lower figure.

In all of this confusion, one study based on a random sample in the Greater Providence area of 1,603 households which contained at least one Jewish member goes a long way toward introducing some order. The total rate of intermarriage found was 4.5 percent, of which only 0.1 percent was between a Jewish female and a non-Jewish male. While these findings appear to be considerably lower than that of many other communities, they do square with studies in New Haven, Connecticut; Rochester, New York; and Camden, New Jersey. The authors broke down their findings in terms of age and generation and found that the lowest rate of intermarriage occurred in the oldest, largely first-generation group, the highest in the youngest, third-generation group. However, the proportion

---

[5] See Nathan Glazer and Daniel P. Moynihan, *Beyond the Melting Pot.* Cambridge, Massachusetts, M.I.T. Press, 1963.
[6] "Social and Demographic Aspects of Jewish Intermarriages," *Social Problems,* Vol. 13, No. 4, Spring, 1966.
[7] United States Bureau of the Census, *Current Population Reports,* Series P-20, No. 79, February, 1958.

of conversions to Judaism rises in direct ratio to the rise in rate of
intermarriage—in families where the male spouse was sixty or over
none of the partners had been converted; in the 40–59 age group,
four out of ten had converted, and in cases where the husband was
under forty years old, the percentage of conversions rose to 70
percent. To be sure, the statistics do not indicate how many Jews
are lost to the community so that they cannot be located at all.
Possibly, the fact that only 0.1 percent of intermarriages are between a Jewish female and a non-Jewish male reflects the fact that
in this kind of mating the family merges completely into the non-
Jewish community.

The Providence data also show that intermarried couples have
smaller families than couples in which both partners are born
Jewish; however, this is truer for the older than for the younger
couples studied, suggesting that eventually the fertility rates may
even out. In all cases where the non-Jewish partner had been converted, the children were being raised as Jews; in those cases where
there was no conversion, 84 children were being raised as Jews
against 60 who were not. In all, only 22 percent of the total number of children were being raised as non-Jews.

These findings are in direct contradiction to Rosenthal's—those
on which the *Look* article was based. It appears necessary to have
exhaustive studies of a great many communities before it will become possible to project the future of the American Jewish community in terms of numbers. The major value of such a study as
the one conducted in Providence is to point up the danger of
generalizing from findings in such atypical communities as Washington or Iowa.

Some keep describing a low rate of Jewish fertility in comparison to that of the population as a whole. Here, again, we have a
kind of generalization that is easier to make than to support. Jews
are largely members of the middle class. When Jewish fertility is
compared with that of middle-class Protestants, rather than with a
national sample including Catholics, the working class, the unemployed—the differences disappear. It would seem reasonable to
conclude that as the population generally moves into the middle
class, the fertility patterns for all groups will converge.

We have explored some of the data dealing with the social patterns of American Jews. The portrait that emerges is of a group

determined to retain its separateness, yet equally determined to "be like everyone else." We find little reason to be pessimistic about the physical disappearance of Jews, but what is Jewish, after all, is not biological. Judaism and Jewishness revolve around a long tradition—remembrances, attitudes, value systems, and disciplines, making up a singular culture. There is some evidence that older cultural patterns of Jews are still persisting, influencing such things as low delinquency, lack of alcoholism, and even their voting patterns. This latter is particularly interesting because studies have thus far indicated that Jews *do not* vote for Jewish candidates but for liberal candidates. Of all the groups studied, only the Jews do not fall into line by switching to the Republican Party when their economic status rises.[8] Civil rights, welfare, aid to education—these were the key issues that determined how Jewish voters cast their ballots. It would appear that for Jews, moral-political questions and ideological concerns still outweigh their own economic interest and status.

While it is heartening to know that Jews have not yet become "just like everybody else," that their unique history has retained its power to direct their decisions in a positive manner, the cultural survival this represents hardly connotes the survival of Judaism! It is, in a sense, derivative, a vestige of a past experience which is beginning to fade for lack of new reinvigorations.

The enduring qualities of a culture can only be transmitted through folkways, rites, the sacred and secular mores that are symbolized in festivals, prayers, poetry, songs. In short, the matrix of survival is education—the passing on of the uniquely Jewish values, gathered together over centuries, through teaching and practice. The evidence we now have in this area points in two directions. On the one hand, Jewish education has been considerably upgraded in the last number of years, and the great majority of the present young generation has far more Jewish education than its parents. Indeed, the growth of the intensive Jewish school —the all-day school—is a major development.[9] On the other hand, Jewish education, even in these day schools, with few exceptions

[8] W. Allingsmith and B. Allingsmith, "Religious Affiliation and Political-Economic Attitude: A Study of Eight Major United States Religious Groups," in *Public Opinion and Propaganda*, D. Katz et al., eds., 1954.

[9] Today over fifty thousand, or about 8 percent of all children receiving a Jewish religious education, are enrolled in the Jewish day school.

terminates at the elementary level, and Jewish students come to college with a child's knowledge of their culture and heritage.

In the European past the situation was reversed: Many Jews had the benefit of higher Jewish learning, but were denied the advantages of a general university education. In such circumstances, their cultural loyalties to Jewish life were firmly grounded in the roots of Jewish knowledge. While there has been a new and growing emphasis in the contemporary American Jewish community upon a more intensive elementary education, very few Jewish college graduates can boast of having received a *higher Jewish education*. It is already apparent that even their intensive elementary Jewish education cannot stand up to their new sophistication as college graduates; they rarely unlearn or relearn the Jewish materials they have been taught as children, in childish ways. Indeed, the more general learning they achieve, the more critical and secularized their thinking process grows. And if they have not complemented their new knowledge with an approach to Judaism equally adult and equally sophisticated, it is likely that they will forever identify its teachings only with the naïve and "primitive" meanings they were taught as children. Thus, the fact that American Jews will soon comprise a community consisting almost completely of college graduates poses new threats to their creative survival as a vital cultural group. Clearly, more strenuous efforts at developing programs to strengthen secondary and higher Jewish education are called for.

There are some signs on the horizon that do indicate a new orientation in this direction. Jewish students on the college campuses are turning in increasing numbers to the Hillel Foundations, the collegiate religious organizations sponsored by B'nai B'rith since 1925. There are today over 70 such full-time Foundations, in addition to almost 150 part-time Hillel Counselorships. These groups offer Jewish students on the American campus a wide variety of cultural, religious, and academic opportunities. The lectures, discussion groups, seminars, and classes they provide make Judaism available to the college student, on a level more proximate to his own intellectual status. Hillel also publishes high-caliber books on Judaism which further serve to advance the Jewish cultural level of the college student. The growing popularity of its program is attested to in the remarkable fact that, as of 1967, over two hundred American colleges were on Hillel's waiting list, looking forward to the future establishment of its service on their own campuses. The Hillel Foundation has thus become an integral part of the landscape of American higher education, by the side of Wesley, the Methodist student organization, and Newman, the organization of Catholic college students.

8. THE CHALLENGE OF THE CITY

Most of us are inhabitants of the modern city. The city is central to the destiny of modern man. He thinks, feels, and responds differently in the city than outside it. To an astonishing degree, studies of modern city man tend to be pessimistic, and at their core there is an unspoken nostalgia for the past, when life was simpler. A black vision emerges—the metropolis is seen as the necropolis, the city of the dead. The urbanite is presented as segmented, dehumanized, mechanized, outerdirected, depraved, lost. For many the city is portrayed as the image of the physical and moral ruin of mankind.

Now there is no doubt that as the city grows, there is a continuous breakdown of older traditional, social, and economic structures based on family ties, on local association, on culture, on caste, or status. All traditions are moderated in and modified by the city. Substantive values and traditional patterns are continually discarded, because the multiplication of the numbers of persons involved in interaction radically alters the nature of that interaction. A city is not a village multiplied a thousand times! It is different, and the challenges it presents are different.

The real surprise in this study, then, is not that change has taken place in religious attitudes, but the degree to which traditional ideas appear to have held! It is no accident that the statistics reveal that the big-city-dwellers, the most highly educated, and the young, are the groups who are challenging traditional religious beliefs in the greatest numbers. In a very real sense they are the men and women of the future; they represent the direction in which we are all going. Is this a trend to be accompanied by despair on the part of religious leaders, or is it a direction that needs to be properly evaluated, in order for the challenge to be taken up by the leaders of our churches and synagogues?

For Harvey Cox the challenge is exhilarating. "Urbanization," he writes, "contributes to the freedom of man. . . . He must exercise choice more frequently. . . ."[1] Urban man is delivered from obedience to conventions; he must choose to be anonymous to nine tenths of the people he meets, and he must carefully select those among the mass who will be his friends, those with whom he will enter into close relationship. "It is the chance to be free," says Cox.

Hand in hand with urbanization goes mobility. But mobility, we know, plays havoc with traditional forms of religion, for it is closely related to social change, which in turn generates intellectual and psychological changes. All of this adds up to the growing secularization of American society. This means that we are arriving at a genuinely free society based upon plural choices. For a long time America was conceived of as divided into three large segments—Protestant, Catholic, and Jewish, or what Martin E. Marty has termed the "American Shinto." But it becomes increasingly clear that American society also includes a great many people who do not fit into any of the three categories. And even within the three religious groupings, as the study reveals, are to be found great numbers whose beliefs depart drastically from the traditional formulations. In the secular city, man is free to choose his religion or none, just as he is free to choose his associates, his pleasures, and his foibles. Religion must now compete openly with all the other stimulations offered by the modern metropolis—intellectual, spiritual, and material—and win its adherents on the basis of what it has to offer that is true, what it has to say that is relevant to the condition of man today.

For those who throw up their hands in despair at the challenge presented by change, who retreat behind a barricade of ancient values and refuse to face the challenge, it is well to point out that the Judeo-Christian tradition implies constant movement, constant change. The primitive gods of ancient times were tied to place; they were the gods of a village or town, or resided in mountains, caves, in the sun, thunder, the ocean. They were gods who acted in accordance with the cycles of nature and, as such, could never transcend it. The great breakthrough of the Hebrew people under the leadership of Moses was the discovery of the God who

[1] *The Secular City.* New York, Macmillan, 1965, pp. 40–41.

exists in time. He acts in history, in fact, he reveals himself through history and thus cannot be tied to any place. He is a hidden God who is everywhere at once. It is surely no accident that monotheism was adopted by a people on the move, by a people whose life style was mobility and wandering, for whom sedentary gods could have no spiritual meaning. The God of history discovered by the Hebrew tribes in the desert above all implies freedom for man; freedom from subservience to an enchanted and demonic nature, and freedom to act in accordance with what he believes to be the will of God.

This is clearly seen in the Hebrew idea of the covenant. A covenant is a pact, an agreement between two partners. Thus the covenant implies that God and man together will cooperate in creating the future history of mankind. "God is transformed from an 'absolute' into a 'constitutional' monarch," Erich Fromm suggests. "He is bound, as man is bound, to the conditions of the constitution. God has lost his freedom to be arbitrary, and man has gained the freedom of being able to challenge God in the name of God's own promises, of the principles laid down in the convenant."

A careful reading of the Hebrew Bible makes it clear that it is essentially a series of documents defining the nature of man. Man is seen as free because he is regarded as a partner of God. In essence, the Hebrew Bible is a call to freedom.

Much of the crisis of America in the 1960's lies in the agonizing conflict between the vestigial strength of sacral definitions and interests (reinforced by already shaky group self-image and identity) and the move toward the secular, open, free society. Paradoxically, the Jews who have always opted for the freedom and possibilities inherent in the emancipated climate of the secular city, and who have made no small contribution in promoting and supporting its development, now find themselves increasingly American. Instead of remaining marginal, they try to assimilate culturally.

This survey, along with many others, points to the waning of stereotyped notions, the clear gains for tolerance and acceptance in American life—and yet all may not be as well as supposed.

The intersection of and the conflict between older sacral notions and current secular trends and aspirations may give rise to explosive tensions and irritabilities between groups on either side or in the middle. Historically, Jews have been not only the promoters of change, but very often its victims, as well.

Perhaps all this is best summed up by Ben Halpern: "In cold fact, the acceptance of Judaism as an American faith, when voiced by Christians, frequently implies a degree of confidence that Judaism is progressing toward submergence. . . . In Jewish mouths, talk of a Judeo-Christian civilization or of a peer relationship among Catholics, Protestants, and Jews often tacitly anticipates an eventual merger in a joint American religion. . . . The most significant novel element in the Jewish experience today is not the relatively limited changes which these developments have so far wrought in gentiles' attitudes towards Jews; it is the attitude changes that are needed among Jews themselves. . . ."[2]

Jews, in America, are free to change, as never before. They are changing. They will change. Most will remain Jews. All of these things we know—and the survey retells them.

But will their future be worthy of their past? Will they still be partners in the covenant?

[2] "Three Soliloquies on a Colloquium," in *Jewish Frontier*, February, 1967, pp. 7–11.

BIBLIOGRAPHY

American Jewish Committee, "Baysville" and "Southville," two unpublished studies sponsored by the AJC.

Bogue, Donald J., *The Population of the United States.* Glencoe, Illinois, The Free Press, 1959.

Dinnin, Samuel, "The Quest for Identification," a mimeographed paper.

Free, R., Whelpton, P. K., and Smith, J. W., "Socio-Economic Factors in Religious Differentials in Fertility." *American Sociological Review,* 1961.

Greenberg, M., "Social Characteristics of the Jewish Students at the University of Maryland." *Jewish Social Studies,* Vol. XXIII, January, 1961.

Jospe, A., *Judaism on the Campus: Essays on Jewish Education in the University Community.* B'nai B'rith Hillel Foundation, 1963.

Kallen, Horace M., "American Jews, What Now?" *The Jewish Social Service Quarterly,* Vol. XXXII, No. 1, 1955.

Lee, Robert, and Marty, Martin E., eds., *Religion and Social Conflict.* New York, Oxford University Press, 1964.

Minkin, Jacob S., *The World of Moses Maimonides.* New York, Thomas Yosseloff, 1957.

Montefiore, C. G., and Loewe, H., *A Rabbinic Anthology.* Philadelphia, The Jewish Publication Society of America, 1960.

Moore, George F., *Judaism in the First Centuries of the Christian Era, the Age of the Tannaim.* Cambridge, Massachusetts, Harvard University Press, 1954.

Rosenberg, Stuart E., *America Is Different*. New York, Thomas Nelson and Sons, 1964. (Also published by Doubleday Anchor as paperback 1965 under the title, *The Search for Jewish Identity in America*.)

Sanua, Victor D., "Jewish Survival and Jewish Education: A Review of Empirical Studies." *Orot*. Jerusalem, 1965.

Sklare, Marshall, ed., *The Jews: Social Patterns of an American Group*. Glencoe Illinois, The Free Press, 1958.

Slawson, John, "Quest for Jewish Identity in America," a mimeographed paper of the American Jewish Committee.

Stein, Maurice R., *The Eclipse of Community*. New York, Harper Torchbooks, 1964.

Vidich, A. J., and Bensman, Joseph, *Small Town in Mass Society*. Garden City, New York, Anchor Books, 1958.

PART THREE

by

Andrew M. Greeley

1. CONTINUITY AND CHANGE
IN AMERICAN RELIGION

This essay on the study of religious change addresses itself to the question of how much permanency in religious beliefs and religious organization can be expected in a highly dynamic American society. The basic sources of information are two national surveys, one taken in 1952 and the other in 1965. The principal analytical technique used will be a comparison of the responses of American Protestants, Catholics, and Jews in 1965 to the responses of the same three religious groups in 1952. Since this section is written by a professional sociologist, it will lean much more heavily on the actual statistical tables than do the other two essays. When one determines to stay very close to the statistical data, one runs the risk of producing a volume which is neither easy nor exciting reading. Nonetheless, there are so many spacious generalizations about American religious behavior in the mass media at the present time that there seems to be some considerable merit in remaining very close to empirical data whenever one possibly can.

There are five major findings which will be discussed in this essay:

1. There is little evidence of major doctrinal change or major decline in religious activities among American gentiles, but there seems to be a rather notable doctrinal decline among American Jews while at the same time there has been an increase in religious activity in the Jewish group.

2. There is some evidence of major structural strain in American Catholicism.

3. The religious-school question continues to be a lively one in

American society, but there is no evidence that American Catholics are disenchanted with Catholic education.

4. There is a decline of anti-Jewish feeling among gentiles; and there is also a decline of anti-Catholic feeling among Protestants; but there is an increase of anti-Catholic feeling among Jews.

5. Religious differences between young people and adults, at least as measured by the indicators available to this study, are not very great; there is therefore no evidence of a massive defection from religion among those under twenty-five.

The data with which we are working in this report have one major advantage and a number of disadvantages of greater or lesser importance. The advantage is that the data provide an extremely rare commodity in social-science research—time series information. Since exactly the same questions were asked by the American Institute of Public Opinion in 1965 as were asked by Ben Gaffin and Associates in 1952, we were able to measure quite precisely the change in expression of religious attitudes and beliefs. When Father John Thomas wrote his *Religion and the American People*[1] as a report of the 1952 research, he had no information as to how the questions would have been answered in 1942 or 1932 or in any previous time in the history of American religion. It was therefore necessary for him to speculate on whether the 1952 data represented an increase or a decrease in religious activity. Thomas' response was a very subtle and sophisticated one, but other commentators are not so skillful in avoiding the "good old days" fallacy. They immediately concluded that there was a decline in religious faith since an unnamed date in the past, but that presumption has no social scientific validity. We simply do not know what the precise percentages of the American population were that went to church on a given Sunday in 1920 or the precise percentages of American gentiles who believed in the divinity of Christ in 1920. Speculation is fun but hardly precise. However, the 1965 survey makes it possible for us to speak meaningfully about the changes that have occurred between 1952 and 1965. Guesswork about certain dimensions of religious change tapped by the survey questionnaire is eliminated. The findings of such precise analysis may not be very spectacular (though surely

[1] John L. Thomas, S.J., *Religion and the American People*. Westminster, Maryland, The Newman Press, 1963.

some of the changes reported in this volume are very spectacular) or capture newspaper headlines, but they have a distinct advantage of being based on statistical documentation instead of guesswork or fantasy.

Such an advantage is one that is rather infrequent in social research, though increasingly social scientists are recognizing the value of precise replications of previous studies. But we must also honestly note the disadvantages under which this volume labors.

First of all, there are numerous problems involved in all survey research, more specific problems occur in the sociology of religion, and finally, there are some distinct disadvantages in the material made available in the present project.

Survey research is based on the rather broad assumption that an interviewer decending upon the house of a randomly selected American is able to learn through perhaps an hour of questions and answers significant and valuable information about the attitude and the behavior of the respondent. It further assumes that when a properly chosen random sample is assembled, the respondents interviewed will be representative of broad categories of the total American population. Both of these assumptions are taken for granted by most educated Americans, and only when sample survey findings violently conflict with one's own beliefs or prejudices, are the assumptions called in question. It is perhaps unfortunate that more Americans do not understand the rationale behind these assumptions so that they could be more nuanced in their reactions to sample surveys.

The second assumption is the easier to establish for those who are capable of understanding the complexities of probability mathematics. If a sample is properly random, then it can within certain limits of confidence be taken to represent accurately the larger population. The important question for the student of the survey is not Does sampling work? but Was the sampling in the particular survey well executed? Since most Americans cannot be expected to understand the methodology involved in sample surveys, they must rely on the integrity and competence of the international sampling organizations. Without at this time attempting to give a quality rating to sampling agencies, we can be content by saying that both the polling organizations which provided material for the present volume were and are reliable.

The assumption that the interviewer can get at reality is a more difficult one to establish. What does the response to a question really mean? Does the question itself adequately measure the attitude or behavioral dimension in question? Is the respondent telling the truth? Or even if he thinks he is telling the truth, will he behave according to what he has said in his response? The answers to these questions are not particularly easy, and while those who are engaged in social research are constantly striving to improve their techniques, it must be understood that, at least in its present stage of development, survey research still must stand halfway between art and science. One can place a reasonable amount of trust in a questionnaire which has been carefully prepared by one of the major commercial or academic survey-research organizations. It gets at *something* "out there," but it is likely to be still a rather crude and imperfect tool. One would be mistaken to reject out of hand the findings of survey research, but also one would be mistaken to think that there is no need for caution or reservation in accepting and interpreting the results of such research. It is a careful, systematic, and relatively economic way to measure certain rather broad aspects of behavioral and attitudinal reality. It can collect information which is infinitely superior to personal impression or personal opinion, but the reader of this volume and indeed the reader of any survey-research report must not think that the neat and orderly statistical tables are an indication that human behavior has been precisely measured. What we are reporting in this volume is the change in the responses to questions between 1952 and 1965. It is safe to assume that the changing patterns of response also represent some sort of change in reality. Gentiles' religious beliefs do not appear to be undergoing great change, while Jewish attitudes toward Catholics do appear to be undergoing great change. Beyond these assertions, which we can make rather confidently, one must necessarily be very cautious, at least on the basis of the data herein analyzed, in saying what precisely the nature of continuity and change in American religious belief and practice really is.

There are also special difficulties in the survey-research approach to religion. The questions that survey-research technology has so far devised to measure religious attitude and behavior seem to be particularly ill suited for coping with the subtle nature of religious beliefs. Thus in the present survey, when the respondent was asked whether he thought of God as a loving Father or some kind of infinite power, it probably appeared to such a respondent that the question really had little connection to his own notion of the nature of the Deity. Similarly, when he was asked to say whether the Bible was the inspired word of God or merely great literature, he might have felt a necessity for clarifying what he would mean by either answer. Both the professional theologian and the interested lay reader can easily criticize the wording of the questionnaire (in this survey as well as in other religious surveys), but they will find it somewhat harder to rephrase the questions in such a way as to be confident that a better format has been found. Progress has been made in the last decade and a half in measuring religious attitudes. In a sense it is both fortunate and unfortunate that the 1965 survey did not include some of the new "standard items" in religious research; the responses to such questions would have provided a base line for measuring changes fifteen years hence.

There are particular problems in measuring religious behavior of American Jews, as is pointed out in Mr. Rosenberg's essay. The religious values and norms of the Jewish community differ radically from that of the gentile community. Those measures which would be important indicators of religiosity for gentiles would be considerably less important indicators for Jews. The questionnaire used in the present research was essentially a gentile questionnaire. Thirdly, since Jews are only 3 percent of the American population, even a fairly large national sample such as the 1965 sample would contain a relatively small proportion of Jewish respondents; 128 Jews are actually a rather thin base on which one can make broad generalizations. One is forced to limit oneself to saying that the changing patterns in the Jewish population are so extremely interesting that further research with a larger sample of Jews is clearly indicated.

Finally, there are problems peculiar to the two surveys on which this volume is based. The questions on religious belief are few and relatively superficial. There is no measure of the depth of religious commitment or of the meaningful nature of religious experience. There are no personality variables which might explain or at least give a hint of an explanation of the meaning in the respondent's life of his religious behavior. Lastly, the IBM cards on which the 1952 material was recorded have unfortunately been lost, and while it is possible for us to say, for example, how many Jews

believed in God in 1952 and how many college graduates believed
in God in 1952, it is impossible for us to say how many Jewish
college graduates believed in God in 1952 and thus impossible
to make any meaningful comparisons between the responses of
such subgroups in the 1952 survey and the 1965 survey. We are
able to affirm that the Jewish belief in God has declined, but we
are not able to affirm whether this is merely a result of an increase
in educational level among Jews or whether the belief in God has
declined among Jews no matter what their educational background is. For sociologists this inability is a particularly severe
handicap.

The basic analytical technique to be used in this volume is called
multivariate analysis, and a word should be said about this
method. The sociologist sees that Jewish faith in God has declined
from 1952 to 1965, while gentile faith has not so declined, but he
also realizes that Jews are far better educated than gentiles and he
suspects therefore that the difference in faith and belief in God
may well be a function of this higher educational level. He therefore separates Jews and gentiles into (at least in this volume)
three groups—those who did not go beyond grammar school, those
who went to high school but not college, and finally those who
went to college. He then compares members of the three religions
within each educational group on their belief in God. The finding
is that college-educated Jews are much less likely to believe in God
than Jews who did not go to college but that there is little difference among the gentile educational groups. He therefore determines that there is a relationship between not believing in God
and higher education among Jews, and that higher education has
an impact on the faith in God of Jews that it does not have on the
faith of gentiles. Whether college-educated Jews today are less
likely to believe in God than they were in 1952 is impossible to say
in the absence of the 1952 IBM cards.

How seriously can one be expected to take the findings of this
volume in view of the qualifications and reservations which we
have discussed in this chapter? The proper response is neither to
reject them completely nor accept them unreservedly. Like all
survey research, the findings reported in this book tell us something, and they tell us something rather important, and relatively
inexpensively. They give important hints but they tell us considerably less than everything we need to know. For example, we have

learned that the anti-Catholic feeling among Jews seems to have increased noticeably. This finding cannot simply be dismissed. It ought to be a matter for grave concern and for more careful research, but neither can it be asserted as a phenomenon proved beyond all reasonable question.

Most of this first chapter has been spent in establishing that the world to be reported in this volume is a gray and probabilistic world. In such a world, one is often (to use the phrase of a national news magazine about another survey) "mired in qualifications." Nonetheless, it seems appropriate in dealing with the highly delicate and controversial matter presented in this book to warn the reader at the very beginning that, if he is not prepared to be mired in qualifications, he should stay away from not only this book but from all survey-research reports, or at least all that have any claim to integrity. On the other hand, the fact that our findings are necessarily mired in qualifications, a mire which we have clearly pointed out in this first chapter, may persuade some readers that the report may come fairly close to the world as it really is, a world which, whether we like it or not, is filled with qualifications.

2. THE GOD WHO WOULD NOT STAY DEAD

In whatever segment of the hereafter the shade of Friedrich Nietzsche is to be found, he must be somewhat amused (or perhaps violently angry) at the outburst of "God Is Dead" publicity.[1] Whether the radical secular theologians realized that they had such a marvelous public-relations gimmick in announcing considerably more than a century after the late Herr Nietzsche that the Deity had departed is problematic. Nevertheless, they touched what apparently is an important aspect of the American personality, the willingness, even eagerness, to believe that everything is rapidly going to hell, a pilgrimage which one can reasonably expect to be reported even on the cover of *Time* magazine.

---

[1] One wonders what Nietzsche would think of the craze of bumper stickers commenting on the death of the Deity: "God Is Not Dead, He Just Doesn't Want to Get Involved," "God Is Alive and Well in Argentina," and "God Is Alive in Jerusalem."

If one is to believe the radical theologians and their more moderate fellow travelers, the secular theologians, and the journalistic popularizers of both, belief in God is no longer relevant in human society. It is not always immediately obvious what such an assertion means. It might mean that people may profess belief in God but fail to take his existence or his presumed prescripts seriously in their daily lives. It may mean that religion has less direct influence over other social institutions than it did in the Middle Ages. It may mean that the intellectual elite of the nation is not comfortable with organized religion or even religious beliefs. It may finally mean that major segments of the general population can no longer live with the religious beliefs of their predecessors. This volume can only deal with the last assertion, though it is worth remarking that the first assertion has probably been true through the course of history and that the second and the third, while they may be true, are of themselves hardly very new. If the radical or secular theologians are merely reporting any of the first three assertions, one is permitted to wonder what the fuss is all about. If, on the other hand, the fourth assertion is true, then indeed we are in the midst of a major social change and perhaps even revolution.

The first of the many tables in this report (Table 2.1) does not provide much consolation for those who would have us believe that God is dead or dying in the minds of the general population. Among American gentiles there are only negligible changes between 1952 and 1965 in the percentage believing in God, the Divinity of Christ, the Trinity, life after death, and the existence of heaven. Similarly, there are only minor changes in those who pray at all or pray frequently or consider themselves active church members. One is a bit at a loss to say how important changes of one or two percentage points, or even three percentage points, actually are. In Table 2.1 there are more minus signs than plus signs in the columns representing gentile respondents. If these small attritions were to continue over a century, or even half a century, then we surely would have a major religious change, but the differences in gentile responses in 1952 and 1965 are not such that one can evaluate them as being important, much less revolutionary, and they may well be simply minor fluctuations without any importance whatever. One will only be able to say for certain when the study is done once again, perhaps in 1980.

But if the changes among the gentiles are relatively minor, the

changes among the Jews are striking. Jews are 21 percentage points
less likely to believe in God, 19 percentage points less likely to
pray, 18 percentage points less likely to believe in life after death,
and 15 percentage points less likely to believe in heaven. While
propositional faith may well not be nearly so important for Jews as
it is for gentiles, it still would seem that there are major religious
changes going on within the Jewish population, changes which,
however, do not necessarily indicate that Jews are less likely to
consider themselves Jews or even less likely to be affiliated with a
Jewish congregation. Thus, as the last item on Table 2.1 indicates,
despite the changing shape of Jewish religious belief in the thir-
teen-year period under investigation, Jews are 12 percentage
points more likely to consider themselves active church members.

While there are therefore certain basic continuities among
American gentiles in their religious beliefs and practices, there are
also some interesting changes which are summarized in Table 2.2.
All three religious groups—Protestants, Jews, and Catholics—were
less likely to report in 1965 that religion was important in their
own personal lives than they were in 1952. They were also—at
least Jews and Protestants—less likely to believe that the Bible is
the inspired word of God. On the other hand, there has been a
general increase in church attendance among all three groups
(annual church attendance for Jews having been chosen as a
somewhat more important indicator of Jewish religious behavior
than weekly attendance at the synagogue). Furthermore, even
though they are apparently not so committed to the Bible's being
the explicit word of God, all three groups are much more likely to
report that they read the Bible at least once weekly. We have thus
the interesting paradox that Americans are less likely to think
religion is important in their lives but more likely to attend
church, less likely to think that the Bible is the inspired word of
God but more likely to read it.[2]

One is somewhat hard put to find an explanation for these phe-

[2] The percentages claiming to read the Bible at least once weekly are
extremely high. The writer is inclined to suspect that the change reported in
Bible reading may have to do with the fashion rather than a change in
behavior. It may very well be that Americans are more likely to think
they *ought* to read the Bible and hence more likely to report that they in
fact do read it.

nomena, particularly among gentiles. It may be that a greater religious sophistication has emerged and that Americans are more rigorous in their norms of what constitutes an important religious influence. It may also be that they are more sophisticated in their notions of the theology of inspiration, or it could conceivably mean that more exposure to the Bible has forced them to modify somewhat the concept of inspiration. In any case, it is clear from Table 2.2 that within the broad continuities in American religious behavior, particularly among gentiles, there are also forces of change at work, changes which are paradoxical and difficult to understand but whose long-run impact, while yet hard to calculate, may be extremely important.

We therefore have two unsolved problems emerging from Tables 2.1 and 2.2: (1) What is the explanation of the major changes in religious attitude and behavior among Jews? and (2) What is at the root of the somewhat paradoxical changes which are occurring within the broad context of continuity among American gentiles?

Table 2.3 is an attempt to add to our understanding of changing religious patterns among the Jewish population. Younger Jews are less likely to believe in God than older Jews, with a 30 percent difference between those under thirty-five and those over fifty. Similarly, the younger Jews are less likely to pray and so those between thirty-five and fifty are quite similar to those under thirty-five. However, it is the middle-aged group which is least likely to believe in life after death, while both younger and older Jews have higher percentages (approximately one fifth) reporting a belief in an afterlife. It is precisely this same middle-aged group that is also most likely to report church affiliation, with almost three quarters of the Jews between thirty-five and fifty describing themselves as members of congregations.

The second panel in Table 2.3 reports basically similar information. There is a negative relationship between education and belief in God, prayer, and a belief in life after death among American Jews. Furthermore, it is precisely the high-school-educated Jews who are the most likely to report congregational affiliation.

In both panels the case bases are relatively thin and one attempts generalizations and explanations with great caution, but it would appear that middle-aged Jews and Jews with a high-school education may well represent that element in the Jewish population where a decline in acceptance of doctrinal propositions can coexist with an increase in congregational affiliation; as a number of authors have suggested, congregational affiliation has become synonymous among "suburban" Jews with the maintenance of Jewish ethnic identity without demanding any specifically religious convictions.

The final panel in Table 2.3 lends some confirmation to this explanation. The Jews in the higher-income groups are less likely to believe in God, less likely to pray, and less likely to believe in life after death, but they are considerably more likely to report congregational affiliation. The picture that emerges, however tentatively, from Table 2.3 is that as the Jewish population becomes more successful, better educated, and more integrated into American life, its readiness to affirm specific doctrinal propositions decreases, while its congregational membership increases, as, at least in part, a means of maintaining a Jewish identity. Among the younger Jews, however, and the college-educated Jews, there does seem to be some decline in congregational membership, though it is possible that younger Jews will increase their level of congregational affiliation as their children become of school age and the problem of the maintenance of a Jewish identity in their children becomes more serious. If this explanation is correct, then it would follow that the future of religious affiliation among American Jews is closely tied to the importance of the maintenance of Jewish identity. If ethnic identity should become less important among the younger generation of American Jews, then we might expect that congregational affiliation would be in very serious straits indeed.

We find few hints of an explanation of the paradoxical changes among American gentiles in Table 2.4. Younger Catholics and Protestants are less likely than older ones to say that religion is important in their lives, and they also are less likely to attend church weekly, though in both instances there is to be observed what sociologists call a U-curve. That is, the middle group, those between thirty-five and fifty-five, are more likely to report weekly church attendance than either the younger or older groups, leading us to suspect that we are dealing with a phenomenon that has largely to do with age and not with generational change. The young people are too busy to go to church, and older people do not have the health to attend quite so frequently, but it is very

likely that when the middle-aged become older, their church attendance will decline somewhat, and when the younger become
middle-aged, their church attendance will increase.

It is also the youth who are more skeptical of the Bible being
the word of God, but also, at least among Protestants, it is the
young who are more likely to report reading the Bible weekly
than the old. There is therefore in the first panel of Table 2.4
not much that will help us to explain the paradox of increased
church attendance and increased Bible reading with greater skepticism about the inspiration of the Bible and the importance of
religion in one's own personal life. In the last two panels of Table
2.4 we attempt to discover whether the social class variables such as
income and education are any help in understanding the para-
doxes. Those with higher income are more likely to think of religion as important and to attend church weekly. They are also,
among the Protestant groups, simultaneously less likely to give
credence to the inspiration of the Bible but more likely to read the
Bible. Those with a college education are less likely to think religion is important and considerably more likely to attend
church. Similarly, they are less likely to think of the Bible as inspired if they are Protestants and more likely to read it.

We therefore can find no explanation in age or social class variables for the paradoxical changes occurring among American gentiles. One is inclined to suspect (until another survey fifteen years
hence makes possible a table comparable with Table 2.4) that
whatever the changes are, they run more or less uniformly through
the whole religious culture and do not affect one age or social class
group more than any other.

Religion is still very important to Americans, particularly of the
upper social classes and middle-aged groups; and religious behavior, both church attendance and Bible reading, is, if anything,
more important than it was a decade and a half ago. On the other
hand, the persistent criticism of religion as a means of social
location, which began with Will Herberg and has persisted for
the last decade and a half, has made Americans somewhat more
skeptical of how meaningful external religious conformity really
is. Such a suggestion, of course, is subject to further testing, but if
it is correct, it probably represents some sort of net gain for organized religion.

In this chapter we have sketched in broad outline the continuities and changes in religious attitudes and behavior in the American population. Although there are some puzzling changes within the gentile group, the broad picture of doctrinal belief and organizational practice did not change for gentiles appreciably between 1952 and 1965. Not only did not God die for the general population, but he does not even seem to be appreciably ill. On the other hand, there have been major changes in propositional religion among the Jews, which has meshed paradoxically enough with an increase in congregational affiliation. God is not dead for the Jews either, but there is some evidence that he may be dying; however, *religion* among the Jews seems to be improving.

3. STRESSES AND STRAINS WITHIN CATHOLICISM

We need only to glance casually at newspaper headlines to realize that there are major changes within the Roman Catholic community in the United States. The Mass is said in English, with the priest facing the people. The Protestants have stopped being heretics or schismatics and have become separated brothers. Ecclesiastical leaders no longer have unquestioned respect. On the contrary, it often seems that the leadership of the brothers is treated with a great deal more reverence than Catholic leadership. Theological formulations of the past are openly reexamined, and moral teachings which were once thought to be completely immutable have become the subject matter for public debate. An institution which was once conceived of as stable and almost stagnant is suddenly swept by vigorous currents of reform and perhaps even revolution.

It is fashionable to credit this dramatic change in the posture of Roman Catholicism to the charismatic genius of Pope John XXIII. There is no doubt that this great man captured the imagination of the world as few leaders ever have, nor is there any doubt that his summoning of the Vatican Council and the style of leadership he manifested for his all-too-brief reign were of major moment in shaking Roman Catholicism to its very roots. But Pope John's refusal to take the prophets of doom seriously and his eagerness to engage in dialogue with the modern world served more as a catalyst than a cause. The forces making for change in counterreformation Catholicism were at work in Europe for almost a half century. Renewal of interest in positive theology, Scripture, church history, and modern philosophy, combined with social-action commitments and attempts to recapture the lost working class probably would have occasioned remarkable changes within Western Catholicism in any event. Pope John's genius was to recognize that the forces of change demanded release.

Catholicism has therefore put aside the frozen immobility of the counterreformation and entered into the relatively open dialogue of the ecumenical age. The ghetto walls appropriate in the garrison church have collapsed at least in principle and have been replaced by an eagerness for discussion and conversation which Protestant ecumenists in their relaxed and off-the-record moments will admit is something of an embarrassment. The change, of course, is anything but complete, and the forces of conservatism and reaction in the Roman Church have yet to give up the battle; but the winds that were blowing outside of Pope John's windows when he opened them were powerful, and now that they have swept into the Church it does not seem very likely that the windows can be closed once again.

Within American Catholicism the change from the counterreformation to the ecumenical age has been complicated by the fact that American Catholics have finally come abreast of the rest of the population socially and economically. Catholics under forty are just as successful occupationally and financially, just as likely to have gone to college and even to have gone on to graduate school as American Protestants. The election of a Catholic President was but symbolic evidence that the immigrant experience was over, that the American Catholics were now full-fledged junior partners of the American experiment.

But the immigrant journey was a long one, and the habits Catholicism in this country acquired during the process are not easily put aside. The early Catholic Church in the United States under the leadership of the aristocratic John Carroll was thoroughly native American. The establishment of lay trustees to own the parish, Carroll's insistence that he and his coadjutors be elected by their colleagues in the clergy, and the policy laid down by Carroll of being as American as possible were all based partly on the need to adjust to American society but partly on Carroll's conviction that the American way, after all, was the best for the Catholic Church in this country and quite possibly in any part of the world. Carroll was part of the early American Establishment. He once went to Canada on a mission with Benjamin Franklin during the Revolutionary War in an attempt to persuade the Canadians to join the patriot cause. His brother was a signer of the Constitution, and his cousin was Charles Carroll of Carrollton, who was the last to die of the signers of the Declaration of Independence, was also a close business associate and personal friend of George Washington and was briefly considered as Washington's successor as President. When John Carroll saw fit to address congratulations to the newly elected President Washington, he did so indeed as a leader of a minority religious sect, with hardly thirty thousand members out of the three million Americans, but he also spoke as a member of the Maryland aristocracy, an acquaintance of the President, and a cousin of one of the President's close friends. The early American Catholicism may have been looked upon with suspicion by non-Catholic Americans because of its Roman allegiance, but it was not viewed basically as a church of foreigners, nor did it consider itself to be particularly threatened by a xenophobic society.

But when the waves of immigrants began to wash up on the American shores in the nineteenth century, the situation drastically changed. Catholicism was no longer a small sect, nor was it any longer politically harmless. The American Protestants were unhappy and even frightened by tens of thousands of "foreigners" of Catholic allegiance who entered their cities every year. The Catholic reaction to nativism was one of suspicion and hostility, even though an occasional genius like John England, first bishop of Charleston, clearly demonstrated that American political democracy provided an ideal format for the governance of the Catholic Church in the United States. The more typical reaction was that of the paternalistic and militant archbishop of New York, John Hughes, who fought the Protestants tooth and nail every inch of the way and won at least as many battles as he lost. Deeply afraid of the threat to the faith of the immigrant, Catholicism in the United States retreated behind ghetto walls.

By the end of the century, under the leadership of the so-called Americanists, particularly James Gibbons, John Lancaster Spalding, John Ireland, and John Keane, the liberal wing of the Ameri-

can Catholic Church made a dramatic attempt to thoroughly
Americanize Catholicism and, indeed, to bear the gospel of Americanism to the rest of the Church. While not officially condemned
by Rome, they were nonetheless warned quite clearly in a condemnation of the so-called heresy of Americanism; well into the
middle of the twentieth century a defensive and inward-looking
style was still typical of the organized ecclesiastical structure.

A compromise was reached between the Americanizers and the
anti-Americanizers, with ecclesiastical leaders being loyal sup-
porters of American democracy and American foreign policy,
vigorous in their affirmation of patriotism but autocratic and
paternalistic in their government inside the Church, on the
grounds that such use of authority was essential if the Church was
to survive in a culture that was basically hostile and unfriendly
and a threat to the faith of the poor and ignorant immigrants.

The Al Smith campaign in 1928, even though it represented, by
the very fact that a Catholic had been nominated, a major step for
the Catholic population, still convinced American Catholics, and
particularly their leaders, that anti-Catholic feeling was as strong
as it ever was. The economic disaster of the great Depression
slowed to a halt the upward climb of the immigrant groups and
led many social-science observers to conclude that Catholics would
be an almost permanent part of the working-class population,
since they lacked, it seemed, sufficient amounts of the "Protestant
ethics" to achieve parity with Protestants in American society.

It was only with the end of the Second World War and the
two decades of prosperity which followed it that it became possible
for the final Americanization of the Catholic population to take
place, an Americanization which ·came to a fitting climax with
the inauguration of John F. Kennedy. But even though by 1960
Catholicism had become a middle-class religion and was rapidly
becoming a religion of the upper middle class, the styles of ecclesiastical government, the relationships between clergy and laity,
the approach to moral and doctrinal problems, and the attitude
toward culture and society beyond the Church were relatively little changed since the beginning of the century. Even without the
Vatican Council, the strains and pressures generated by this in-
congruity would have certainly increased, but the coincidence of
the transition of the Church universal from the counterreformation to the ecumenical age, with the transition of the American

Church from the slum to the suburb, apparently made the strains and stresses within the Catholic community even greater. We are therefore forced to ask whether the 1965 survey indicates any major changes within the Roman Catholic population in their religious attitude and behavior. Some Catholic observers are inclined to say that American Catholicism is such a rapidly changing phenomenon that three years ago is almost ancient history and the positions taken by American Catholics in 1965 are no indication of what their position might be today. Without intending to deny the very unstable condition apparently existing in Roman Catholicism in the United States today, we are skeptical that large masses of the population will change greatly in the space of two or three years; elite groups, particularly those in close touch with the key communication networks, may change very rapidly. The masses of the population will change more slowly. We can be reasonably confident that a large mass of American Catholics will have changed only very little in the last three years.

Data reported in the previous chapter would also suggest that as far as basic doctrinal commitment, church attendance, and organizational participation are concerned, there occurred only very minor changes in the Catholic population from 1952 to 1965. Thus, at the conclusion of the Vatican Council, the doctrinal faith and religious activity of the Catholic population of the United States were not very different from the early 1950's.

But the major changes in Catholicism, or at least the changes most likely to hit the front page of the newspapers, have not been doctrinal changes but rather the restructuring of relationships inside the institutional church and open questioning of ethical stands which were previously considered inviolable.

The fertility studies done at the University of Michigan and Princeton University in the last decade have clearly demonstrated that a substantial segment of the Catholic population was either unwilling or unable to honor the Church's teaching on birth control. In 1952 a *Catholic Digest*'s study created something of a sensation when it reported that only about half the Catholics in the United States reported themselves in agreement with the Church's teachings on both divorce and birth control. Table 3.1 indicates a substantial change in the thirteen years between 1952 and 1965, with only a little better than a third of the Catholic respondents disapproving of divorce or "mechanical means" of birth control. The forces of change in American Catholicism have not yet produced mutations in acceptance of essential creedal propositions, but they have very clearly led to dramatic change in ethical norms. It should be noted that the survey in 1965 was taken before the deliberations of the papal birth-control commission and before the widespread publication of articles by many Catholic theologians indicating that a change in the Church's position on birth control was feasible. If such a change does, in fact, occur, there would be reason to think, on the basis of Table 3.1, the change in the official stand of the Church will follow and not precede a change in opinion on the part of the general Catholic population.

In addition to dramatic shifts in ethical position, Table 3.1 also indicates that rather major changes may be taking place in the organizational structure of American Catholicism. In the Protestant and Jewish groups there was little change in attitude toward their respective clergy in the thirteen years between 1952 and 1965. However, Catholics are rather less likely in the latter time to describe their clergy as very understanding and as preachers of excellent sermons than they were in 1952 and rather more likely to accuse them of being too concerned about money. While these items may not be perfect indicators of shift in attitudes toward the clergy, they do, nonetheless, strongly suggest that the strains of changing Catholicism have substantially weakened the position and the respect that the Catholic clergy have previously enjoyed. No longer the unquestioned social leader of his community, nor one of the best-educated men in the community, the Catholic priest frequently finds himself dealing with the problems of the present by using the techniques and vocabularly of the past. He is well aware, at least in principle, that his people are no longer uneducated immigrants, but he has been unable to adjust himself in practice to the implication of this change. Even though he may be making more effort to be understanding, working harder on his sermons, and using a much softer sell on parish finances, he has not changed nearly so much as his people and is hence subject to stronger criticism than he was in years gone by.

The survey material on which we are reporting was, of course, not designed specifically to measure the impact of the post-conciliar reform on American Catholicism, and the five indicators reported in Table 3.1 are indicators and nothing else; but they are indicators that strongly suggest that momentous changes are oc-

curring in American Catholicism and that these changes are producing severe organizational and ethical strains.

Our data also suggest that the truth lies somewhere in between
two possible extremes in evaluating the post-conciliar Church. It
would not be true to say that as of 1965 American Catholicism was
falling apart. The basic organizational participation, Church attendance, and doctrinal orthodoxy of Catholics were, at least in
1965, relatively unaffected by the forces set in motion at the Vatican Council. But neither would it be true to say that the change
and ferment in the American Church is limited to a small group of
malcontents, no larger, let us say, than the circulation of the *National Catholic Reporter*. The general Catholic population may
not be sophisticated enough to understand the implications, let us
say, of new questions in Christology, and they may be quite unaffected by the writings of the radical or secular theologians. Nev-
erthless, they are anything but unaware that their Church is
changing. Other surveys show clear examples of their enthusiasm
about the English liturgy and that they would not be opposed to a
married clergy. Our data indicate that in addition there has been a
drastic change in their attitude toward birth control and divorce
and there is a great deal more restlessness toward their clergy. It is
too early at this time to say what the future portends for Roman
Catholicism in the United States, but it seems unlikely that the
forces set in motion by the dual transition we have discussed in
this chapter will not abate in the foreseeable future.

There is also considerable reason to think that the changes, at
least in attitudes toward sex, are fairly general throughout the
Catholic population. We observe in Table 3.2 that both the
youngest and the oldest in the Catholic population are less likely
to disapprove of divorce and birth control than are the middle-
aged, and that the college-educated and the grammar-school educated are somewhat more strongly opposed to divorce and to birth
control than are those who attended high school. Exactly what
these patterns mean is not immediately clear, but they would suggest that neither income nor youth nor superior education by
themselves are a sufficient explanation for changing Catholic attitudes toward divorce and birth control. The young and the old,
the well-educated and the poorly educated, all seem to have rather
different ideas on these subjects than they apparently had in
1952.

Criticism of the clergy, however, does correlate directly with youthfulness and education, with younger Catholics almost more likely to be critical of their clergy than older Catholics, and college- and high-school-educated Catholics very substantially more inclined to be anticlerical than Catholics who only attended grammar school. If we look in Table 3.2 at some of the comparable Protestant percentages, we also note that youthful Catholics and college-educated Catholics are considerably more critical of their clergy than are Protestants in the same demographic or socioeconomic categories. At one time it would have been safe to say that the Catholic clergy were far more secure from criticism than their Protestant counterparts, but Table 3.2 suggests not only that they are now considerably more likely to be criticized than their Protestant colleagues, but that, as the socioeconomic position of the Catholic population improves even more, and as the younger Catholics mature, the level of criticism of the clergy is very likely to become even more substantial than it is.

Periodically, Catholic journalists have announced the appearance of native American anticlericalism. Until now, there has been almost no strong statistical evidence to support the claim. While the indicators reported in Tables 3.1 and 3.2 are obviously something less than completely satisfactory measures of anticlericalism, and further research would be necessary before any definitive judgment could be made, it nonetheless would seem, on the basis of these data, that something extremely important is taking place in the relationship between laity and clergy in the Roman Catholic Church, and that the clergy have lost, probably permanently, their immunity to criticism.

Since both youth and education generally indicate a change in Catholic attitude toward sexual reality and toward their clergy, one wonders if a combination of the two would provide us with any more information about the changes within American Catholicism. Table 3.3 would indicate that there is no simple and clear interrelation between age and education and sexual morality; thus in 1965 the youthful college graduates were more likely to see birth control as wrong than their coreligionists who had college educations but were middle-aged, while on the other hand the middle-aged high-school graduates were more likely to see birth control as being wrong than either the young or old Catholics who attended high school. Furthermore, the middle-aged grammar-school graduates were also more likely than those with the same education in the younger or older groups to agree with the official teaching of the Church. The differences among the college graduates can be explained by the fact that the younger collegians have not yet amassed for themselves large families and to the older ones birth control is a relatively unimportant practical question, but the opposite patterns for the grammar- and the high-school Catholics are somewhat more difficult to understand.

For the college-educated group there is an increased opposition to divorce with age, the youngest of the collegians being the most sympathetic toward divorce, though a U-shaped curve exists among the high-school graduates, with the middle-aged most likely to be opposed to divorce. The U-curve in the high-school Catholics' attitudes toward divorce is similar to the U-curve in their attitudes toward birth control, suggesting that middle-aged Catholics who went to high school are more or less, as a matter of principle, likely to be in accord with the Church's teachings, without much concern for whether these teachings could be a source of potential difficulty for them, since the birth-control teaching undoubtedly involves some personal difficulties for far more people than does divorce. On the other hand, the college graduates seem, as a matter of principle, to be more sympathetic toward divorce the younger they are but demonstrate a U-curve in attitude toward birth control. Why young Catholics who went to college would be much more vigorous in their support of the Church's teaching on birth control than they are in support of the teaching on divorce is not immediately evident.

There is some reason to think that what is shown in Table 3.3 is a very complicated set of interactions among the influences of age, education, ethnicity, and Catholic schooling, a series of phenomena which, with the resources available to us from the present questionnaire, we are not able to analyze more fully.[1]

Data on attitudes toward the clergy are not much clearer than those toward birth control. The younger college-educated people do show a rather dramatic difference in attitudes toward the clergy from their older confreres, but at all age levels the college-educated find the clergy more sympathetic than do the high-school-educated. One notes that among those over fifty-five, there is a 20 percent

---

[1] My colleague Michael Schiltz and I are, however, engaged in a careful study of these phenomena.

differences within education groups. The middle-aged college-Catholics in attitudes toward the clergy, the latter being less critical of the clergy's understanding, whereas among the youthful population the difference is narrowed down to 10 percent, with college-educated Catholics under thirty-five being as likely to say that the clergy are not understanding as were high-school graduates thirty-five and older.

However, the concern over poor sermons seems to be concentrated at the younger end of the population, with relatively minor differences within education groups. The middle-aged college-educated Catholics are least critical of clerical sermons. Finally, the youngest Catholics are most likely to object to the Church's concern over money, but in the younger population the college-educated are less critical than the other two groups, while in the population over thirty-five the college-educated are the most critical.

We are forced to say once again that education and age by themselves do not explain the changing patterns of attitude toward ethical norms and toward the clergy in the Catholic Church. Young Catholics and college-educated Catholics tend to be more critical of the clergy and more "liberal" in their notions of sexual morality, but college-educated young people seem, if anything, relatively less anticlerical than high-school- and grammar-school-educated young people and also more orthodox in their ethical attitudes, whereas middle-aged college people are more liberal on birth control, less liberal on divorce, more tolerant of the clerics' sermons and lack of understanding, but more critical over their concern over money than are the grammar-school and high-school Catholics in the same age group. College education obviously has a notably different impact on the relationship of the younger generation to the Church than it does on the relationship of the older generation. Within their own generation, younger Catholic college graduates seem to be more rigorous ethically and more tolerant of their clergy. One can conclude the analysis of Table 3.3 with the paradox that while there is a decline among young people in acceptance both of the clergy and the Church's attitude toward birth control, and that while this decline is also most precipitous in the college population, nonetheless college-educated young Catholics are still more sympathetic toward their Church than are those young Catholics who did not go to college.

We finally turn to the intriguing question of whether the Church's attitude on birth control is related to the dissatisfaction Catholics are feeling toward their clergy. It has been claimed frequently that the reluctance of the Church to modify its stand on birth control has led to the alienation of large segments of the Catholic population. Obviously, the measures available to us in the present report are anything but precise measures of alienation from the Church. Nonetheless it does appear from Table 3.4 that those Catholics who do not accept the teaching of the Church on birth control are more likely to say that the clergy are not understanding or that the sermons are not excellent or that the clergy are too concerned about money. But the differences are relatively very small—in all three instances around 5 percentage points. The relationship therefore between critical attitudes toward the clergy and rejection of the Church's teaching on birth control seems somewhat weak; one of course cannot say on the basis of the present data which direction the relationship goes—whether it is those who are more critical of the clergy who feel freer to disagree with the Church's birth-control teaching, or whether those who are dissatisfied with the birth-control teaching for that reason turn against the clergy. But we are able to say that the relationship is so weak between the two that there would have been a substantial increase in anticleric feeling if there were not a birth-control issue and a substantial change in the birth-control attitude if there were no changes in attitudes toward the clergy. The two phenomena are, of course, related, but there is no major pattern of change going on in the Church. Rather, the nature of the relationship is such as not to relate the two of them closely to one another.

This chapter must end on something of an ambiguous note. We have established that there are major institutional strains within Catholicism, leading to changes in attitudes toward sexual morality and toward the clergy, and we also see that this change is related to the changing educational makeup of the Catholic population and is apparently most pronounced among the younger generation of Catholics. Finally, there is some kind of weak relationship between anticlericalism and liberal sexual attitudes, but the patterns of changes and strains within Catholicism do not clearly emerge. The college-educated group under thirty-five, which one would expect to be the most rebellious, is not nearly as disaffected as is the high-school group, although the college-educated young Catholic is clearly far more unhappy with his Church than are his college-educated predecessors. This would suggest that at least part of the change of American Catholicism has been brought about by the increased education of the Catholic population, but that to some extent education is a self-balancing mechanism as far as Catholics' relationships to their Church go. The young are more critical than the old within the Church, and they are critical in part because they are better educated. Nonetheless, paradoxically the better their education, the less likely they are to be critical. American Catholicism can, therefore, look to the future expecting far more criticism and discontent, but also finding that its most articulate members, that is to say, those who have gone to college, may be also more sympathetic to it.

4. THE PERSISTENCE OF CATHOLIC SCHOOLS

Since the very beginning, American Catholic schools have been perhaps the most controversial practical issue separating Catholics from other Americans. In Ireland, where American Catholicism has its very strongest organizational roots, the state schools were viewed as proselytizing agencies for the established Church, and the independent and frequently illegal "hedge schools" were defined as heroic manifestations of the solid faith of the Irish people. The public schools in the United States in the early part of the nineteenth century were, from the point of view of Catholic religious leaders, very obviously nondenominational Protestant.

Under such circumstances it was perfectly natural for Catholic leaders such as the truculent John Hughes in New York to strive to establish their own school system with as much state support for the schools as they possibly could obtain. We have no record of how seriously the faith of the immigrants was in fact harmed by the public schools, though it does not seem that many immigrants left the Church, at least in the large immigrant centers where there was social support for the maintenance of the Catholic faith. Surely in more recent times there is no evidence in available data to indicate much of a leakage from the Catholic Church among those Catholics who attend public schools. The common school was then not in fact a threat to Catholicism, but it appeared a very strong threat in the 1830's and 1840's. When it became clear that state support would not be forthcoming for religious schools, as in Canada, American Catholicism set out on its incredible mission of having "every Catholic child in a Catholic school." What is surprising is not that the Catholic school system has fallen far short of this immense goal but that it has accomplished as much as it has. It is also quite astonishing that the greatest increase in the relative size of the Catholic schools occurred not at the height of the immigrant era but between 1940 and 1965, when the proportion of Americans in Catholic schools rose from somewhat over 6 percent to somewhat over 12 percent. Whatever rationale was developed to justify Catholic schools as a defense of the faith of immigrants clearly was replaced in the minds of the children and the grandchildren of the immigrants by other goals, which were operating at least as strongly immediately after the Second World War as at any time in the past.[1]

While the proliferation of Catholic schools has been the official policy of the American Catholic Church since the nineteenth century councils of Baltimore, there has always been criticism of the separate school system inside the Church, skepticism about its effectiveness, reluctance to accept the financial and personnel resources it required, and eagerness to seek some kind of compromise or *modus vivendi* with the public schools.

The great Americanizing prelates at the end of the nineteenth century tried mightily to arrive at such *modus vivendi*. Archbishop John Ireland of St. Paul in his famous Faribault experiment attempted to lease some of his parochial schools to a public-school board and to use the buildings after class hours for religious instruction. After controversy with more conservative elements within the Church (led by Bishop Bernard McQuade of Rochester) Ireland finally won Roman toleration for his experiment, but he was much less successful at winning toleration of the Faribault School Board, which canceled the plan long before

---

[1] In *The Education of Catholic Americans* (Chicago, Aldine Publishing Company, 1966), the author suggests with Peter H. Rossi that American Catholics share with all other Americans the desire for religious education. Catholic schools which came into being to protect and develop the faith of the immigrants have been sustained in their existence by a somewhat different rationale, that is to say, the desire of American Catholics for religious education for their children and the fact that the schools were available to provide this education.

Rome was willing to accept it. It is worth noting, however, that the destruction of this serious attempt at accommodation between Catholic and public schools was not the result of ecclesiastical reactionaries but rather of nativist reactionaries. Where there have been in more recent years many experiments with different forms of shared and released time, Catholic and public schools have gone their separate ways, with public educators and many non-Catholic religious groups feeling that every Catholic attempt at obtaining even peripheral support for Catholic schools was violation of this supposedly impenetrable wall of separation between Church and state, with Catholics, and Catholic leaders, increasingly incensed at the suspicion and hostility which non-Catholics have directed at the parochial school system. Many non-Catholics apparently cannot understand how one can be thoroughly American and still not send one's children to public schools, and many Catholics similarly cannot understand how one can be thoroughly American and object to parents sending their children to schools of their choice. The controversy has raged on and on in the ecclesiastical and secular journals, with public authority apparently increasingly ready to give some measure of support to parochial schools if ways can be found to avoid violating the strongly secularist interpretation of the Supreme Court concerning such aid. However, at least some non-Catholic leaders have urged on Catholics, almost as a price for further ecumenical dialogue, the abandoning of pressure for state aid for parochial schools.

Since the opening of the Vatican Council, criticism of Catholic schools has become much more intense within the Catholic liberal elite, and it is jokingly said that one can't really be a Catholic liberal unless one removes one's children from parochial schools. Similarly, some liberal journalists have not bothered to conceal their glee over the slight declines in enrollments in parochial grammar schools in recent years.[2]

Although the writer and his colleague Peter Rossi could find in a 1963 study precious little evidence that this attitude toward Catholic schooling was reflected in the larger Catholic population, it has still been argued that since 1963 there has been a dramatic

---

[2] Declines apparently caused in great part by the closing of small rural schools and the failure to construct new schools at a rapid enough pace in the most recent suburban developments. Enrollment at Catholic high schools, however, has increased.

change in the attitude of Catholics toward their schools and that increasingly major elements of the Catholic population are becoming disaffected with the expenses in the separatism of the Catholic school system.

Table 4.1 provides little evidence, however, of such a change. While American Catholics today are clearly somewhat less likely to favor either direct or indirect state aid for their schools, and demonstrate even somewhat more reluctance to support released time than in 1952, there is no evidence that they are particularly critical of parochial schools. Only 2 percent think that Catholic schools are bad for the country, and only 5 percent do not think they are as good academically as public schools, while almost half the American Catholics are convinced that parochial schools are better academically than public schools. (Interestingly enough, about one fifth the Protestants and Jews would agree with them.) It is also interesting to note that Protestant attitudes toward Catholic schools have improved somewhat since 1952. Even at that time, only a relatively small minority of Protestants was likely to think that religious schools were bad for the country and that they were not as good academically as public schools. However, this group has grown even smaller in the ensuing thirteen years. American Jews, on the other hand, have grown considerably more critical of religious schools, with approximately a third of them thinking that such schools are bad for the country and not as good academically as public schools.[3] Furthermore, American Jews have dramatically diminished their support for indirect and direct state aid to religious schools, a phenomenon which may very well be related with the sharp increase in anti-Catholic feeling among American Jews which we will discuss in the following chapter.

It could be argued that the enthusiasm of Catholics for their schools will wane with the passage of time, as younger and better-educated Catholics become more and more skeptical of the need for a separate school system. Table 4.2 does not sustain such an expectation. Younger Catholics are indeed less likely to favor di-

[3] It should be noted that the question on which Table 4.1 is based has to do with religious schools and not specifically Catholic schools. Since there is rather strong religious-school movement among American Jews, it is possible and even likely that some Jewish respondents also had such schools in mind. Presumably, however, the religious schools that would be most salient for American Protestants would be Catholic schools.

rect tax support for Catholic schools, but there is not much evidence of an increase in unfavorable attitude toward these schools among younger Catholics. Similarly, there is but a slight change between the grammar-school-educated Catholics and college-educated Catholics in their attitude toward the parochial school, although the college-educated Catholic is only half as likely as his colleague with a high-school education to support tax aid for parochial schools.

It thus seems that four generalizations might be hazarded on the basis of the suggestions of Tables 4.1 and 4.2:

1. American Catholics are still strongly committed to a parochial school system.

2. Sympathy for both direct and indirect support for religious schools seemed in 1965 to be decreasing.[4]

3. Protestant opposition to separate religious schools was rather small in 1952 and has declined somewhat since then.

4. Jewish opposition to separate religious schools, at about the same level as Protestant opposition in 1952, has sharply increased since then.

It seems very likely therefore to suggest that in the future Catholic-Protestant controversy over religious schools will cease to be very important and that the "school issue," which was for so long a bone of contention among Christian denominations, may be a happy casualty of the ecumenical age—at least among gentiles. It also seems, however, that Catholic-Jewish controversy over religious schools may increase—a prospect made even more ominous by the data to be reported in subsequent chapters which indicate a somewhat notable increase in anti-Catholic feeling among Jews.

5. INTERRELIGIOUS ATTITUDES

While many more sophisticated Americans have grown somewhat tired of hearing the glories of our nation's pluralism extolled, it nonetheless remains true that the success of the pluralistic experiment in American society is remarkable and perhaps phenomenal.

---

[4] Other data, however, suggest that it may have increased somewhat in the years since 1965.

The four "conspiracies" (to use the late John Courtney Murray's word) of Protestant, Catholic, Jew, and secularist have managed to compete in American society within a generally accepted framework of rules which have prevented them from tearing the fabric of the society apart. American Protestants have not been overwhelmingly happy as they have watched a country, which they can rightfully argue they founded, cease to be what was for all practical purposes a Protestant nation. Nonetheless, they have borne the burden of this drastic change with what must be considered on balance a surprising lack of intolerance; convents were indeed burned, Catholics were indeed killed, other Catholics were barred from political office, but American Protestants did not use their majority position to prevent Catholics from becoming full-fledged and successful members of American society.

Catholics, on the other hand, have crawled their way up the ladder to social and economic success with what must be described on balance as a remarkable amount of sophistication. Their leaders, and occasionally the Catholic people themselves, may have been alternately defensive and truculent, they may have built up powerful urban political organizations on which to base their battles for recognition as Americans. They may have at times engaged in orgies of superpatriotism, but nonetheless the attitude of Senator McCarthy from Minnesota toward American society is far more typical of the vast majority of Catholics than was the attitude of the late Senator McCarthy from Wisconsin. The first Catholic to become President of the United States was anything but a militantly aggressive Catholic.

Finally, American Jews, having very quickly achieved financial and social success in American society, and having lived through the horror of suffering imposed upon their brothers in the concentration camps of Europe, have reacted to the residue of anti-Semitism still to be found in American culture with remarkable tolerance and forbearing. Religious conflicts have torn nation after nation apart; that they have not torn this nation apart is a tribute to the constitutional and customary inhibitions which American society has placed on religious conflict.

Since most Americans are philosophical optimists, there is a strong tendency in the United States to believe that the conflicts and divisions which separate man from his fellow men are slowly declining and that religious animosity and bigotry will shortly be a thing of the past. While it is no doubt true that at least in some respects man's moral conscience does develop with passage of time, and while it is also true that interracial attitudes have notably improved in the last quarter century, it does not follow that bigotry, prejudice, and misunderstanding automatically decrease.

In this chapter we shall be forced to report the rather unpleasant information that if our data are accurate, there has been an increase of religious tension in one set of relationships in American society in the last decade and a half.

We should carefully note at this point that all we have proposed to assert in this chapter is the increase or decrease of antireligious *feeling*. We will not contend that our indicators measure either religious bigotry or are even an accurate reading of reality. Some items used (for example, the questions of members of religious groups "sticking together too much") are probably rather good measures of bigotry, while the worth of other questions tapping the prejudice dimension cannot be so well established. But we will not contend that an increase in the number of Jews who assert that Catholics are not honest in public office is an increase in prejudice. We will rather say that it is merely an increase in anti-Catholic feeling. Nor will we contend that a decline in the percentage of Catholics who think that Jews are getting too much power in the United States is a sign of decrease in anti-Semitism. We will be content with arguing much more generally that it is a sign of decrease in anti-Jewish feeling. We will leave to other and more detailed research the question of whether anti-Semitism among Catholics is declining and anti-Catholic prejudice among Jews is increasing, since at least in theory one might wish to argue, for example, that Jews are merely reporting more accurate preceptions of, let us say, dishonesty of Catholics in public office.[1]

The first panel of Table 5.1 indicates a response to the question in which the person interviewed is asked whether he thinks there is much ill feeling toward other religious groups among the members of his own religious denomination. Catholics are less likely to think that they are prejudiced against Protestants or Jews than

[1] The restraint described in this paragraph is based on the author's skepticism about the use of most opinion items for measuring prejudice and bigotry. More important in the author's judgment than the absolute percentages responding to the questions considered in this chapter are the relative changes to the responses in the thirteen years between the two studies.

they were in 1952, and similarly there has been a decline in the Protestant perception of internal prejudice toward members of other groups. Jews agree that they are less likely to be anti-Protestant than they were a decade and a half ago but are more likely to report that they detect anti-Catholic feeling among their fellow Jews. The decline in perceived anti-Jewish feeling among Catholics and the increase in perceived anti-Catholic feeling among Jews leads to a situation where Jews are twice as likely to say their own group is prejudiced against Catholics than Catholics are to say that their own group is prejudiced against Jews.

The pattern described in Table 5.1A will persist through almost every table in this chapter. Anti-Jewish feeling declines among Catholics and Protestants, anti-Protestant feeling declines generally among Jews, and anti-Catholic feeling increases among Jews. Thus, in Table 5.1B almost half the Jews (44 percent) think that Catholics look down on them, an increase of 14 percentage points, where only 14 percent of the Catholics think that Jews look down on Catholics, a decrease of 4 percentage points. Nineteen percent of Jews argue that Catholics are likely to interfere with their religious beliefs (an increase of 6 percent), while only 3 percent of the Catholics accuse Jews of the same behavior.

However, there are some alternatives in the picture; 28 percent of the Protestants and 23 percent of the Catholics are inclined to say that Jews are not fair in business practice, although only 1 percent of the Jews will say this of Catholics, and none of the Jews in the sample would make the same accusation against Protestants. The percentage accusing Jews of sharp business practices has declined since 1952 (11 percent for Protestants and 8 percent for Catholics) but still indicates that approximately one quarter of the gentile population is fearful of Jewish business acumen and is inclined to accuse Jews of not being fair in business practices. However, Table 5.1D at least indicates no increase in antireligious feeling, but Table 5.1E returns to the previous pattern. While most Americans are not inclined to accuse members of other religious groups of being more dishonest in public office, there is an 8 percent increase among Jews in the implication of dishonesty in Catholic officeholders and a 5 percent decrease among Catholics making the same accusation against Jews. In this table, as in others, the Catholics and Jews seem to have passed each other since 1952. At that point Catholics were more likely to accuse Jews of disreputable behavior than Jews were likely to accuse Catholics. In the ensuing decade and a half the positions have been reversed.

The Catholics are, perhaps somewhat naïvely, disinclined to think that either their Protestant or Jewish brothers do not respect others' religious beliefs, but 28 percent of the Protestants and 45 percent of the Jews believe that Catholics are not good in respecting the religious beliefs of others, a decrease of 7 percent for Protestants and increase of 10 percent for Jews. The Protestant response may be somewhat more realistic, given the considerable changes in Catholicism in recent years, but the Jewish response may indicate greater Jewish uneasiness about Catholic practices in the past which were deemed more tolerable at one time than they are today (such as the placing of Christmas crèches on public property).

The Kennedy election has clearly improved the political climate of American religious interaction, with more than 80 percent of both Catholics and Jews quite willing to vote for a member of the opposite religion for presidency of the United States. However, it is interesting to observe that there are 35 percent of American Protestants who are still not willing to say that they would vote for a Catholic President and almost 50 percent of Protestants who will not affirm that they could cast their vote for a Jewish presidential candidate.

There is surely no more sensitive issue in interreligious behavior than the question of intermarriage. When someone marries outside of his religious group, he assaults not merely the traditional religious piety but also the very fabric and structure of family life. Mixed marriages have never been particularly popular in American society, and the fragmentary data that are available would suggest that the proportion of religiously mixed marriages has not notably increased in the last half century. However, Table 5.1H provides evidence for us to conclude that among gentiles the opposition to religious intermarriage is decreasing, with approximately half the Catholic population objecting neither to marriage to Protestants nor marriage to Jews. On the other hand, Jewish opposition to intermarriage, always high, has increased considerably in the last decade and a half. As a rather small minority group in American society and one that does not have the tight bonds of ecclesiastical organization which are at the disposal of Catholicism, Jews will inevitably consider intermarriage more of a threat to the homogeneity of their religion or ethnic community. The striking fact is not that the Jews are against intermarriage but rather that as they become more acculturated into American society they are apparently even more opposed to it than they were a decade and a half ago.

The patterns we describe continue relatively unchanged through most of the rest of the tables in the 5.1 series. Jews are more likely to expect discrimination from Catholics than they were thirteen years ago, while Catholics are less likely to expect discrimination from Jews. Jews are more likely than in the past to say Catholics stick together too much; Catholics are less likely to say that Jews stick together too much, with the result that now a higher proportion of Jews accuse Catholics of clannishness than do Catholics accuse Jews. Jews are dramatically more likely than in 1952 to say that Catholic clergymen do not give intelligent leadership to their followers, while few of any Catholics will say this of Jewish rabbis. Similarly, there has been a considerable increase in the number of Jews who do not think that the Catholic clergy provide a fluid understanding among religious groups and who assert that Catholic leaders do not work for the civic common good; however, few, if any, Catholics are willing to make such charges against the Jewish religious leaders and those that do are less in number than they were a decade and a half ago. Neither group is very likely to accuse the others' religious leaders of not giving good personal examples, but, nonetheless, Jews are more inclined to say this of Catholics than Catholics of Jews, and the Jewish proportion making such an assertion has gone from 5 to 10 percent in the last thirteen years. Jews are also more inclined to accuse Catholics of trying to influence the secular press in their own favor and of being unfair in their own magazines to Jewish religious beliefs. In both instances, these assertions by Jewish respondents represent an increase in the proportion making the charges since 1952. The only bright spot is to be found in Table 5.1K, where there is a decline in both Catholic and Jewish proportions asserting that the other group is getting too much power in the United States, though the decline in the Catholic population is 21 percent and in the Jewish population only 16 percent, leaving a situation in which Jews are more than twice as likely to say that Catholics are getting too much power as Catholics are to say that Jews are getting too much power.

Finally, in Table 5.1R, we note that only a handful of Americans report that they personally have had unpleasant experiences with members of other religious faiths, though once again there is a slight increase in the proportion of Jews who report unpleasant experiences with Catholics. It would appear that the criticisms most Americans have with other religious groups are based on the things they read and the things their religious leaders tell them and not on their own personal experiences. One can, of course, lament that misunderstandings and ill feelings persist in the absence of any actual unpleasant experiences, or one can rejoice that the feelings of antipathy toward members of other religious groups are not based on personal experiences and hence can perhaps be more readily extirpated than if they were based on actual incidences which have occurred in peoples' lives.

One cannot, however, look through the tables discussed so far in this chapter and escape the almost overwhelming conclusion that Jewish ill feeling toward Catholics is increasing. In summary Table 5.2 we notice that in only one instance (the question of the "other side's" respecting "our" beliefs) has anti-Jewish feeling increased among Catholics, but that in only three instances has anti-Catholic feeling failed to increase among Jews. At the very time when Catholics are becoming more friendly toward Jews it would appear that Jews are becoming less friendly toward Catholics. This phenomenon is not only paradoxical but also not a little disturbing.

One may well wonder when this increase in anti-Catholic feeling among Jews is likely to reverse itself in years to come. If the younger Jew and the better-educated Jew were less anti-Catholic than his older and more poorly educated counterpart, then we could be reasonably optimistic about future prospects for a change for the better. However, as Table 5.3 indicates, it is precisely the young Jew and the college-educated Jew who is most likely to display anti-Catholic feelings, while younger Jews are not as likely as their older coreligionists to think that Catholics will discriminate against them. On every item in Table 5.3 there is a direct relationship between youth and anti-Catholic feeling. Younger Jews are more likely to think that Catholics look down on them, more likely to think they will interfere with their liberty, more likely to say they don't respect the faith of others, more likely to say that Catholics stick together too much, more likely to say that

Catholics are after power (though here differences are small across generational lines), more likely to think the Catholic clergy do not provide intelligent leadership and do not promote goodwill toward members of other religious faiths. Similarly, in every item in Table 5.3 it is the college-educated Jew who is most likely to have anti-Catholic feelings, though on the item concerning Catholics' sticking together too much, the differences are quite small.

We must enter here a caution which we have repeated before in discussing the Jews in the two surveys. The Jewish sample is quite small because the Jewish segment of the American population is quite small; one would not want to arrive at any definite conclusions concerning American Jews on the basis of a sample of 128, no matter how excellent the sample design might be. One would therefore even be much more careful about drawing any definitive conclusions from cross-tabulations which reduce this sample into subgroups. The findings being reported about the Jews in this book and particularly in this chapter are therefore highly tentative, and we are very careful to enter the qualification once again: *If our sample is representative of the Jewish population and if it continues to be representative when the Jews are divided into educational and age subgroups, then not only is there an increase in the anti-Catholic feeling among American Jews, but this increase is most marked among college graduates and among younger Jews and therefore seems very likely to grow worse instead of better.* A minimal conclusion from the findings reported in this chapter is that considerably more research is necessary on the subject of Catholic-Jewish relationships.

We are still faced with the intriguing question of why there has been an apparent change in Jewish attitudes toward Catholics in the last decade and a half. It is possible to argue that along with the decline in doctrinal orthodoxy among Jews there has been an increase in "nationalist" feeling, and to some extent anti-Catholic feeling is a substitute for religious faith. If this were true, then one would expect the Jews who did not believe in God and who are not affiliated with the congregation to be the strongest in their anti-Catholic feelings. However, Table 5.4 indicates exactly the opposite is the case. Leaving aside those nine Jewish respondents who are affiliated with congregations but who do not believe in God, we see that there is a direct relationship between religiousness of Jews and anti-Catholic feelings. It is those who believe in

God and who belong to congregations who score highest on each
of the items on the list (with two exceptions) and those who
neither believe in God nor belong to a synagogue scoring the
lowest on all items—with those in between, who do believe in God
but who are not affiliated with the congregation, scoring somewhere in between on most items. It would, therefore, seem that we
are dealing with a phenomenon that is indeed *religious*. The more
religious a Jew is, the more likely he is to have anti-Catholic feelings. If our respondents are truly representative, we are therefore
faced with attempting to find explanations for the increase in
anti-Catholic feeling among Jews in the last thirteen years which
would be *religious,* since the nonreligious Jews show much less
sign of an increase. Many explanations can be advanced, of course:
the confusion of the Vatican Council over the condemnation of
anti-Semitism; the increased tension between Catholics and Jews
in suburban areas around the large metropolitan areas of the
country; decline in Jewish self-hatred and increase in national
pride, which makes them more alert and sensitive to affronts; an
increasing consciousness in Judaism as a "third partner" in American society, and, hence, possessing the same rights in the society
as the other religions.

Given the very limited and uncertain nature of our data, however, such speculations would be based on very shaky foundations.
Other sociologists have claimed, we think without the proper
qualification, that there is a relationship between religiousness and
anti-Jewish feeling among gentiles (particularly among Protestants). We are not prepared to state on the basis of our data that
there is a relationship between religiousness among Jews and the
increase of anti-Catholic feeling, if indeed there be such an increase, but we are prepared to affirm that our data are strong
enough to justify further research. If the phenomena reported in
this chapter are indeed valid representations of reality, a very notable problem in Catholic-Jewish relationships may be facing us in
years to come, particularly when Catholics, whose attitudes toward
Jews have apparently improved substantially in the last ten years,
discover that the very reverse is happening within the Jewish population. Such a discovery might lead to a resurgence of anti-Jewish
feeling among Catholics. Optimism that an era of religious goodwill in the United States is about to begin seems quite unjustified
if our data are valid. Perhaps it would not be inappropriate to

suggest that Catholic and Jewish agencies ought to join together in studying relationships between their two religious groups and that in such future studies it would be a mistake to concentrate merely on anti-Jewish feeling among Catholics.

6. YOUNG PEOPLE: THE FUTURE OF GOD

The subject of youth and religion has always been an exciting one for Americans, partly because Americans are inclined to be sentimental about youth and partly because youth is taken realistically to represent the future. It is therefore not surprising that the religious optimists and pessimists have often issued announcements that youth is undergoing a religious revival and the future of religion looks promising indeed, or that youth is deteriorating in religious faith and that even though God might still be alive for adults, young people don't believe in his relevance. More recently the pessimists have had a field day by suggesting that the hippie movement or the civil-rights movement, or even the volunteer movement represents a new alternative for young people in addition to religion.

The unbiased observer is entitled to remain skeptical; religious recessions or revivals of the past have neither put religion out of business nor made it the vital, dynamic force that the leaders think it ought to be. Young people are, of course, very different from their parents, but in focusing on the difference we overlook the much more impressive similarities. Human religion may inch forward or inch backward with the passage of generations, but dramatic changes in religion, like dramatic changes in most human behavior, will generally occur very, very slowly.

In Table 6.1 we attempt to glean some impression as to what the religion of the future will look like by comparing our respondents who were under twenty-five in 1965 with members of those religious groups who were over twenty-five (the Jews are not considered in this table because the very small samples make it impossible to find enough under twenty-five for serious analysis). Catholic young people are, if anything, more orthodox than their predecessors in the matter of the inspiration of the Bible. They are as likely to believe in God and more likely to believe in life after

death and heaven and hell. They are as opposed to mixed marriage and to divorce as the members of the older generation, but
only one fifth of them accept the official teaching on birth control.
Furthermore, they are more likely to be critical of the Church's
quest for money, of the sermons, and of the understanding and
sympathy of the clergy. They are also slightly less likely to consider
themselves church members, though this may simply be due to the
fact the young people have not yet settled down into a parish in
which they can consider themselves formally involved.

Catholic young people, therefore, demonstrate quite a bit of
consistency with general Catholic population as we described it in
previous chapters. Their religious faith and their religious practice suggest that the relatively high level of devotion and of doctrinal orthodoxy currently existing in the American Catholic
Church will continue into the future. Furthermore, their attitude
toward the clergy and birth control seems to suggest that opposition to the status of the clergy and the Church's sex morality will
continue to increase within American Catholicism. Young Catholics are both doctrinally stable and ethically and organization-
ally restless. Their restlessness represents a continuation and an
expansion of a problem that has notably increased in American
Catholicism since 1952. If one wishes to project into the future of
Catholic young people, one can say that church attendance,
church affiliation, and doctrinal orthodoxy will continue to be
high among American Catholics for the remainder of the century,
but that the willingness to accept the Church's sexual teachings
and respect for the privileged status of the clergy will continue to
decrease between now and the year 2000. If young Catholics represent the most revolutionary elements of the Church, it must then
be admitted that the revolution is a highly selective one.

The picture among Protestant young people is somewhat more
ambiguous. We remember in the early chapters that the differences between Protestants in 1952 and 1965 were generally slight
but represented in most instances a downward trend in orthodoxy
and loyalty. Younger Protestants demonstrate to some extent a
continuation of this trend; while they are more likely to believe in
God (all four hundred of our respondents under twenty-five believed in God), they are somewhat less likely to pray and to believe in life after death and to accept the existence of heaven,
though, curiously enough, they are more willing than their elders

to subscribe to the possibility of hell. They are less opposed to mixed marriage than their predecessors but still a trifle more unsympathetic to mixed marriage than younger Catholics. They are also less impressed with the sympathy and sermons of their clergy than are previous generations of Protestants, though their criticisms do not represent such a dramatic shift of attitude as is going on in the Catholic population.

Insofar as our very sketchy indicators are any adequate measure of reality, the future outlook for American Protestantism is one of relative stability with some doctrinal erosions.

The data reported in Table 6.1 substantiate our contention in the earlier chapters that there is no revolutionary religious change to be observed among American gentiles despite the overwhelming publicity to the contrary. Whatever its "crises of faith" might have been, young American Protestants and Catholics are, if anything, more likely to believe that God is not dead than are their parents. How can we explain the apparent diversity between the statistical data and popular impressions?

First of all, it could well be that the measures available in the 1965 survey do not tap the dimensions of religious restlessness and revolution that actually exist. Secondly, it could be that the revolutionary elites are so small as not to turn up in a national sample. Those who have been seriously influenced by atheistic theology may be too small a portion of the national population of young people to affect any change on *average* figures of religious attitude and behavior. Thirdly, it may be that our impressions are based on the "dog bites man" approach to reality. That most young people differ very little in their religious attitudes from their parents is not news and we do not notice it; but that some think very differently from their parents is news and we do notice it, though the group that represents disagreement and change may be a very minute part of the total population. It is also possible, of course, that there have been very dramatic changes between 1965 and now. However, the sociologist is always skeptical of such dramatic changes because the general behavior of large populations tends to be relatively stable. When someone says to a sociologist, "Things have changed since your data were collected," he is forced to reply, "They may have, but there was no indication in my data that such a change was impending, and I am skeptical of it until I see data as strong as mine indicating that the change has occurred." It is also possible that considerable numbers of young people go through agonies over their religious faith but somehow or other manage to subside the agony without changing very much their basic orientation on religious doctrine and practice. Table 6.1 may merely be an indication that while the crises of faith are more serious and more frequent in our time, they are, in most instances, not the beginning of the loss of faith or the departure from organized religion.

The problem of growing up religiously may be more acute in contemporary American society, or it may simply be more explicit, but its ultimate resolution seems not to differ with the generation under twenty-five from the solution arrived at by the generations over twenty-five.

Obviously, if the churches are concerned about not understanding the problems of their young people and also about projection of the meaning of the future in the behavior of the young, it will be required that they do far more research on the attitudes of the young than they have in the past and surely far more detailed and precise research than the surveys on which this volume is based. Nonetheless, it would seem to the writer that two warnings about this research ought to be made. First of all, it should not start from the premise that the younger generation is less religious than their parents. However popular that premise may be in certain religious magazines which are fond of predicting the demise of the institutional church, there is no evidence for it in our data, and one would think that there would be at least some evidence. Secondly, the researchers must be wary of the "good old days" fallacy. They should not decide on a priori grounds that the basic religious problems and religious solutions of the present generation of young people are all that different from the generations that went ahead of them. A difference there surely is, of course, and the difference is important. But it does not follow therefore that human nature has changed with the passage of time. The continuity between the past and the present is far stronger than many of the possessors of prophetic voices would be willing to admit.

From one point of view, of course, it is omission of the failure on the part of organized religion to say that its young people are no worse than their parents. Christianity is supposed to be an evolutionary and dynamic religion, and none of the data reported in this book indicates much in the way of religious progress on the part of the churches (and data also make us skeptical about the alleged religious revival of the past decade and a half). Between 1952 and 1965 and between the older and the younger generations, things religious have not changed very much. Religion has, indeed, been able to survive, and survive with a great deal of vigor; but it has not demonstrated enough vigor to improve its relative position. There may be more or less prophetic charisma in the church than there was in the past, but the unfortunate part about prophets is that there aren't very many of them, not nearly enough to notably affect a national sample. Perhaps at no time have either the hot or the cold been strong enough to change national averages. This leaves the field then to the meek or the lukewarm, depending on your preference in labels.

7. THE ROLE OF RELIGION IN AMERICAN SOCIETY

There seems to be no way of avoiding a certain dullness in the writing of sociological analysis. When one is working with the materials of survey research, one is pretty much tied to describing and commenting on statistical tables. Rarely do these tables provide anything in the way of sensational information. In many instances the sociologist is faced with the reaction to his findings that no survey was needed to establish what people already knew. Such a reaction is usually caused not by the fact that people did in fact already know what the sociologist was reporting but that his findings are so undramatic that most people *thought* they already knew it. If someone were to say in summary of this volume, for example, that there is no major shift away from traditional religion among American gentiles, the findings could easily be dismissed as obvious. But before that dismissal takes place, the one who dismisses should remember the vast outpouring of headlines, feature articles, worried or pompous editorials in church magazines, and journalistic essays recounting either a religious revival or a religious decline. Our data suggest that decline and revival represent probably only minor shifts within small groups of the population and not major changes. Such a finding is dull and hence obvious, whereas the sensational headline reporting "God is dead," or that

the Church has become secularized is not dull and therefore cap-
tures the popular attention. An author who claims that a new kind
of being, secular man, is emerging in the metropolises of our nation, is able to make the claim because he has not been tied to the
rigorous evidences statistical tables provide. His argument will become part of the folklore of American society so rapidly that few
would dare to question its validity or utility as an analytic tool.
The sociologist therefore is in a peculiar position of arguing,
before the fact, that he needs evidence before he can be persuaded
that there is secular man, and being dismissed as a "counter of fruit
flies"; after the fact of having gathered evidence which demonstrates that there are apparently very few of the new species *homo
saecularis,* he is told that he has merely established what everybody
already knew. He can only reply, "If you knew it, why didn't you
say so before?"

Social research does not, of course, claim to be the only way that
man views reality, and there may very well be insights that the
headlines, the feature articles, and the worried or pompous editorials provide which the statistical table cannot match. There
are surely exciting things going on in American religion which
sociological research will not be able to tap, but it must also be
recognized that as far as the systematic collection of concrete evidence is concerned, social research is far superior to journalism. I
remember once being on a platform for a discussion of religious
education. I very carefully described the findings of a three-year
study done with a representative national sample. Another member of the platform dismissed my findings with the simple statement, "My experience is different." What she was saying was that
twenty or fifty or one hundred nonrepresentative people with
whom she had interacted provided her with information superior
to that provided me by three thousand people in a representative
sample. Herein, I suppose, is the difference between the social-
science report and the journalistic article. The journalist is dealing
with his impressions, and they may be very astute and pene-
trating impressions, but the evidence on which he bases his impressions is very thin and dubious. The social scientist has impressions
too, but he is not speaking of impressions but rather of propositions based on very carefully and systematically collected evidence.
The journalist is strong on impression and weak on evidence. The
social scientist chooses to be rather weak on impressions and very

strong on evidence. Both methods of discourse have their advantages, and both are necessary in any society, but it ought to be noted that one's own personal experience is not an effective response to the carefully collected evidence of the sociologist.

This somewhat long introductory comment seems to be necessary since the data analyzed in this book provide very little support for sweeping religious movements that many writers and religious leaders would have us believe are occurring. The reader must decide for himself whether the dull and uninteresting changes that are reported in this volume are a more adequate description of the American religious scene than are the editorials and sermons and feature articles to which he has been exposed. The reality described in the latter is a reality of lights and shadows, of rapidly changing colors, of great and dramatic new perspectives. The reality which we are describing, alas, in this volume tends to be very gray, very complicated, and relatively dull. We can only say that the history of the human race suggests that reality is far more often gray and dull than it is dramatic and sensational. Man generally has been conservative in matters of religion, especially because religion deals with some of the most intimate aspects of human life and because it is passed on from generation to generation in the very early years of existence. If we are correct in arguing, as we will in this concluding chapter, that religion's basic function is to furnish an explanation for life and that in addition in American society it also provides an important means of social identification and location, and if both this interpretation and identification are acquired in great part before a young person passes his tenth birthday, it does not seem so surprising that religious change would move very slowly indeed.

We conclude this introduction to our conclusion therefore by arguing that the rather dull and undramatic shifts in religion which we have reported in this volume are exactly what somebody who accepts the sociological theories about the nature of human religion would expect. We would also suggest that anyone who takes a careful look at the nature of religion in his own life and the life of his friends would be inclined to expect the same thing.

How then can we proceed to tie together into a coherent form the findings that have been reported in this volume? What can be said of the three main American religious groups?

The Protestants, first of all, can be described as a collection of denominations which show, at least in the overall national average, a rather high degree of stability. There seems, as Dr. Marty points out in his essay, to be slow erosion of both doctrinal orthodoxy and religious observance. The changes between 1952 and 1965 would not be of sufficient magnitude to persuade the present writer that such erosion was going on if the same phenomenon could not be observed in the comparison of younger Protestants with older Protestants in the previous chapter. The magnitude of this erosion is not very startling, and it would have to go on for perhaps another century before American Protestantism would be in the seriously debilitated condition of, let us say, its English counterpart. In addition, it is possible that the changes, both across time and across generations, represent but minor fluctuations which are part of the long-term religious cycles, the nature of which we do not understand. One might say that if the indicators used in this volume—or even more sophisticated indicators—were used to test the Protestant population fifteen years into the future, and these indicators showed even more erosion, then Protestantism might at that point decide that it was having the serious troubles that a great number of popular writers are affirming it has today. In the midst of the general continuity of stability, however, Protestants representing the mainstream of American religion have apparently adjusted to the fact that the United States is no longer a Protestant society. Anti-Catholic and anti-Jewish feeling has considerably declined among Protestants in the last decade and a half, though one third of the Protestant population would, even after the Kennedy victory, still be skeptical of voting for a Catholic presidential candidate. American Catholics, on the other hand, show almost no signs of doctrinal or devotional erosion either across time or across generations. At the present time, on the basis of the data of this volume, it must be affirmed that both the doctrinal and devotional position of Roman Catholicism in the United States seems almost impregnable. Nonetheless, there are troubles within Catholicism, marked by a general increase in dissatisfaction toward the clergy, particularly in the better-educated and younger Catholic population, and also a very notable shift away from the Church's ethical position on sexual matters. While there is a general relationship between these changes and both youth and education, the patterns are complicated and one cannot make the simple affirmation that as the Catholic population becomes better educated and more assimilated into American society, the internal strains that we discovered will continue to grow. At least, one cannot assert this on the basis of the present data. There seems some reason to think that they may continue to grow, but the complexities of our data, which probably reflect the complexities of the later stages of the assimilation and acculturation of the Catholic population to American life, make any simple projection into the future rather difficult.

However, Catholics have become secure enough in American society and do feel accepted enough so that militant suspicion and distrust of other American religious groups seems to be generally declining. As a matter of fact, other research, particularly that carried on by Charles Glock and his associates at the University of California at Berkeley, seems to indicate that Catholics are relatively less prejudiced than Protestants toward Jews and have been so perhaps for some time.

In many ways the small Jewish segment of the American population, if it is validly represented in this sample, is the most interesting group of all. It would appear, on the basis of our data, that there have been dramatic changes in the proportion of Jews assenting to the doctrinal propositions that were used in our two surveys, though it should be noted that, as we said before, these doctrinal propositions may be of less importance in the Jewish faith than they are in other faiths. Nevertheless, even on something as basic as the existence of God, which presumably is quite central to the Jewish faith, there has been considerable change among American Jews in the last decade and a half. But, curiously enough, combined with the decline in propositional orthodoxy, there has been an increase in both attendance at religious services and affiliation with religious congregations, with the latter phenomenon taking place among the somewhat better-educated and the more well-to-do groups within the Jewish population. The other two religious groups have lessened their opposition to intermarriage and are inclined to take more tolerant views of their fellow Americans who profess different faiths. The exact opposite seems to be true of the Jews in our sample: They are more opposed to intermarriage, slightly more anti-Protestant, and quite notably more anti-Catholic in their feelings. This increase in anti-Catholic feeling is especially pronounced among the younger and better-educated Jews and among the more religious Jews. Our evidence did not permit us to seek further explanation, though we did suggest that an increasing pride in Jewishness and an increasing awareness that Judaism has become the third major religion in American society may have made Jews more sensitive to discriminations which in the past would have produced only repressed ill feeling.

Is there some more general explanation into which these various findings can be fitted in a coherent pattern? We think that such an explanation can be deduced, though it represents an ordering of the findings into a speculative theory and not an explanation which is so closely connected to the empirical data as to be unchallenged.

Religion in American society seems to play twin roles. It is first of all an interpretative scheme (and here we follow the writings of such authorities in sociology of religion as Thomas Luckman, Clifford Geertz, and Talcott Parsons). Religion purports to be an explanation of ultimate reality or at least those dimensions of ultimate reality for which other cultural systems such as science and common sense cannot provide explanations. Religion is a meaning-giving system which is designed particularly to cope with uncertainty, sickness, suffering, death—those harsh and unpleasant realities which science and common sense cannot explain and for which there must be an explanation if life is not to be dismissed and is ultimately to become meaningless and cruel. This "interpretative scheme" is learned in part, of course, by formal education, by reading religious books, newspapers, listening to sermons, and attending church; but it is learned much more profoundly in the family experience. We may not be born Protestants, Catholics, Jews, or humanists, but it is a fair bet that we have become one of these before the first day we set foot in a classroom. These ultimate interpretations of reality are extremely important to those who adhere to them, just as the questions which the interpretation strives to answer are extremely important. It is a rare parent who would not want to share his interpretation of reality with his children, or who would risk the possibility that the child's own interpretative scheme or cultural system would suggest the possibility that the parent might be wrong.

But in addition to providing meaning, in the United States religion also provides belonging. In the American society, religion is highly organized and also pluralistic; by affiliating oneself with one or the other religious denominations an American obtains, as Will Herberg has pointed out, a social location and a social identity. He is able to answer the question "Who are you?" with the response that he is a Protestant or a Catholic or a Jew. In a less pluralistic society than the United States such social location against other groups would not be either necessary or possible. In a nation where there is but one ethnic group and one religion, one is born into the religion, and there is neither the necessity nor the opportunity for joining a church, and hence affiliation or non-affiliation can be casual, informal, and ambiguous. Church membership is not "a big thing," save in a society where there are many churches to which one might belong and the choice of the church puts one in a definite social category.

Again, one has become not only a Protestant, Catholic, or Jew in one's interpretative scheme before entering grammar school, but also, and perhaps more importantly, in one's organizational membership; the grammar-school child may have only vague ideas of how his interpretative scheme differs from that of his Protestant, Jewish, or Catholic classmate. But even in this ecumenical age, when diversities in interpretative schemes, at least among gentiles, appear less formidable than they did in the past, the grammar-school child still knows that if he is a Catholic he is different from Protestants and Jews, different because he *belongs* to a different church. Both religion as an interpretative scheme and the church as a defining organization have become very much a part of the child's life long before his tenth birthday.

We would suggest that against these twin forces of meaning and belonging the so-called secularization of society will make very little headway. Secularists may argue that religion no longer has a direct influence on politics or art or science in American society, but one must reply to them, "So what?" The secular philosophies and theologies provide neither an interpretation of ultimate reality that is adequate for most men nor a community to which one can belong and which would provide significant element in one's self-definition. Since it is extremely difficult to persuade men to give up that which they have learned in their youth, particularly when one has nothing in the way of a viable and appealing alternative, secularism, however important it may be in American culture, cannot yet be considered a serious threat to either the religious faith or the church affiliation of American Protestants and

Catholics. We suspect that the more important of the two elements at work is the belonging element, because it is this element which seems to differentiate precisely American societies from European societies, where church affiliation and religious belief have apparently declined much more rapidly than they have in the United States. We would suggest that far from weakening church affiliation in the United States, religious pluralism has unintentionally strengthened it because of its "social locating" function.

Such a theoretical explanation enables us to understand why Harvey Cox's "secular man" does not appear in the data reported in this book save perhaps among American Jews. Many theologians and scientists have drastically overestimated the incompatibility of science and myth. Even though man may very well realize now that thunder is not the sign of God's anger (one wonders how many people in the past thought it was), this particular knowledge and all the scientific knowledge like it does not provide man with an interpretative scheme that answers the most difficult questions he must face, nor does it provide American man with a socioreligious community which will give him some kind of identity in the midst of a vast and apparently impersonal industrialized culture. In the rarefied atmosphere of academia it may well be true that religion and science seem incompatible and that secularized religion is really the only solution; but the battle between religion and science has not been settled for the general population, in part because many people have not yet decided that there ought necessarily to be a battle. It is also possible—and some of the more recent writings in the philosophy of science at least give some hints of this—that the self-proclaimed victory of science over religion even in *academia* might result from a misunderstanding of the terms of an argument which could have more appropriately been a dialogue.

It may very well be that there is a very long-run trend toward the erosion of religious faith and practice when it is not reinforced strongly by organizational loyalty. The relative security and stability of American Protestantism as the biggest and senior partner in the American religious scene may actually weaken it, since such a posture does not demand vigorous organizational loyalty, and in the absence of such loyalty the long-run influences of secularism have more of a chance to operate. It is also possible, of course, that the stimulus of the secularization trend, if it is realistically faced, may provide an opportunity for the churches for authentic renewal, which would move them out of the position where they are content with merely being stable and holding their own. Surely this is a claim of many who are reporting on the secularization revolution, and we do not wish at this point to dispute their claim that the secular city, should it ever come into existence, would be an extraordinarily challenging and fruitful place for the churches. But we are compelled to observe that neither the empirical evidence collected in these studies, nor the theoretical perspectives within which we are attempting to integrate the evidence, give much indication of a revolution.

We have then sufficiently explained the relative stability and slow erosion of the Protestant position in American society, but we will have to spend somewhat more time trying to fit the Catholic and Jewish phenomena into our theorizing. Perhaps the most important event that happened to American Catholicism was the identification of religion and immigrant origins. Many of the Catholic bishops of the nineteenth century felt that the exposure of the immigrant to the pressures of a non-Catholic society would lead to a decline in religious faith. But such leaders did not understand the dynamics of human behavior quite as well as we do today. When the host society chose to equate an immigrant's ethnic origins with his religion, far from posing a threat to religion, they actually reinforced it. The immigrants were perhaps ashamed of their poverty and their inept ways in American society. They were ashamed of being the lowest people on the socioeconomic ladder, but man needs something to be proud of, something with which he can identify himself in the inner core of his personality to give him self-respect and dignity. For the Catholic immigrants, religion was precisely that essential element of self-definition—partly, one supposes, because of the deep religious faith that they had in the countries from which they came, but more so because in an American society which already was religiously pluralistic, religion had already been established as an important means of self-definition.

Thus the Irish immigrants to England were much more likely to drift from the Church than the Irish immigrants to the United States, precisely because in the United States, to a far more important extent than England, religion had already become, because of Protestant multidenominationalism, a means of self-description which it had never become in England. The great loyalty and the strong organizational control which exists in American Roman Catholicism—or existed at least until the Vatican Council—were made possible by the fact that the immigrants, with great help from their non-Catholic fellow Americans, decided that being vigorously and militantly Catholic was essential for them to be anything.

There are some indications in our data and many indications in the public events since 1965 that would suggest that the intense loyalty of the immigrant era has come to an end. There seems to be much less respect for Canon Law and also a tendency for a kind of ecclesiastical underground to appear which organizes some members of the Catholic elite in extracanonical organizations which still, nonetheless, claim to be loyal to the basic principles of Catholicism and the general Catholic community. There are some hints of the possibility of the emergence of such an underground in the data on which we have reported. Clearly there has to be a substantial change in both internal structure and the external posture of Roman Catholicism as the last traces of the immigrant experience become merely a memory. We would be inclined to suspect that the long-run trend in American Catholicism is for it to become more "Protestant" in its organizational structure and style, and perhaps eventually, over several generations, for the slow doctrinal and devotional erosion that we observed in Protestantism to begin also to affect American Roman Catholicism, though it must be stressed that our data show no signs of this happening as of 1965. It is also possible, though unlikely, given what we have said about the way a child learns his religious faith and his religious membership, that the process of Protestantization of American Catholicism will be greatly accelerated by the pressures of the postconciliar and ecumenical age.[1]

It is relatively easy for someone who stands within the American

---

[1] It is interesting to observe how the Protestantization of other churches affects the role of the religious functionary. Both the priest and the rabbi in the United States have taken on many, if not most, of the functions and responsibilities of a Protestant minister, so that the general behavior and responsibilities of a priest or a rabbi are much more similar to that of their Protestant counterparts than they are of that of priests or rabbis in other countries. I have been told that in Hawaii, with its substantial Buddhist population, the Buddhist religious leader is also required to behave in fashions roughly similar to that of a minister or a parish priest.

Catholic experience to speculate on the meaning of our data for American Catholicism. It is obviously somewhat more difficult for an outsider to attempt to evaluate the implications of the data for Jewish tradition. But one can at least try, subject to correction by one's Jewish brothers.

First of all, it seems reasonable to assert that Judaism is not a denomination in the sense that, let us say, Catholicism or Lutheranism is, but is rather, as Jewish observers are careful to point out, "a people." Jewish unity is constituted not merely by church membership, but by a whole series of relationships to various welfare and religious organizations (many of which interlock) and also by a profound loyalty to historic tradition. Thus, formal congregational affiliation would be, in American Judaism, much less important in constituting one as a Jew than it would be for other religious groups. The outside society seems to agree with this, because it is pretty hard to be considered a Catholic unless one makes some nominal attempts at Catholic behavior, but one is a Jew even if one never sets a foot inside a synagogue or a temple. It therefore is possible to ask whether the increase in congregational affiliation among Jews represents a strong Americanizing— that is to say, Protestantizing—tendency. In the larger American society, influenced as it is by the multidenominationalism of its Protestant past, formal membership in a church is important if one is actually to be considered a member of a religious group. There is, we think, no particular reason to suspect that with the increased acculturation of Jews into American society, they would be immune to the need of formal religious affiliation.

But there is still another question that we may ask in attempting to understand the rather dramatic changes in Jewish orientations that we have discovered in this study. First of all: Is it possible that in Judaism membership in the religious community (either formal or informal) and propositional faith are less closely connected than they are in the other two American religions? If it was possible in the past to accept a Jewish interpretative scheme without conscious and formalized choice of church membership, it may also be equally possible in the present to maintain a formal choice of congregational membership without an explicit acceptance of an interpretative scheme. If such an explanation is accurate, then one could say that the Americanizing impact on the Jews has produced two quite diverse tendencies. Since the inter-

pretative scheme was much less important to being a Jew than it
was to Protestants or Catholics, there were no organizational barriers to protect the interpretative scheme from the powerful on-
slaught of scientific secularism which occurred in American society. But, on the other hand, since being a Jew is still important,
and since being anything religious requires congregational affiliation, it was also possible in American society for Jews to become
much more conscious and formalized in their religious adherence
than they had been in the past, despite the simultaneous decline in
propositional orthodoxy. We are thus suggesting that it might be
possible that the looser connection between membership and interpretative scheme in Judaism, faced with the acculturating and
assimilating influences in American society, made possible the
situation where conscious and formal affiliation would increase,
while adherence to the interpretative scheme would decrease. Such
a paradox is not possible in the Protestant or Catholic groups
because of the much more intimate connection between the interpretative scheme and affiliation in these groups.

We would see then the increase in anti-Catholic feeling as quite
possibly being part of the Americanization of Judaism. The old
animosities between Catholics and Jews are not the real cause of
the present increase in tension, but they may provide a useful
occasion for such tension as Jews recall what was done to them in
years gone by. But the real cause would be the increased necessity
for formalized membership, which in its turn is both a cause and
an effect of the increasing self-consciousness of Jews as members of
a *third American religion.* Both because of the historic background and because of the close physical juxtaposition of Catholics and Jews in a handful of American cities, Catholics are perceived as the primary obstacle to the Jews' obtaining the same
acceptance of the larger society *as a religious group* that Catholics
have previously received. We might therefore hopefully hypothesize that if indeed the increase in anti-Catholic feeling that we
reported early in the book is valid, then it represents a relatively
short-run trend and that with increased acceptance of Judaism as
an *American* religion the anti-Catholic feeling might decline.

It therefore seems to us faily likely that some kind of formalized
identification with their religion or a religious cultural group will
become more and more characteristic of American Jews. We are
less hopeful of our ability to predict what will happen to the other
element in man's religious behavior, his interpretative scheme.

Humanism does seem to be an adequate faith for large numbers of American Jews. Whether it will continue to be so is problematic, though one suspects that given the strong tendency of American ethnic groups to return periodically to the founts of wisdom in their past, it is not impossible that we shall witness, sometime before the end of the century, a rather dramatic resurgence of Jewish theologizing. What such a resurgence would mean to the younger generation of Jews at that time is uncertain. However, if our theorizing in this chapter is correct, and since the American way means a strong linkage between interpretative schemes and church membership, then the previously rather weak link in Jewish tradition may grow much stronger, and, at some point in the future, Jews—seeing that Protestants and Catholics have a highly developed theology to which most of their members assent in at least broad outline—may want this also for themselves. This sort of speculation is so far from our empirical data that it ought not to be taken too seriously.

Thus, we are arguing in this chapter that the experience of Americanization differentially affects the minority American religious groups according to their different histories and their different internal structures. This different reaction to the Americanizing (or "Protestantizing," if one wishes) tendency explains the rather different postures of the two minority religious groups at the present time. We are also suggesting that eventually we will witness an increased Protestantization (in organization and style, though not necessarily in creed) of the minority religious groups. Such influence might be easier for Catholics to cope with because Protestantism represents an emphasis which Catholic leadership is now prepared to admit was long present in the Catholic tradition and without which the tradition is in some way incomplete. Ecumenical movement may, therefore, facilitate the Protestantization of Catholicism in this country and in passing may also facilitate the Catholicization of Protestantism.

This final point should be stressed. Acculturation is not a one-way street, and while American Protestants and Jews are very likely to take on the religious styles of American Protestantism, (though each in his own way) as they adjust to American society, Protestantism in its turn is likely to be influenced by Catholicism and Judaism. It is difficult at this time to project with any degree of confidence how these interchanges will occur, but the student of American religion in years to come will have an interesting time.

Table 2.1. Continuities in Religious Beliefs and Behavior
(Percent)

	1965			Change from 1952		
Continuities	Protestant	Catholic	Jewish	Protestant	Catholic	Jewish
Believing in God	99	100	77	0	0	-21
Believing Christ is God	73	88	-	-1	-1	-
Believing in Trinity	96	86	-	-2	-1	-
Believing in prayer	94	99	70	0	0	-19
Praying three times a day or more	23	25	5	+2	-3	-4
Believing in life after death	78	83	17	-2	-2	-18
Believing in heaven	71	80	6	-4	-3	-15
Active Church member	75	80	62	0	+3	+12
N	(3,088)	(1,162)	(128)			

Table 2.2. Changes in Religious Beliefs and Behavior
(Percent)

	1965			Change from 1952		
Changes	Catholic	Protestant	Jewish	Catholic	Protestant	Jewish
Believing religion important in own life	76	74	30	–7	–2	–17
Attending Church weekly	33	67	4	+8	+5	–8
Attending Church at all			61	–	–	+17
Believing Bible inspired	82	85	17	–6	0	–28
Reading Bible at least once weekly	37	47	31	+15	+7	+17
N	(1,162)	(3,088)	(128)			

Table 2.3. Religious Changes Among Jews
(Percent)

Religious Changes	Age			Education			Income		
	18-34	35-55	Over 55	Grammar School	High School	College	High	Medium	Low
Believing in God	64	74	93	87	87	67	67	80	83
Praying	69	67	75	80	77	63	56	81	66
Believing in life after death	22	10	20	27	16	13	14	14	50
Church membership	47	71	59	47	70	60	73	60	33
N	(35)	(62)	(29)	(15)	(44)	(69)	(48)	(70)	(6)

Table 2.4. Religious Change Among Gentiles
(Percent)

a. Age

| | 18–34 | | | 35-55 | | | Over 55 | | |
Religious Change	Cath-olic	Protes-tant	Jewish	Cath-olic	Protes-tant	Jewish	Cath-olic	Protes-tant	Jewish
Religion important	68	62	11	75	76	33	88	81	44
Attend Church weekly	63	26	0	69	44	3	67	32	10
Bible inspired	77	81	5	82	84	12	89	89	37
Read Bible weekly	33	46	20	37	49	41	46	37	27
N	(379)	(881)	(36)	(530)	(1,219)	(62)	(253)	(989)	(29)

b. Income

| | High | | | Medium | | | Low | | |
Religious Change	Cath-olic	Protes-tant	Jewish	Cath-olic	Protes-tant	Jewish	Cath-olic	Protes-tant	Jewish
Religion important	74	67	27	76	72	32	70	80	33
Attend Church weekly	77	34	2	66	33	4	61	30	16
Bible inspired	79	75	4	83	85	21	81	89	83
Read Bible weekly	34	51	33	36	44	30	43	40	32
N	(197)	(528)	(48)	(669)	(1,382)	(70)	(281)	(1,130)	(6)

c. Education

| | Grammar School | | | High School | | | College | | |
Religious Change	Cath-olic	Protes-tant	Jewish	Cath-olic	Protes-tant	Jewish	Cath-olic	Protes-tant	Jewish
Religion important	86	83	33	75	73	39	70	67	23
Attend Church weekly	55	31	7	66	30	9	78	39	0
Bible inspired	88	92	40	83	87	29	72	72	4
Read Bible weekly	36	38	27	37	45	37	39	44	27
N	(203)	(719)	(15)	(703)	(1,671)	(44)	(246)	(705)	(69)

Table 3.1. Changing Attitudes Among Catholics

	1952	1965
A. Sex Mores		
Percent disapproving divorce	51	36
Percent disapproving mechanical means of birth control	51	37
B. Attitudes Toward Clergy		
Percent describing clergy as "very understanding"	72	62
Percent saying sermons are "excellent"	43	30
Percent thinking clergy too concerned about money	11	19

Table 3.2. Trends in Attitudinal Change Among Catholics by Age and Education
(Percent)

	Age			Education		
Trends in Attitudinal Change	18–34	35–55	Over 55	Grammar School	High School	College
Disapproving divorce	31	41	33	41	32	41
Disapproving birth control	33	41	35	38	33	43
Clergy not "very understanding"	53 (40)*	44 (38)	32 (30)	30 (30)	50 (35)	28 (45)
Sermons not "excellent"	85	67	68	60	73	74
Too "concerned about money"	26	14	5	10	18	20
N	(329)	(530)	(253)	(203)	(703)	(246)

*Percentages in parentheses indicate comparable Protestant responses.

Table 3.3. Catholic Attitudes on Sex and Anticlericalism by Age and Education

	18–34			35–55			Over 55		
	Grammar School	High School	College	Grammar School	High School	College	Grammar School	High School	College
Birth control sinful	40	21	48	42	43	31	36	25	61
Divorce sinful	50	28	34	39	40	45	44	16	52
Clergy not "very understanding"	20	56	47	41	46	39	24	47	27
Sermons not "excellent"	90	84	88	65	70	59	70	65	68
Too much concern over money	30	30	23	13	12	20	6	5	12
N	(10)	(253)	(111)	(83)	(343)	(101)	(109)	(102)	(34)

Table 3.4. Attitudes toward Clergy Among Catholics by
Attitudes Toward Birth Control

	Birth Control Sinful	Birth Control Not Sinful
Percent clergy not "very understanding"	34	40
Percent sermons not "excellent"	70	75
Percent clergy too concerned about money	14	18
N	(427)	(742)

Table 4.1. Attitudes Toward Religious Schools
(Percent)

Attitudes	1965			Change Since 1952		
	Catholic	Protestant	Jewish	Catholic	Protestant	Jewish
Bad for country	2	14	37	0	−6	+9
Not as good academically	5	16	34	−1	−5	+15
Better academically	46	22	23	−2	+4	+2
In favor of bus, textbook aid	73	40	25	−6	−1	−17
In favor of tax support	55	32	17	−8	−2	−14
In favor of released time	71	44	35	−5	−5	−8

Table 4.2. Trends in Attitudes Toward Religious Schools
by Age and Education

a. Age

Item	18–34			35–50			Over 50		
	Protes-tant	Cath-olic	Jewish	Protes-tant	Cath-olic	Jewish	Protes-tant	Cath-olic	Jewish
Bad for the country	11	2	40	14	2	37	15	1	34
In favor of tax support	37	47	8	30	54	14	29	68	35
N	(881)	(379)	(36)	(1,219)	(530)	(62)	(988)	(253)	(29)

b. Education

Item	Grammar School			High School			College		
	Protes-tant	Cath-olic	Jewish	Protes-tant	Cath-olic	Jewish	Protes-tant	Cath-olic	Jewish
Bad for the country	15	1	40	13	2	27	14	3	42
In favor of tax support	40	66	40	35	60	30	17	31	4
N	(719)	(203)	(15)	(1,671)	(703)	(44)	(705)	(246)	(69)

Table 5.1 A. "Do you think there is much ill feeling toward——— among most people of your religious preference or not?"

Toward	Percent Yes			Change Since 1952		
	Protestant	Catholic	Jewish	Protestant	Catholic	Jewish
Protestants	–	6	2	–	–5	–3
Catholics	19	–	30	–5	–	+15
Jews	30	14	–	–14	–7	–

Table 5.1 B. Do you think———look down on people of your belief?

	Percent Yes			Change Since 1952		
	Protestant	Catholic	Jewish	Protestant	Catholic	Jewish
Protestants	–	17	16	–	–5	0
Catholics	32	–	44	–2	–	+14
Jews	14	14	–	–6	–4	–
look down						

Table 5.1 C. Do you think that———as a group try to interfere in any way with your religious beliefs or personal liberties?

	Percent Yes			Change Since 1952		
	Protestant	Catholic	Jewish	Protestant	Catholic	Jewish
Protestants	–	6	9	–	–6	+5
Catholics	13	–	19	–2	–	+6
Jews	2	3	–	–2	–1	–
interfere						

Table 5.1 D. Compared with most people of your religious beliefs would you say that most———are about the same, better, or not as good in being fair in business?

	Percent Not as Good			Change Since 1952		
	Protestant	Catholic	Jewish	Protestant	Catholic	Jewish
Protestants	–	3	0	–	0	–
Catholics	5	–	1	–1	–	–2
Jews	28	23	–	–11	–8	–
are being fair in business						

Table 5.1 E. Compared with most people of your religious beliefs would you say that most———are about the same, better, or not as good in being honest in public office?

	Percent Not as Good			Change Since 1952		
	Protestant	Catholic	Jewish	Protestant	Catholic	Jewish
Protestants	–	4	0	–	–2	–1
Catholics	6	–	11	–2	–	+8
Jews	9	7	–	–7	–5	–
are honest in public office						

Table 5.1 F. Compared with most people of your religious beliefs would you say that most——are about the same, better, or not as good in respecting beliefs of others?

	Percent Not as Good			Change Since 1952		
	Protestant	Catholic	Jewish	Protestant	Catholic	Jewish
Protestants	–	9	18	–	–1	+10
Catholics	28	–	45	–7	–	+10
Jews	11	5	–	–5	–5	–
respect beliefs of others						

Table 5.1 G. Would you vote for a——for President of the United States as for someone of your own religious faith?

	Percent Yes			Change Since 1952		
	Protestant	Catholic	Jewish	Protestant	Catholic	Jewish
vote for a						
Protestant	–	94	92	–	+2	+2
Catholic	65	–	86	+23	–	+27
Jewish	51	83	–	+20	+26	–
President						

Table 5.1 H. Would you just as soon have a member of your family marry a——as someone of your own religion?

	Percent No			Change Since 1952		
	Protestant	Catholic	Jewish	Protestant	Catholic	Jewish
marry a						
Protestant	–	46	80	–	–9	+12
Catholic	53	–	85	–10	–	+17
Jew	60	55	–	–15	–17	–

Table 5.1 I. Do you think most——employers would discriminate against you because of your religion or not?

	Percent Expecting Discrimination			Change Since 1952		
	Protestant	Catholic	Jewish	Protestant	Catholic	Jewish
Protestant	–	6	26	–	–2	–1
Catholic	12	–	37	–8	–	+6
Jewish	11	8	–	–7	–6	–
employers discriminate against you						

Table 5.1 J. Do you think——stick together too much?

	Percent Yes			Change Since 1952		
	Protestant	Catholic	Jewish	Protestant	Catholic	Jewish
Protestants	—	9	9	—	–2	–10
Catholics	28	—	47	–12	—	+3
Jews	37	43	—	–4	–5	—
stick together too much						

Table 5.1 K. Do you think——are getting too much power in the United States?

	Percent Yes			Change Since 1952		
	Protestant	Catholic	Jewish	Protestant	Catholic	Jewish
Protestants	—	5	8	—	–3	+3
Catholics	30	—	30	–11	—	–6
Jews	14	12	—	–20	–21	—
are getting too much power						

Table 5.1 L. Compared with most clergymen of your religious preference, would you say most——clergymen are about the same, better, or not as good in giving intelligent leadership to their followers?

	Percent Not as Good			Change Since 1952		
	Protestant	Catholic	Jewish	Protestant	Catholic	Jewish
Protestant	—	5	0	—	–1	–1
Catholic	10	—	25	–3	—	+17
Jewish	3	2	—	0	0	—
give intelligent leadership						

Table 5.1 M. Compared with most clergymen of your religious preference, would you say most——clergymen are about the same, better, or not as good in promoting understanding between their group and others?

	Percent Not as Good			Change Since 1952		
	Protestant	Catholic	Jewish	Protestant	Catholic	Jewish
Protestant	—	7	4	—	0	+1
Catholic	24	—	31	–6	—	+17
Jewish	11	6	—	–1	3	—
are promoting understanding						

Table 5.1 N. Compared with most clergymen of your religious preference, would you say most————clergymen are about the same, better, or not as good in cooperating with leaders of other religions for the common civic good?

	Percent Not as Good			Change Since 1952		
	Protestant	Catholic	Jewish	Protestant	Catholic	Jewish
Protestant	—	4	0	—	+1	−4
Catholic	19	—	25	−5	—	+13
Jewish	9	2	—	−1	−4	—
are cooperating for common good						

Table 5.1 O. Compared with most clergymen of your religious preference, would you say most————clergymen are about the same, better, or not as good in setting a good personal example?

	Percent Not as Good			Change Since 1952		
	Protestant	Catholic	Jewish	Protestant	Catholic	Jewish
Protestant	—	4	0	—	−2	−1
Catholic	14	—	10	−4	—	+5
Jewish	6	3	—	−2	−1	—
setting good personal example						

Table 5.1 P. Do you think————try to influence the press too much in favor of their religion or not?

	Percent Yes			Change Since 1952		
	Protestant	Catholic	Jewish	Protestant	Catholic	Jewish
Protestants	—	7	6	—	−6	−5
Catholics	25	—	43	−5	—	+7
Jews	4	5	—	−5	−5	—
influence						

Table 5.1 Q. Do you think————magazines try to be fair to your religious beliefs or not?

	Percent No			Change Since 1952		
	Protestant	Catholic	Jewish	Protestant	Catholic	Jewish
Protestant	—	12	2	—	—	−12
Catholic	24	—	29	−7	—	+12
Jewish	12	13	—	−2	−2	—
magazines are fair						

Table 5.1 R. Have you or your family ever had any unpleasant personal
experience that might have made you dislike————?

| | Percent Yes | | | Change Since 1952 | | |
	Protestant	Catholic	Jewish	Protestant	Catholic	Jewish
unpleasant *personal* *experience* *with*						
Protestants	–	4	9	–	0	+2
Catholics	7	–	15	–2	–	+4
Jews	5	5	–	–3	–1	–

Table 5.2. Changes in Jewish and Catholic Attitudes Toward Each Other
1952–1965
(+% = favorable change; –% = unfavorable change)

Item	Catholics Toward Jews	Jews Toward Catholics
Prejudice against other	+7	–15
Prejudice from other	+6	–14
Interfere with our liberties	+1	–6
Unfair in business	+8	+2
Dishonest in public office	+5	–8
Don't respect our belief	–5	–10
Would vote for the other as President	+26	+27
Would not want intermarriage	+17	–17
Employers would discriminate	+6	–6
Stick together too much	+5	–3
Getting too much power	+21	+6
Clergymen not intelligent	0	–17
Clergymen don't promote understanding	+3	–17
Clergymen don't promote civic cooperation	+4	–13
Clergymen don't set good personal example	+1	–5
Try to influence press	+5	–7
Their magazines not fair	+2	–12
Have had unpleasant experience with other that caused dislike of other	+1	–4

Table 5.3. Anti-Catholic Feeling Among Jewish Groups

	Young	Middle	Old	Grammar School	High School	College
Catholics look down	44	29	13	33	41	48
Catholics interfere	25	17	10	6	13	25
Catholics don't respect faith of others	56	46	28	13	31	60
Catholics discriminate	51	36	44	33	25	44
Catholics stick together	61	33	58	46	45	47
Catholics after power	31	27	31	20	27	33
Clergy not intelligent	36	22	14	7	12	38
Clergy doesn't promote goodwill	36	29	28	20	15	43
N	(36)	(42)	(29)	(15)	(44)	(69)

Table 5.4. Jewish Attitudes Toward Catholics by Belief in God
and Congregational Affiliation

	Believe in God Belong to Congregation	Believe in God Do not Belong	Do not Believe Do not Belong
Catholics look down on us	57	36	36
Catholics try to interfere	30	34	7
Catholics don't respect our beliefs	62	63	22
Catholics discriminate	50	29	29
Catholics stick together too much	57	37	43
Catholics are getting too much power	33	34	27
Clergy not intelligent	40	29	12
Clergy doesn't promote understanding	43	32	27
N	(40)	(38)	(41)

Table 6.1. Religious Attitudes of Young People

	Catholic		Protestant	
	18–25	Over 25	18–25	Over 25
There is a God	100	99	100	97
Bible is inspired	76	83	74	86
Pray	99	99	90	94
Life after death	85	81	72	77
Heaven	84	79	68	70
Hell	76	70	57	54
Against mixed marriage	62	62	65	74
Birth control	21	38	17	18
Divorce wrong	37	36	12	10
Church member	87	90	62	76
Clergy not very understanding	59	43	58	50
Sermons not "excellent"	93	70	76	68
Church too concerned about money	23	16	12	15
N	(135)	(1,027)	(259)	(2,829)

APPENDIX

Study Conducted for
The Catholic Digest

OBJECTIVES OF THE STUDY :

The objectives of this study were :   (1) to measure the religious beliefs and practices of American adults, and attitudes of members of the three main religious groups toward each other, and (2) to determine what changes, if any, have come about since a comparable study in 1952.

DESIGN OF THE RESEARCH :

This study is based on 2,783 personal interviews with a representative cross-section of U. S. adults 18 years of age and over. The interviews were conducted during November, 1965.

The recent study was made comparable to the one conducted in 1952 (by Ben Gaffin and Associates) in as many respects as possible. The questions have been repeated exactly, the sampling method is comparable, and approximately the same number of persons have been interviewed.

The study in 1952 was based on 2,987 personal interviews with a representative cross-section of U. S. adults 18 years of age and over. The interviews were conducted during June and July, 1952. A description of the design of the sample for the 1952 study is found in Religion and the American People, by John L. Thomas, S.J., published by The Newman Press, Westminster, Maryland, 1963. Briefly, the sample is what is termed technically a "quota sample".

The composition of the sample for the 1965 study is to be found at the end of the report. It is followed by a description of the design of the sample and by tables of recommended sampling tolerances to have in mind when reading the report.

The national adult civilian population, 18 years of age and older, excluding the institutional population, was estimated as of November, 1965, at 120.5 million. This estimate can be used for the purpose of projecting percentages into number of people.

IMPORTANT NOTE :

Results for "non-labor force" under the category of "occupation", have not been included for the 1952 tables in this report. Persons in the non-labor force in the 1952 study were reclassified in terms of the Chief Wage Earner in the family. In the 1965 study, results for the non-labor force are provided. Included in this group are persons who are unemployed themselves and live in families where no one else is employed.

1a.   Do you think people in general today lead as good lives - honest
and moral - as they used to?

	1965			1952		
	Yes %	No %	Undec. %	Yes %	No %	Undec. %
TOTAL	39	52	9	47	46	7
RELIGION						
Roman Catholic	48	43	9	54	37	9
Protestant total	33	58	9	44	49	7
Baptist	26	64	10	34	60	6
Methodist	33	58	9	45	49	6
Lutheran	41	51	8	52	40	8
Presbyterian	50	43	7	57	39	4
Episcopal	49	42	9	50	38	12
Congregational	51	43	6	65	33	2
Other denominations	30	64	6	40	53	7
Jewish	59	32	9	58	34	8
Other and None	47	43	10	50	43	7
SEX						
Men	43	50	7	49	45	6
Women	35	55	10	45	46	9
AGE						
18-24 years	34	61	5	46	48	6
25-34	40	51	9	49	45	6
35-44	41	51	8	48	44	8
45-54	41	51	8	52	40	8
55-64	37	53	10	47	45	8
65 & over	35	52	13	34	58	8
RACE						
White	40	51	9	49	44	7
Non-White	30	63	7	27	68	5
EDUCATION						
0-8th grade	32	58	10	40	51	9
1-3 years' high school	31	59	10	45	47	8
High school graduate	41	51	8	52	42	6
1-3 years' college	45	49	6	57	37	6
College graduate	49	42	9	53	41	6

	1965			1952		
	Yes %	No %	Undec. %	Yes %	No %	Undec. %
OCCUPATION						
Professional	48	43	9	55	39	6
Proprietor or manager	46	48	6	56	36	8
White-collar worker	38	52	10	49	44	7
Service worker	37	54	9	42	51	7
Manual worker	35	57	8	44	48	8
Farmer	27	62	11	45	49	6
Non-labor force	37	52	11	*	*	*
INCOME						
Upper	46	48	6	56	36	8
Middle	41	50	9	49	44	7
Lower	30	60	10	39	54	7
CITY SIZE						
Over 1 Million	42	48	10	50	43	7
100,000 - 1 Million	40	53	7	48	46	6
25,000 - 100,000	45	49	6	52	37	11
10,000 - 25,000	40	52	8	39	53	8
Under 10,000	35	55	10	48	46	6
Rural, farm	30	61	9	42	49	9
REGION						
New England	51	45	4	49	41	10
Middle Atlantic	45	45	10	50	41	9
South Atlantic	31	59	10	44	49	7
East South Central	28	63	9	32	62	6
West South Central	32	56	12	47	44	9
East North Central	40	52	8	48	44	8
West North Central	40	54	6	49	43	8
Mountain	44	45	11	44	48	8
Pacific	37	55	8	48	48	4

1b. Do you think that young people today have as strong a sense of right and wrong as they did, say, fifty years ago?

	1965			1952		
	Yes %	No %	Undec. %	Yes %	No %	Undec. %
TOTAL	41	46	13	57	34	9
RELIGION						
Roman Catholic	46	42	12	56	34	10
Protestant total	39	48	13	57	35	8
Baptist	41	47	12	51	38	11
Methodist	37	48	15	62	32	6
Lutheran	41	46	13	55	36	9
Presbyterian	43	45	12	62	30	8
Episcopal	41	49	10	57	28	15
Congregational	41	46	13	68	30	2
Other denominations	32	52	16	56	37	7
Jewish	52	37	11	73	20	7
Other and None	44	41	15	51	37	12
SEX						
Men	45	44	11	56	36	8
Women	37	48	15	58	33	9
AGE						
18-24 years	41	48	11	55	34	11
25-34	41	46	13	59	33	8
35-44	43	45	12	60	31	9
45-54	45	42	13	57	34	9
55-64	39	48	13	57	34	9
65 & over	36	47	17	47	45	8
RACE						
White	41	46	13	57	34	9
Non-White	42	45	13	47	44	9
EDUCATION						
0-8th grade	39	46	15	50	40	10
1-3 years' high school	39	44	17	58	32	10
High school graduate	40	48	12	60	32	8
1-3 years' college	48	44	8	67	26	7
College graduate	45	43	12	56	36	8

	1965			1952		
	Yes %	No %	Undec. %	Yes %	No %	Undec. %
OCCUPATION						
Professional	41	48	11	58	34	8
Proprietor or manager	42	44	14	62	30	8
White-collar worker	45	44	11	60	34	6
Service worker	49	37	14	57	35	8
Manual worker	40	48	12	55	35	10
Farmer	38	42	20	60	31	9
Non-labor force	37	49	14	*	*	*
INCOME						
Upper	44	43	13	64	28	8
Middle	42	45	13	59	33	8
Lower	38	49	13	50	40	10
CITY SIZE						
Over 1 Million	41	44	15	56	36	8
100,000 - 1 Million	41	48	11	55	35	10
25,000 - 100,000	46	44	10	58	31	11
10,000 - 25,000	40	43	17	54	37	9
Under 10,000	42	46	12	59	33	8
Rural, farm	36	44	20	58	34	8
REGION						
New England	41	49	10	53	35	12
Middle Atlantic	41	46	13	59	33	8
South Atlantic	45	41	14	60	30	10
East South Central	37	46	17	53	38	9
West South Central	43	41	16	59	36	5
East North Central	41	47	12	55	35	10
West North Central	39	51	10	57	33	10
Mountain	38	49	13	54	37	9
Pacific	39	47	14	55	36	9

2a. How important would you say religion is in your own life --
very important, fairly important, or not very important?

	1965 Very Impt. %	Fairly Impt. %	Not Very Impt. %	Undec. %	1952 Very Impt. %	Fairly Impt. %	Not Very Impt. %	Undec. %
TOTAL	70	22	7	1	75	20	5	*
RELIGION								
Roman Catholic	76	20	3	1	83	14	3	*
Protestant total	74	20	5	1	76	20	4	*
Baptist	82	14	3	1	84	13	3	-
Methodist	65	28	7	*	74	22	4	*
Lutheran	66	25	7	2	70	24	6	*
Presbyterian	71	21	8	*	72	23	5	*
Episcopal	61	35	4	-	67	26	6	1
Congregational	62	27	11	-	57	41	2	-
Other denominations	80	14	5	1	77	20	3	*
Jewish	30	50	17	3	47	37	15	1
Other and None	30	30	36	4	37	27	30	6
SEX								
Men	63	26	10	1	68	22	8	2
Women	77	18	4	1	79	18	3	*
AGE								
18-24 years	57	32	10	1	64	30	6	*
25-34	61	29	10	*	71	24	5	*
35-44	72	22	5	1	71	23	6	*
45-54	74	20	5	1	77	15	6	2
55-64	77	15	7	1	80	14	4	2
65 & over	78	14	7	1	84	11	4	1
RACE								
White	69	23	7	1	75	20	5	*
Non-White	80	13	7	-	78	13	8	1
EDUCATION								
0-8th grade	79	13	6	2	77	16	5	2
1-3 years' high school	72	21	6	1	72	20	6	2
High school graduate	70	24	5	1	73	23	4	*
1-3 years' college	66	25	8	1	73	20	7	*
College graduate	57	26	16	1	67	23	9	1

* Less than one per cent.

	1965				1952			
	Very Impt. %	Fairly Impt. %	Not Very Impt. %	Undec. %	Very Impt. %	Fairly Impt. %	Not Very Impt. %	Undec. %
OCCUPATION								
Professional	62	27	10	1	75	20	5	*
Proprietor or manager	73	20	6	1	72	20	8	*
White-collar worker	67	25	7	1	74	21	5	*
Service worker	74	17	7	1	72	23	4	1
Manual worker	70	23	6	1	73	20	5	2
Farmer	76	20	4	*	81	17	2	*
Non-labor force	75	14	10	1	*	*	*	*
INCOME								
Upper	65	27	7	1	75	20	5	*
Middle	69	24	7	*	75	20	5	*
Lower	75	16	8	1	72	20	6	2
CITY SIZE								
Over 1 Million	65	25	9	1	68	21	9	2
100,000 - 1 Million	68	23	9	*	70	20	9	1
25,000 - 100,000	81	13	5	1	75	21	3	1
10,000 - 25,000	71	19	8	2	77	19	3	1
Under 10,000	73	20	6	1	73	22	5	*
Rural, farm	74	21	5	-	84	14	2	*
REGION								
New England	66	22	11	1	79	15	4	2
Middle Atlantic	68	24	7	1	72	19	7	2
South Atlantic	76	18	5	1	83	13	4	*
East South Central	89	8	2	1	87	11	2	-
West South Central	71	22	6	1	85	13	2	*
East North Central	70	23	6	*	67	27	5	1
West North Central	70	24	6	-	69	24	6	1
Mountain	71	20	9	-	66	25	7	2
Pacific	61	25	13	1	64	27	8	1

* Less than one per cent.

2b. Do you think children should be raised as church members or do you think they should be free of formal religion until they are old enough to make up their own minds?

| | 1965 | | | 1952 | | |
	Raised as Church Members %	Free to Make up Own Minds %	Undec. %	Raised as Church Members %	Free to Make up Own Minds %	Undec. %
TOTAL	76	18	6	72	24	4
RELIGION						
Roman Catholic	90	8	2	91	7	2
Protestant total	75	18	7	67	28	5
Baptist	72	22	6	56	38	6
Methodist	75	18	7	69	25	6
Lutheran	89	8	3	84	16	*
Presbyterian	81	13	6	73	24	3
Episcopal	78	17	5	80	14	6
Congregational	70	17	13	69	22	9
Other denominations	71	21	8	66	29	5
Jewish	80	14	6	67	23	10
Other and None	42	46	12	49	46	5
SEX						
Men	74	20	6	72	24	4
Women	79	16	5	71	24	5
AGE						
18-24 years	70	23	7	66	30	4
25-34	75	18	7	68	28	4
35-44	79	15	6	73	22	5
45-54	80	16	4	75	19	6
55-64	79	17	4	78	18	4
65 & over	72	21	7	71	24	5
RACE						
White	74	26	-	71	24	5
Non-White	77	17	6	69	26	5
EDUCATION						
0-8th grade	72	22	6	69	26	5
1-3 years' high school	75	19	6	72	24	4
High school graduate	79	16	5	74	22	4
1-3 years' college	77	14	9	69	26	5
College graduate	78	16	6	73	21	6

* Less than one per cent.

	1965			1952		
	Raised as Church Members %	Free to Make up Own Minds %	Undec. %	Raised as Church Members %	Free to Make up Own Minds %	Undec. %
OCCUPATION						
Professional	81	13	6	69	24	7
Proprietor or manager	84	11	5	74	23	3
White-collar worker	79	15	6	73	22	5
Service worker	72	21	7	75	20	5
Manual worker	75	19	6	70	26	4
Farmer	68	25	7	65	27	8
Non-labor force	73	22	5	*	*	*
INCOME						
Upper	83	12	5	74	21	5
Middle	79	15	6	73	23	4
Lower	70	25	5	68	28	4
CITY SIZE						
Over 1 Million	82	11	7	75	19	6
100,000 - 1 Million	76	18	6	78	17	5
25,000 - 100,000	87	-	3	78	20	2
10,000 - 25,000	79	15	6	75	21	4
Under 10,000	71	22	7	68	28	4
Rural, farm	66	28	6	66	29	5
REGION						
New England	77	18	5	86	12	2
Middle Atlantic	86	10	4	82	14	4
South Atlantic	70	22	8	70	23	7
East South Central	69	23	8	59	38	3
West South Central	70	23	7	50	47	3
East North Central	79	16	5	72	23	5
West North Central	82	12	6	74	21	5
Mountain	75	24	1	68	28	4
Pacific	69	23	8	70	25	5

3a. Some religious denominations support their own schools, to which members prefer to send their children rather than to public schools. Do you think these religious schools are good or bad for the country, or don't you think it makes any difference?

	1965				1952			
	Good %	Bad %	No Differ. %	Undec. %	Good %	Bad %	No Differ. %	Undec. %
TOTAL	45	11	32	12	42	16	31	11
RELIGION								
Roman Catholic	75	2	20	3	73	2	22	3
Protestant total	36	14	34	16	34	20	33	13
Baptist	39	13	30	18	36	18	29	17
Methodist	30	11	40	19	35	21	33	11
Lutheran	37	15	38	10	46	13	35	6
Presbyterian	31	17	37	15	23	27	34	16
Episcopal	32	9	42	17	34	25	29	12
Congregational	20	25	43	12	22	24	45	9
Other denominations	41	13	31	15	33	21	33	13
Jewish	19	37	30	14	29	28	32	11
Other and None	29	15	46	10	26	21	40	13
SEX								
Men	45	13	32	10	41	18	32	9
Women	44	10	32	14	43	15	30	12
AGE								
18-24 years	48	12	31	9	41	13	36	10
25-34	43	9	38	10	45	15	31	9
35-44	46	11	32	11	41	15	33	11
45-54	46	12	29	13	38	20	32	10
55-64	42	14	27	17	45	19	25	11
65 & over	43	12	30	15	40	17	26	17
RACE								
White	44	12	32	12	42	17	31	10
Non-White	45	9	31	15	51	8	27	14
EDUCATION								
0-8th grade	43	13	31	13	46	13	29	12
1-3 years' high school	42	11	29	18	44	12	33	11
High school graduate	46	9	34	11	42	18	31	9
1-3 years' college	49	10	31	10	36	20	33	11
College graduate	40	19	31	10	33	25	30	12

| | 1965 | | | | 1952 | | | |
	Good %	Bad %	No Differ. %	Undec. %	Good %	Bad %	No Differ. %	Undec. %
OCCUPATION								
Professional	42	16	32	10	35	23	25	17
Proprietor or manager	40	12	34	14	37	21	32	10
White-collar worker	47	10	33	10	41	17	32	10
Service worker	37	14	34	15	48	13	30	9
Manual worker	49	9	32	10	46	13	32	9
Farmer	38	10	30	22	37	18	27	18
Non-labor force	42	13	30	15	*	*	*	*
INCOME								
Upper	40	13	34	13	37	25	28	10
Middle	48	10	31	11	41	16	32	11
Lower	42	12	32	14	46	13	29	12
CITY SIZE								
Over 1 Million	53	10	28	9	55	14	22	9
100,000 - 1 Million	47	10	31	12	43	14	34	9
25,000 - 100,000	47	15	34	4	47	11	33	9
10,000 - 25,000	29	11	43	17	40	15	31	14
Under 10,000	40	13	32	15	36	20	33	11
Rural, farm	33	12	31	24	42	17	28	13
REGION								
New England	42	17	35	6	39	18	38	5
Middle Atlantic	49	10	32	9	48	15	30	7
South Atlantic	38	12	31	19	38	15	31	16
East South Central	39	16	25	20	42	19	23	16
West South Central	39	11	33	17	42	17	28	13
East North Central	50	10	20	10	40	18	31	11
West North Central	40	13	34	13	36	12	40	12
Mountain	32	11	41	16	38	19	30	13
Pacific	50	9	30	11	50	15	28	7

3b.   How would you rate the quality of the general education given in religious grade schools as compared with the public grade schools - about the same, better, or not as good?

	1965				1952			
	About Same %	Better %	Not as Good %	Undec. %	About Same %	Better %	Not as Good %	Undec. %
TOTAL	33	28	14	25	37	25	17	21
RELIGION								
Roman Catholic	38	46	5	11	43	48	6	3
Protestant total	32	22	16	30	35	18	21	26
Baptist	34	26	10	30	36	16	17	31
Methodist	33	18	17	32	37	18	22	23
Lutheran	35	22	21	22	43	22	18	17
Presbyterian	31	22	17	30	29	20	30	21
Episcopal	27	24	27	22	35	17	27	21
Congregational	19	22	42	17	26	22	30	22
Other denominations	31	22	14	33	35	16	20	29
Jewish	23	23	34	20	32	21	19	28
Other and None	29	24	20	27	34	20	14	32
SEX								
Men	35	27	16	22	39	24	18	19
Women	32	29	12	27	36	26	16	22
AGE								
18-24 years	32	31	16	21	38	31	16	15
25-34	33	32	13	22	38	27	14	21
35-44	32	30	14	24	35	27	16	22
45-54	32	28	15	25	41	19	18	22
55-64	38	26	12	24	36	26	19	19
65 & over	33	21	14	32	36	19	19	26
RACE								
White	33	28	14	25	36	25	17	22
Non-White	33	33	13	21	43	29	14	14
EDUCATION								
0-8th grade	42	21	9	28	43	23	12	22
1-3 years' high school	32	28	13	27	38	27	13	22
High school graduate	31	33	13	23	37	26	18	19
1-3 years' college	31	33	14	22	31	29	18	22
College graduate	27	21	29	23	28	22	28	22

	1965				1952			
	About Same %	Better %	Not as Good %	Undec. %	About Same %	Better %	Not as Good %	Undec. %
OCCUPATION								
Professional	29	28	23	20	28	28	25	19
Proprietor or manager	28	30	18	24	32	24	20	24
White-collar worker	34	30	9	27	38	24	18	20
Service worker	42	23	14	21	34	31	16	19
Manual worker	34	32	11	23	41	25	14	20
Farmer	36	21	13	30	40	19	16	25
Non-labor force	31	23	15	31	*	*	*	*
INCOME								
Upper	30	25	20	25	31	23	22	24
Middle	34	31	14	21	38	35	17	20
Lower	34	25	12	29	40	26	14	20
CITY SIZE								
Over 1 Million	30	38	14	18	33	35	14	18
100,000 - 1 Million	33	31	14	22	38	26	17	19
25,000 - 100,000	44	25	16	15	43	28	14	15
10,000 - 25,000	33	22	13	32	38	17	20	25
Under 10,000	32	24	13	31	38	24	17	21
Rural, farm	34	18	14	34	36	22	16	26
REGION								
New England	27	38	18	17	37	26	25	12
Middle Atlantic	35	33	16	16	41	28	17	14
South Atlantic	31	24	12	33	36	22	14	28
East South Central	38	15	11	36	25	27	16	32
West South Central	39	21	11	29	40	18	18	24
East North Central	38	28	14	20	37	25	19	19
West North Central	32	22	20	26	44	20	13	23
Mountain	26	22	14	38	31	19	18	32
Pacific	25	40	10	25	35	31	13	21

4a. Public funds are used in some states to give free bus service and free books to children in the **public** schools. Do you think public funds should also be used to give free bus service and free books to children in religious schools, or not?

	1965			1952		
	Yes %	No %	Undec. %	Yes %	No %	Undec. %
TOTAL	48	41	11	51	40	9
RELIGION						
Roman Catholic	73	18	9	79	12	9
Protestant total	40	48	12	41	50	9
Baptist	51	34	15	47	42	11
Methodist	42	49	9	42	49	9
Lutheran	33	59	8	39	53	8
Presbyterian	32	56	12	32	59	9
Episcopal	27	67	6	25	66	9
Congregational	31	61	8	34	56	10
Other denominations	35	53	12	42	49	9
Jewish	25	60	15	45	44	11
Other and None	47	45	8	42	42	16
SEX						
Men	48	43	9	51	41	8
Women	49	39	12	50	39	11
AGE						
18-24 years	48	44	8	54	38	8
25-34	49	41	10	52	39	9
35-44	50	38	12	51	40	9
45-54	48	42	10	45	43	12
55-64	47	42	11	50	41	9
65 & over	49	38	13	49	37	14
RACE						
White	46	43	11	49	41	10
Non-White	67	23	10	63	21	16
EDUCATION						
0-8th grade	58	28	14	59	28	13
1-3 years' high school	51	37	12	55	34	11
High school graduate	48	42	10	46	46	8
1-3 years' college	40	51	9	38	53	9
College graduate	35	56	9	28	64	8

| | 1965 | | | | 1952 | | |
	Yes %	No %	Undec. %		Yes %	No %	Undec. %
OCCUPATION							
Professional	41	50	9		31	60	9
Proprietor or manager	40	51	9		42	50	8
White-collar worker	44	44	12		47	44	9
Service worker	57	28	15		55	33	12
Manual worker	55	36	9		59	32	9
Farmer	46	37	17		43	42	15
Non-labor force	47	39	14		*	*	*
INCOME							
Upper	40	51	9		37	55	8
Middle	49	41	10		48	43	9
Lower	52	35	13		60	28	12
CITY SIZE							
Over 1 Million	51	39	10		59	30	11
100,000 - 1 Million	50	41	9		50	38	12
25,000 - 100,000	48	42	10		59	33	8
10,000 - 25,000	39	50	11		48	45	7
Under 10,000	48	39	13		45	46	9
Rural, farm	42	41	17		47	40	13
REGION							
New England	52	40	8		63	32	5
Middle Atlantic	57	33	10		57	34	9
South Atlantic	48	35	17		57	34	9
East South Central	59	26	15		48	38	14
West South Central	49	43	8		46	44	10
East North Central	47	43	10		46	44	10
West North Central	38	49	13		44	43	13
Mountain	37	55	8		32	54	14
Pacific	42	49	9		41	49	10

4b. People who send their children to religious schools pay taxes
for the support of the public schools, as well as paying for
the support of the religious schools. Do you think public
taxes should be used to support the religious schools also,
or not?

	1965			1952		
	Yes %	No %	Undec. %	Yes %	No %	Undec. %
TOTAL	38	50	12	40	49	11
RELIGION						
Roman Catholic	55	31	14	63	25	12
Protestant total	32	56	12	34	56	10
Baptist	42	44	14	40	47	13
Methodist	31	55	14	34	55	11
Lutheran	30	63	7	28	61	11
Presbyterian	20	71	9	23	73	4
Episcopal	20	73	7	24	70	6
Congregational	13	77	10	35	57	8
Other denominations	31	57	12	37	54	9
Jewish	17	74	9	35	49	16
Other and None	33	58	9	31	57	12
SEX						
Men	34	56	10	37	53	10
Women	41	45	14	43	45	12
AGE						
18-24 years	42	48	10	46	44	10
25-34	38	52	10	44	46	10
35-44	36	53	11	39	49	12
45-54	37	50	13	34	55	11
55-64	39	48	13	37	52	11
65 & over	34	49	17	39	47	14
RACE						
White	35	53	12	39	50	11
Non-White	57	31	12	57	29	14
EDUCATION						
0-8th grade	46	36	18	47	39	14
1-3 years' high school	47	42	11	48	41	10
High school graduate	39	50	11	38	52	10
1-3 years' college	22	66	12	27	63	10
College graduate	18	75	7	17	77	6

	1965			1952		
	Yes %	No %	Undec. %	Yes %	No %	Undec. %
OCCUPATION						
Professional	23	65	12	20	76	4
Proprietor or manager	31	57	12	32	57	11
White-collar worker	37	49	14	37	52	11
Service worker	48	37	15	48	39	13
Manual worker	45	45	10	48	41	11
Farmer	35	53	12	33	50	17
Non-labor force	35	50	15	*	*	*
INCOME						
Upper	24	64	12	26	66	8
Middle	38	51	11	39	50	11
Lower	43	44	13	49	38	13
CITY SIZE						
Over 1 Million	41	46	13	47	40	13
100,000 - 1 Million	40	50	10	43	45	12
25,000 - 100,000	35	55	10	46	42	12
10,000 - 25,000	31	53	16	37	53	10
Under 10,000	37	50	13	36	55	9
Rural, farm	28	56	16	37	49	14
REGION						
New England	34	57	9	50	43	7
Middle Atlantic	43	45	12	45	44	11
South Atlantic	44	42	14	50	42	8
East South Central	45	34	21	37	44	19
West South Central	37	51	12	38	52	10
East North Central	37	52	11	36	51	13
West North Central	27	62	11	34	54	12
Mountain	23	70	7	24	59	17
Pacific	32	54	14	31	60	9

5a.   In some states, children in public schools are allowed to leave
      school early to attend classes in their own religion, taught by
      religious teachers of their own faith. Do you think this is a
      good idea, a bad idea, or don't you think it makes any difference?

	1965 Good Idea %	1965 Bad Idea %	1965 Indifferent %	1952 Good Idea %	1952 Bad Idea %	1952 Indifferent %
TOTAL	49	24	27	54	22	24
RELIGION						
Roman Catholic	71	10	19	76	10	14
Protestant total	44	27	29	49	26	25
Baptist	42	27	31	45	27	28
Methodist	38	27	35	48	26	26
Lutheran	55	26	19	58	21	21
Presbyterian	35	36	29	50	26	24
Episcopal	36	31	33	53	25	22
Congregational	43	38	19	60	24	16
Other denominations	51	22	27	46	27	27
Jewish	35	39	26	43	31	26
Other and None	32	35	33	39	21	40
SEX						
Men	49	23	28	53	23	24
Women	50	24	26	56	21	23
AGE						
18-24 years	50	21	29	62	16	22
25-34	54	23	23	56	21	23
35-44	53	25	22	56	22	22
45-54	52	20	28	50	25	25
55-64	44	25	31	55	20	25
65 & over	40	27	33	49	27	24
RACE						
White	50	23	27	55	22	23
Non-White	46	24	30	56	21	23
EDUCATION						
0-8th grade	45	23	32	53	21	26
1-3 years' high school	47	23	30	58	18	24
High school graduate	55	22	23	55	22	23
1-3 years' college	51	27	22	54	25	21
College graduate	43	28	29	56	26	18

	1965				1952		
	Good Idea %	Bad Idea %	Indifferent %		Good Idea %	Bad Idea %	Indifferent %
OCCUPATION							
Professional	51	25	24		55	31	14
Proprietor or manager	53	22	25		53	22	25
White-collar worker	55	16	29		55	20	25
Service worker	49	28	23		60	17	23
Manual worker	50	24	26		56	21	23
Farmer	42	25	33		48	21	31
Non-labor force	41	27	32		*	*	*
INCOME							
Upper	45	28	27		50	28	22
Middle	55	22	23		55	21	24
Lower	45	23	32		56	19	25
CITY SIZE							
Over 1 Million	57	19	24		59	17	24
100,000 - 1 Million	55	21	24		59	16	25
25,000 - 100,000	52	25	23		60	18	22
10,000 - 25,000	42	23	35		54	21	25
Under 10,000	43	27	30		51	26	23
Rural, farm	37	32	31		50	25	25
REGION							
New England	53	28	19		64	24	12
Middle Atlantic	62	19	19		67	14	19
South Atlantic	37	30	33		52	21	27
East South Central	41	19	40		43	28	29
West South Central	40	30	30		45	25	30
East North Central	48	23	29		56	24	20
West North Central	56	20	24		55	16	29
Mountain	52	22	26		48	17	35
Pacific	51	23	26		51	28	21

5b. (IF "GOOD IDEA" ON 5 a) Would you be in favor or opposed to holding these religious classes in the public school building, or wouldn't it make any difference to you?

| | 1965 | | | | 1952 | | | |
	In Favor %	No Differ. %	Opposed %	No Opinion %	In Favor %	No Differ. %	Opposed %	No Opinion %
TOTAL	20	16	12	1	24	17	12	1
RELIGION								
Roman Catholic	30	27	11	3	31	30	13	2
Protestant total	18	13	12	1	24	14	10	1
Baptist	19	12	9	2	26	11	8	-
Methodist	16	12	10	*	23	15	9	1
Lutheran	18	12	23	2	25	18	15	-
Presbyterian	12	14	8	1	19	15	12	4
Episcopal	10	12	14	-	23	15	12	3
Congregational	5	25	13	-	26	13	21	-
Other denominations	23	12	15	1	23	13	9	1
Jewish	8	8	18	1	18	9	16	-
Other and None	10	9	11	2	14	11	12	2
SEX								
Men	19	14	14	2	23	16	13	1
Women	21	17	11	1	25	18	11	2
AGE								
18-24 years	20	20	10	*	26	22	13	1
25-34	22	15	16	1	25	20	10	1
35-44	20	17	13	3	29	16	11	*
45-54	21	17	13	1	20	18	10	2
55-64	19	14	10	1	25	15	12	3
65 & over	18	11	9	2	22	15	11	1
RACE								
White	19	17	12	2	24	18	12	1
Non-White	26	9	8	3	38	13	4	1
EDUCATION								
0-8th grade	20	15	8	2	25	18	8	2
1-3 years' high school	22	14	10	1	27	20	9	2
High school graduate	21	20	12	2	25	15	14	1
1-3 years' college	19	14	17	1	25	17	11	1
College graduate	14	12	17	*	18	17	20	1

* Less than one per cent.

	1965				1952			
	In Favor %	No Differ. %	Opposed %	No Opinion %	In Favor %	No Differ. %	Opposed %	No Opinion %
OCCUPATION								
Professional	19	15	16	1	21	15	18	1
Proprietor or manager	20	19	12	2	23	16	13	1
White-collar worker	21	18	14	2	23	17	13	2
Service worker	18	13	16	2	25	18	15	2
Manual worker	22	17	10	1	27	18	10	1
Farmer	18	11	11	2	22	16	9	1
Non-labor force	17	11	10	3	*	*	*	*
INCOME								
Upper	13	15	17	*	22	12	15	1
Middle	22	18	13	2	22	20	12	1
Lower	21	13	9	2	29	16	9	2
CITY SIZE								
Over 1 Million	26	17	11	3	28	19	10	2
100,000 - 1 Million	21	18	15	1	23	21	13	2
25,000 - 100,000	21	22	8	1	28	20	11	1
10,000 - 25,000	15	13	13	1	21	21	11	1
Under 10,000	17	13	11	2	24	14	12	1
Rural, farm	15	9	12	1	27	14	8	1
REGION								
New England	16	25	11	1	23	22	18	1
Middle Atlantic	31	19	10	2	26	25	14	2
South Atlantic	20	9	7	1	31	12	8	1
East South Central	13	15	8	5	28	8	6	1
West South Central	17	12	10	1	23	11	11	-
East North Central	18	18	11	1	27	19	9	1
West North Central	15	20	20	1	17	22	15	1
Mountain	9	15	24	4	16	11	18	3
Pacific	20	13	17	1	24	11	14	2

* Less than one per cent.

6a. Did you yourself happen to receive any religious training as a child?

6b. What was it - Sunday School; religious or parochial school; or instruction by your parents at home?

1965
RECEIVED RELIGIOUS TRAINING

	Sunday School %	Instruction at Home %	Religious or Parochial School %	Other Training %	Received No Religious Training %
TOTAL	69	38	21	1	9
RELIGION					
Roman Catholic	33	28	59	3	5
Protestant total	85	42	8	1	8
Baptist	86	45	5	1	7
Methodist	89	41	5	*	6
Lutheran	78	26	19	3	9
Presbyterian	83	36	10	1	9
Episcopal	94	46	8	-	2
Congregational	87	39	6	-	8
Other denominations	80	49	8	-	12
Jewish	31	31	36	5	14
Other and None	66	29	7	1	21
SEX					
Men	67	35	20	2	11
Women	71	40	22	1	6
AGE					
18-24 years	70	28	26	2	6
25-34	69	31	24	1	10
35-44	68	36	23	1	8
45-54	66	39	20	3	9
55-64	69	41	19	2	9
65 & over	73	49	17	1	9
RACE					
White	67	37	23	2	9
Non-White	86	39	6	1	6
EDUCATION					
0-8th grade	64	41	17	2	14
1-3 years' high school	67	34	20	1	11
High school graduate	70	34	22	1	7
1-3 years' college	75	45	25	1	3
College graduate	72	39	23	2	7

Totals exceed 100 per cent because of multiple answers.
* Less than one per cent.

<u>1952</u>

Sunday School %	Instruction at Home %	RECEIVED RELIGIOUS TRAINING Religious or Parochial School %	Other Training %	Received No Religious Training %
72	37	21	4	6
35	23	62	4	3
86	41	7	5	6
89	47	3	5	6
92	42	4	4	5
76	27	24	7	7
96	47	3	3	1
90	40	7	8	6
89	26	7	-	9
83	39	6	4	9
34	49	36	8	10
59	40	15	4	20
71	35	20	5	8
74	38	21	4	5
66	27	30	6	6
75	34	21	3	5
73	34	21	4	7
71	38	20	4	8
71	45	19	6	6
75	45	15	4	6
72	36	21	5	6
83	44	11	4	8
65	35	20	4	11
69	33	22	5	6
76	36	22	4	4
82	41	18	7	1
81	47	18	4	4

1965

RECEIVED RELIGIOUS TRAINING

	Sunday School %	Instruction at Home %	Religious or Parochial Training %	Other Training %	Received No Religious Training %
OCCUPATION					
Professional	73	38	26	2	4
Proprietor or manager	66	38	26	1	9
White-collar worker	65	36	27	1	7
Service worker	72	29	16	1	12
Manual worker	69	36	21	2	9
Farmer	76	40	7	*	14
Non-labor force	69	42	15	2	11
INCOME					
Upper	71	40	23	1	6
Middle	66	36	25	2	8
Lower	72	38	15	1	10
CITY SIZE					
Over 1 Million	56	29	32	4	6
100,000 - 1 Million	66	34	25	1	10
25,000 - 100,000	70	40	19	1	11
10,000 - 25,000	73	39	19	1	6
Under 10,000	78	44	14	1	8
Rural, farm	79	45	5	*	13
REGION					
New England	69	24	29	1	5
Middle Atlantic	52	30	35	3	7
South Atlantic	76	38	9	1	11
East South Central	85	53	7	*	7
West South Central	74	40	17	1	10
East North Central	68	37	25	2	8
West North Central	72	48	21	*	8
Mountain	77	43	14	-	15
Pacific	73	38	17	2	10

* Less than one per cent.

1952
RECEIVED RELIGIOUS TRAINING

Sunday School %	Instruction at Home %	Religious or Parochial Training %	Other Training %	Received No Religious Training %
78	43	20	3	3
79	39	19	5	5
75	41	20	5	4
69	36	24	5	7
67	30	26	4	7
78	47	11	6	8
*	*	*	*	*
82	45	17	6	2
72	34	23	4	6
68	36	20	4	9
56	36	35	4	6
70	35	23	6	7
67	28	26	4	7
80	27	15	3	5
78	41	17	4	5
76	39	13	5	8
59	26	32	4	6
61	30	31	4	5
87	50	10	6	6
84	46	6	5	8
77	42	10	6	6
69	34	26	3	6
70	34	19	4	9
77	44	22	6	8
76	31	22	3	7

7a. In looking back, is there anything about your own religious training that you wish had been different?

7b. (IF "YES" ON 7a) What?

1965

YES, WISH I HAD

	Rec'd more relig. trg. %	Rec'd better relig. trg. %	Attended church more often %	Rec'd more Bible trg. %	Attended parochial or religious school %	Rec'd less relig. trg. %	Trg. should have been more tolerant %	All other comments, or no opinion %	Religious Training was Satisfactory %
TOTAL	11	5	1	1	1	2	2	3	70
RELIGION									
Roman Catholic	9	7	*	*	2	1	3	2	74
Protestant total	13	5	2	1	*	1	2	2	70
Baptist	13	2	3	1	*	2	1	2	73
Methodist	13	4	2	1	-	1	1	2	73
Lutheran	13	2	2	1	-	3	3	1	71
Presbyterian	6	10	*	1	2	1	1	4	70
Episcopal	5	7	-	1	-	1	3	2	80
Congregational	13	16	-	6	-	6	1	-	57
Other denominations	16	6	2	1	*	1	2	2	64
Jewish	17	12	-	-	-	1	5	4	58
Other and None	9	7	3	1	-	3	6	3	60
SEX									
Men	11	6	2	*	1	1	2	2	70
Women	11	5	1	1	1	2	2	4	71
AGE									
18-24 years	9	6	2	*	-	3	7	4	67
25-34	16	7	1	*	*	2	3	2	65
35-44	12	7	2	2	1	2	1	2	67
45-54	10	5	2	1	1	1	2	2	72
55-64	11	6	1	*	1	1	1	4	71
65 & over	7	2	2	1	*	1	1	3	79
RACE									
White	12	6	1	1	*	2	2	3	69
Non-White	3	6	2	1	1	*	2	1	81
EDUCATION									
0-8th grade	10	3	3	*	1	1	1	2	72
1-3 years' high school	13	2	2	1	*	1	1	2	75
High school graduate	12	5	2	1	1	1	2	3	70
1-3 years' college	11	12	*	-	1	4	5	2	63
College graduate	11	11	-	2	*	1	4	3	66

* Less than one per cent.

1952

YES, WISH I HAD

Rec'd more relig. trg. %	Rec'd better relig. trg. %	Attended church more often %	Rec'd more Bible trg. %	Attended parochial or religious school %	Rec'd less relig. trg. %	Trg. should have been more tolerant %	All other comments, or no opinion %	Religious Training was Satisfactory %
8	4	2	1	1	1	1	6	78
4	2	*	*	2	2	*	4	86
10	4	2	1	-	1	1	6	75
12	6	3	1	-	1	1	4	74
9	4	1	1	-	1	1	5	79
8	3	2	1	1	1	2	7	76
8	4	2	1	-	1	1	6	79
6	1	-	1	-	1	2	5	84
5	2	-	-	-	7	-	10	76
11	4	1	2	*	2	1	9	70
5	10	1	1	-	2	1	8	72
4	1	4	1	-	5	1	11	75
9	4	1	1	*	2	1	4	78
8	9	2	2	1	1	1	7	77
4	3	1	1	1	1	1	5	83
9	3	2	1	1	2	1	6	75
10	4	1	1	*	2	1	7	76
9	3	2	2	1	1	1	5	76
7	4	1	1	*	1	2	5	79
8	3	2	*	-	1	1	5	82
8	4	2	1	1	1	1	6	78
8	4	1	1	1	-	-	4	82
10	3	3	1	*	1	*	6	76
7	4	2	*	*	2	1	5	80
7	3	1	1	1	2	1	3	83
9	7	-	1	1	2	1	7	72
7	6	-	1	1	4	4	10	67

NOTE: The results to this question, nationally : Yes 26%, No 70%, Don't know 4% -- the Don't know category has not been included in these tables.

1965

YES, WISH I HAD

	Rec'd more relig. trg. %	Rec'd better relig. trg. %	Attended church more often %	Rec'd more Bible trg. %	Attended parochial or religious school %	Rec'd less relig. trg %	Trg. should have been more tolerant %	All other comments, or no opinion %	Religious Training Was Satisfactory %
OCCUPATION									
Professional	9	12	*	1	*	3	4	2	67
Proprietor or manager	14	4	1	1	1	1	2	2	71
White-collar worker	11	7	-	*	2	1	2	3	72
Service worker	10	2	*	*	*	4	3	1	71
Manual worker	13	5	2	1	*	2	2	3	68
Farmer	14	3	6	-	-	-	2	1	72
Non-labor force	9	4	2	*	1	1	2	2	74
INCOME									
Upper	11	8	*	2	1	2	4	2	67
Middle	12	6	1	1	1	1	2	3	69
Lower	11	4	2	*	*	1	1	3	73
CITY SIZE									
Over 1 Million	7	5	*	*	*	2	3	4	77
100,000 - 1 Million	11	6	1	*	1	2	2	2	70
25,000 - 100,000	11	7	1	1	-	1	2	1	71
10,000 - 25,000	8	4	1	1	-	2	2	2	79
Under 10,000	15	6	2	2	1	1	2	2	65
Rural, farm	17	5	6	1	-	3	1	2	64
REGION									
New England	9	10	1	2	1	2	5	3	66
Middle Atlantic	8	6	*	1	1	2	1	2	76
South Atlantic	13	3	4	2	1	*	1	2	69
East South Central	11	2	4	2	2	*	1	2	74
West South Central	13	3	1	1	*	3	1	2	69
East North Central	9	6	2	*	*	2	2	4	72
West North Central	16	6	1	*	*	2	3	1	68
Mountain	21	3	1	1	-	4	2	1	65
Pacific	13	8	*	*	1	1	6	3	63

* Less than one per cent.

<u>1952</u>

YES, WISH I HAD

Rec'd more relig. trg. %	Rec'd better relig. trg. %	Attended church more often %	Rec'd more Bible trg. %	Attended parochial or religious school %	Rec'd less relig. trg. %	Trg. should have been more tolerant %	All other comments, or no opinion %	Religious Training was Satisfactory %
9	8	-	2	1	3	2	10	69
7	5	1	1	*	2	2	5	78
7	4	1	*	1	1	1	7	79
9	7	1	*	*	1	*	2	80
9	3	2	1	*	1	*	4	80
13	5	4	3	*	*	1	9	67
*	*	*	*	*	*	*	*	*
8	4	*	1	1	2	2	6	77
7	4	2	1	1	2	1	6	77
10	3	1	1	*	1	*	5	79
4	4	1	1	*	3	*	6	83
9	2	1	*	1	2	2	6	79
7	2	1	1	-	1	*	6	83
9	6	2	1	-	1	1	6	75
8	5	1	1	1	2	1	5	77
12	4	2	2	1	*	1	6	74
2	3	-	-	1	1	1	10	85
4	4	*	*	1	2	*	3	86
12	5	2	3	*	1	1	6	70
14	3	4	*	1	*	1	5	74
12	3	1	*	-	2	1	6	75
9	4	1	1	*	2	1	6	78
9	5	4	1	1	2	2	11	71
9	9	-	1	1	2	-	7	72
7	4	1	1	1	3	1	7	76

<u>NOTE:</u> The results to this question, nationally : Yes 26%, No 70%, Don't know 4% -- the Don't know category has not been included in these tables.

8a.　　Would you want a child of yours to receive any religious
　　　　instruction?

8b.　　What kind - Sunday School, religious or parochial school, or
　　　　instruction at home?

1965

WOULD WANT A CHILD OF MINE TO RECEIVE

	Sunday School %	Instruction at Home %	Relig. or Parochial School %	Other Religious Training %	No Religious Training %	Undecided %
TOTAL	71	41	27	2	2	2
RELIGION						
Roman Catholic	30	24	70	4	1	*
Protestant total	89	49	11	2	2	2
Baptist	90	48	8	1	1	2
Methodist	90	46	8	2	1	3
Lutheran	85	36	22	3	1	1
Presbyterian	88	48	6	2	3	3
Episcopal	96	46	12	2	-	1
Congregational	88	46	11	5	-	-
Other denominations	87	56	16	1	3	2
Jewish	59	37	39	3	2	-
Other and None	54	37	11	3	13	10
SEX						
Men	68	38	26	3	3	3
Women	74	44	27	2	1	1
AGE						
18-24 years	68	41	27	4	2	1
25-34	74	41	23	3	2	2
35-44	70	39	28	2	2	3
45-54	68	37	32	2	2	2
55-64	73	43	24	1	3	1
65 & over	74	47	24	2	3	2
RACE						
White	70	42	29	2	2	2
Non-White	79	36	13	3	3	3
EDUCATION						
0-8th grade	46	81	52	2	7	4
1-3 years' high school	71	31	26	3	2	3
High school graduate	71	40	30	2	1	1
1-3 years' college	70	50	27	3	2	3
College graduate	69	53	19	4	3	3

Totals exceed 100 per cent because of multiple answers.
* Less than one per cent.

<u>1952</u>

WOULD WANT A CHILD OF MINE TO RECEIVE

Sunday School %	Instruction at Home %	Relig. or Parochial School %	Other Religious Training %	No Religious Training %	Undecided %
75	39	25	5	1	1
27	20	74	3	1	1
92	47	9	6	1	1
94	48	9	7	1	1
96	51	8	5	1	*
83	34	21	5	1	2
96	46	2	4	2	1
94	41	11	7	1	1
96	33	9	2	4	-
89	51	7	6	1	1
49	34	40	8	5	1
69	42	11	4	11	6
75	39	23	5	2	2
74	40	27	5	1	*
68	33	29	5	1	2
75	40	25	4	1	1
75	39	24	5	2	1
75	40	25	5	2	2
74	39	25	6	2	1
80	46	22	5	2	*
74	39	25	5	2	1
85	40	21	3	2	2
74	35	25	5	2	2
71	34	30	6	2	1
74	41	26	4	*	2
80	47	21	8	1	1
81	55	19	5	*	3

1965
WOULD WANT A CHILD OF MINE TO RECEIVE

	Sunday School %	Instruction at Home %	Relig. or Parochial School %	Other Religious Training %	No Religious Training %	Undecided %
OCCUPATION						
Professional	72	49	24	3	3	2
Proprietor or manager	70	48	33	3	1	1
White-collar worker	68	40	30	1	1	2
Service worker	69	35	23	6	1	2
Manual worker	71	37	28	2	2	2
Farmer	83	49	13	*	2	1
Non-labor force	45	40	24	2	3	3
INCOME						
Upper	71	41	29	2	3	2
Middle	70	41	29	3	1	2
Lower	74	41	21	2	3	2
CITY SIZE						
Over 1 Million	55	27	39	4	3	2
100,000 - 1 Million	68	40	31	2	2	3
25,000 - 100,000	74	47	22	3	1	1
10,000 - 25,000	71	45	17	4	3	6
Under 10,000	82	49	20	1	2	1
Rural, farm	85	46	12	1	3	1
REGION						
New England	64	34	35	1	*	-
Middle Atlantic	54	25	39	4	2	3
South Atlantic	81	40	16	1	2	3
East South Central	86	55	9	2	3	2
West South Central	82	45	19	2	1	3
East North Central	67	41	33	3	3	1
West North Central	74	54	27	1	2	1
Mountain	79	58	23	2	2	6
Pacific	79	47	20	2	2	2

* Less than one per cent.

1952

WOULD WANT A CHILD OF MINE TO RECEIVE

Sunday School %	Instruction at Home %	Relig. or Parochial School %	Other Religious Training %	No Religious Training %	Undecided %
79	50	23	6	1	2
80	43	23	6	2	1
75	40	25	5	1	1
74	40	26	5	1	2
70	33	29	5	1	1
88	53	16	6	1	2
*	*	*	*	*	*
81	48	21	7	2	1
74	39	27	5	2	*
73	36	25	5	2	2
55	29	44	3	3	2
74	37	27	5	1	1
65	30	31	4	2	1
80	29	17	4	1	1
81	46	20	5	2	1
83	47	16	7	1	1
59	22	37	3	1	1
59	26	39	3	2	1
90	57	13	8	2	*
88	46	14	7	*	1
83	50	17	8	2	1
71	39	27	3	3	1
76	38	22	9	1	2
81	59	26	7	2	1
80	34	24	2	1	1

9a.   Did you happen to attend any Sunday or Sabbath church services during the last 12 weeks?

9b.   About how many times would you say you attended Sunday services during the last 12 weeks?

1965
ATTENDANCE AT SUNDAY CHURCH

	Don't Attend %	Once a Month or Less %	About Twice a Month %	About 3 Times a Month %	Every Sunday %
TOTAL	32	13	7	10	38
RELIGION					
Roman Catholic	13	8	4	8	67
Protestant total	33	14	9	11	33
Baptist	35	12	11	12	30
Methodist	41	13	9	13	24
Lutheran	29	17	10	11	33
Presbyterian	30	18	8	12	32
Episcopal	40	9	6	10	35
Congregational	31	27	-	14	28
Other denominations	26	14	10	8	42
Jewish	39	43	10	4	4
Other and None	81	10	1	2	4
SEX					
Men	37	14	7	8	34
Women	27	12	8	11	42
AGE					
18-24 years	30	18	8	9	35
25-34	32	16	11	9	32
35-44	31	12	6	12	39
45-54	30	12	6	10	42
55-64	29	11	7	10	43
65 & over	38	10	7	8	37
RACE					
White	30	14	7	10	39
Non-White	41	10	10	9	30
EDUCATION					
0-8th grade	42	9	7	9	33
1-3 years' high school	37	13	8	9	33
High school graduate	28	13	8	11	40
1-3 years' college	24	17	6	8	45
College graduate	26	17	6	10	41

1952

	Attendance At Sunday Church			
Don't Attend %	Once a Month or Less %	About Twice a Month %	About 3 Times a Month %	Every Sunday %
32	11	12	13	32
18	6	6	8	62
32	14	13	16	25
26	13	15	18	28
37	13	14	16	20
36	12	17	18	17
31	14	14	23	18
30	25	12	13	20
42	30	7	11	10
34	13	10	12	31
56	11	17	4	12
81	9	2	3	5
36	12	11	12	29
29	11	12	15	33
30	14	12	10	34
31	12	11	14	32
32	14	11	13	30
32	11	14	11	32
32	11	11	15	31
42	5	8	14	31
32	11	12	13	32
31	12	12	17	28
39	9	11	11	30
33	11	11	15	30
29	13	13	14	31
31	14	12	15	28
25	15	9	15	36

1965

	ATTENDANCE AT SUNDAY CHURCH				
	Don't Attend %	Once a Month or Less %	About Twice a Month %	About 3 Times a Month %	Every Sunday %
OCCUPATION					
Professional	26	17	6	8	43
Proprietor or manager	22	16	7	11	44
White-collar worker	27	13	7	10	43
Service worker	44	12	6	5	33
Manual worker	35	12	8	11	34
Farmer	31	13	13	10	33
Non-labor force	38	13	5	7	37
INCOME					
Upper	26	13	9	11	41
Middle	30	14	7	9	40
Lower	38	12	8	9	33
CITY SIZE					
Over 1 Million	32	14	7	6	41
100,000 - 1 Million	32	15	5	9	39
25,000 - 100,000	29	11	7	11	42
10,000 - 25,000	36	11	9	7	37
Under 10,000	32	11	9	13	35
Rural, farm	31	12	11	11	35
REGION					
New England	29	12	4	4	51
Middle Atlantic	30	13	6	9	42
South Atlantic	32	13	11	12	32
East South Central	23	13	13	12	39
West South Central	31	15	7	12	35
East North Central	30	12	7	11	40
West North Central	25	16	7	11	41
Mountain	41	12	11	4	32
Pacific	46	13	5	6	30

<u>1952</u>

ATTENDANCE AT SUNDAY CHURCH				
Don't Attend	Once a Month or Less	About Twice a Month	About 3 Times a Month	Every Sunday
%	%	%	%	%
23	14	12	13	38
33	12	11	17	27
29	15	10	14	32
34	13	9	16	28
35	10	12	12	31
30	11	14	15	30
*	*	*	*	*
25	15	10	17	33
31	12	12	15	30
38	9	11	12	30
35	11	9	9	36
38	15	11	12	24
32	11	11	9	37
31	14	12	16	27
30	11	11	15	33
28	10	14	16	32
27	8	11	9	45
31	11	10	13	35
29	12	13	20	26
30	12	13	17	28
23	9	16	15	37
32	13	12	12	31
35	11	12	16	26
30	21	7	9	33
50	12	7	9	22

10a.   Do you believe in a God?

10b.   How strong would you say this belief is? Are you absolutely
       certain there is a God - fairly sure there is - not quite sure,
       but like to think there is - or, not at all sure, but not sure
       there isn't?

1965

BELIEVE IN A GOD

	Abso-lutely Certain %	Fairly Sure %	Quite Sure %	Not at all Sure %	Do Not Believe %	Don't Know %
TOTAL	81	12	3	1	2	1
RELIGION						
Roman Catholic	88	10	2	*	-	*
Protestant total	85	11	2	1	*	1
Baptist	89	7	2	1	1	*
Methodist	81	13	3	2	*	1
Lutheran	82	13	2	1	1	1
Presbyterian	76	16	4	2	1	1
Episcopal	74	20	5	-	-	1
Congregational	73	19	7	-	-	1
Other denominations	90	8	1	1	-	*
Jewish	39	31	5	9	9	7
Other and None	45	20	10	5	17	3
SEX						
Men	75	16	3	2	3	1
Women	87	8	2	1	1	1
AGE						
18-24 years	71	17	4	3	4	1
25-34	80	14	3	*	2	1
35-44	81	12	3	1	1	2
45-54	83	11	2	2	2	*
55-64	85	8	4	1	2	*
65 & over	86	9	2	2	1	*
RACE						
White	82	12	3	1	1	1
Non-White	83	10	3	1	3	-
EDUCATION						
0-8th grade	87	9	2	1	1	*
1-3 years' high school	85	10	2	1	2	*
High school graduate	82	12	2	1	2	1
1-3 years' college	78	14	4	1	2	1
College graduate	66	17	6	4	4	3

* Less than one per cent.

Abso-lutely Certain	Fairly Sure	Quite Sure	Not at all Sure	Do Not Believe	Don't Know
%	%	%	%	%	%
87	10	2	*	1	*
92	7	1	-	-	*
87	10	2	-	1	*
93	6	1	-	*	*
86	11	2	-	1	*
80	17	2	-	1	-
90	8	2	-	*	*
77	17	4	2	-	-
72	20	8	-	-	-
89	9	2		*	*
70	18	9	1	1	1
55	21	7	2	12	3
84	11	3	-	2	*
89	9	2	-	*	*
87	9	2	1	1	*
85	11	3	-	1	*
85	11	2	-	1	1
87	10	2	-	1	*
88	9	2	-	1	-
91	7	1	-	1	*
87	10	2	-	1	*
87	8	4	-	-	1
87	9	2	-	1	1
87	10	2	-	1	*
87	10	2	1	*	*
85	8	4	1	2	-
78	13	3	1	4	1

BELIEVE IN A GOD — 1952

* Less than one per cent.

	BELIEVE IN A GOD	1965				
	Absolutely Certain %	Fairly Sure %	Quite Sure %	Not at all Sure %	Do Not Believe %	Don't Know %
OCCUPATION						
Professional	72	15	5	4	3	1
Proprietor or manager	84	11	1	1	2	1
White-collar worker	81	10	5	1	1	2
Service worker	91	4	1	*	2	2
Manual worker	81	14.	2	1	2	*
Farmer	87	11	2	-	-	-
Non-labor force	84	10	2	2	2	*
INCOME						
Upper	73	17	4	3	2	1
Middle	83	10	3	1	2	1
Lower	84	11	2	1	1	1
CITY SIZE						
Over 1 Million	81	9	2	2	4	2
100,000 - 1 Million	78	13	4	2	2	1
25,000 - 100,000	90	6	3	-	1	-
10,000 - 25,000	81	10	4	3	1	1
Under 10,000	83	13	2	1	1	*
Rural, farm	83	16	1	-	-	-
REGION						
New England	72	17	5	-	4	2
Middle Atlantic	81	11	2	2	3	1
South Atlantic	85	10	3	1	1	*
East South Central	89	10	1	-	-	*
West South Central	85	11	1	2	1	*
East North Central	84	10	3	1	1	1
West North Central	82	12	2	3	1	-
Mountain	80	13	4	-	2	1
Pacific	74	16	5	1	3	1

* Less than one per cent.

			1952		

BELIEVE IN A GOD

Abso-lutely Certain %	Fairly Sure %	Quite Sure %	Not at all Sure %	Do Not Believe %	Don't Know %
84	11	2	-	3	*
83	12	3	1	1	*
88	9	2	-	1	-
88	10	2	-	-	-
87	10	2	-	1	*
91	8	1	-	*	*
*	*	*	*	*	*
86	10	2	1	1	*
86	10	3	-	1	*
87	9	2	-	1	1
81	14	3	1	1	*
84	11	3	-	2	*
86	10	2	1	1	*
81	14	5	-	-	-
89	9	1	-	1	*
92	6	1	-	1	*
85	12	1	-	2	-
84	12	2	1	1	*
91	7	2	-	*	*
97	3	-	-	*	*
93	5	1	-	1	-
83	12	3	*	1	1
81	15	3	-	1	*
78	17	2	1	2	-
84	11	4	-	1	-

* Less than one per cent.

10a.　Do you believe in a God?

10c.　How do you think of God - as a loving Father who looks after us; as some kind of supernatural power but don't know what; or how?

	1965 THINK OF GOD AS			Do Not	1952 THINK OF GOD AS			Do Not
	A Loving Father %	Some Kind of Power %	Other %	Believe in God or Don't Know %	A Loving Father %	Some Kind of Power %	Other %	Believe in God or Don't Know %
TOTAL	73	19	7	3	79	17	5	1
RELIGION								
Roman Catholic	76	19	6	*	81	19	3	*
Protestant total	77	17	6	1	82	14	5	1
Baptist	84	11	5	1	88	10	2	*
Methodist	74	20	6	1	82	14	4	1
Lutheran	73	19	9	2	77	18	5	1
Presbyterian	70	21	8	2	77	16	7	*
Episcopal	58	32	10	1	76	12	13	-
Congregational	56	30	13	1	61	30	11	-
Other. denominations	82	16	5	*	82	14	5	*
Jewish	20	46	21	16	40	40	20	2
Other and None	41	27	12	20	50	27	8	15
SEX								
Men	66	23	9	4	73	20	6	2
Women	79	16	5	2	84	13	4	*
AGE								
18-24 years	67	21	9	5	80	16	4	1
25-34	68	22	9	3	80	15	5	1
35-44	74	18	6	3	77	18	5	2
45-54	75	18	7	2	76	19	5	1
55-64	77	18	5	2	77	17	5	1
65 & over	74	20	7	1	81	14	5	1
RACE								
White	73	19	7	2	79	17	5	1
Non-White	75	18	6	3	79	17	5	1
EDUCATION								
0-8th grade	81	15	4	1	79	17	4	2
1-3 years' high school	82	13	5	2	84	13	3	1
High school graduate	75	18	6	3	80	17	4	*
1-3 years' college	64	26	11	3	75	19	7	2
College graduate	47	35	13	7	63	22	12	5

Totals exceed 100 per cent because of multiple answers.

* Less than one per cent.

| | 1965 THINK OF GOD AS | | | Do Not Believe in God or | 1952 THINK OF GOD AS | | | Do Not Believe in God or |
	A Loving Father %	Some Kind of Power %	Other %	Don't Know %	A Loving Father %	Some Kind of Power %	Other %	Don't Know %
OCCUPATION								
Professional	58	29	11	4	70	20	10	3
Proprietor or manager	70	18	10	3	74	18	8	1
White-collar worker	72	18	9	3	78	18	5	1
Service worker	81	13	4	4	77	20	3	-
Manual worker	78	16	5	1	81	15	3	1
Farmer	84	10	6	-	88	8	4	*
Non-labor force	70	25	5	2	*	*	*	*
INCOME								
Upper	63	27	9	3	76	16	8	1
Middle	71	20	8	3	79	17	4	1
Lower	80	14	6	2	80	16	5	2
CITY SIZE								
Over 1 Million	62	25	9	6	69	23	8	1
100,000 - 1 Million	70	21	8	3	73	22	5	2
25,000 - 100,000	82	13	4	1	79	15	5	1
10,000 - 25,000	75	21	5	2	82	15	4	-
Under 10,000	79	16	6	1	81	16	4	1
Rural, farm	84	12	4	-	85	11	4	1
REGION								
New England	62	27	5	6	80	19	1	2
Middle Atlantic	68	23	7	4	73	22	5	1
South Atlantic	84	11	5	1	84	13	4	*
East South Central	86	13	2	*	91	8	3	*
West South Central	80	10	11	1	85	12	2	1
East North Central	73	19	7	2	76	18	6	2
West North Central	71	21	9	1	76	15	9	1
Mountain	79	18	2	3	62	20	16	2
Pacific	60	29	10	4	76	19	5	1

Totals exceed 100 per cent because of multiple answers.

* Less than one per cent.

10a. Do you believe in a God?

10d. Do you believe in the Trinity - The Father, Son and Holy Ghost?

| | 1965 | | | | 1952 | | | |
| | BELIEVE IN THE TRINITY | | | Do Not Believe in God or Don't Know** | BELIEVE IN THE TRINITY | | | Do Not Believe in God or Don't Know** |
	Believe in the Trinity %	Do Not Believe in the Trinity %	Undec. %	%	Believe in the Trinity %	Do Not Believe in the Trinity %	Undec. %	%
TOTAL	83	7	7	3	89	6	4	1
RELIGION								
Roman Catholic	96	1	3	*	98	1	1	*
Protestant total	86	6	7	1	87	8	4	1
Baptist	89	4	6	1	95	2	3	*
Methodist	83	6	10	1	90	3	6	1
Lutheran	88	4	6	2	93	3	3	1
Presbyterian	82	8	8	2	89	5	6	*
Episcopal	87	11	1	1	89	7	4	-
Congregational	80	11	8	1	83	4	13	-
Other denominations	85	9	6	*	89	7	4	*
Jewish	2	79	3	16	8	81	10	1
Other and None	41	18	21	20	62	12	11	15
SEX								
Men	80	9	7	4	86	8	4	2
Women	86	6	6	2	91	5	4	*
AGE								
18-24 years	80	11	4	5	90	6	3	1
25-34	83	8	6	3	87	7	5	1
35-44	84	6	7	3	88	6	4	2
45-54	83	8	7	2	86	8	5	1
55-64	82	8	8	2	92	4	3	1
65 & over	84	7	8	1	90	4	5	1
RACE								
White	83	8	7	2	89	6	4	1
Non-White	82	7	8	3	91	3	5	1
EDUCATION								
0-8th grade	84	5	10	1	90	5	3	2
1-3 years' high school	87	6	5	2	90	5	4	1
High school graduate	85	6	6	3	91	6	3	*
1-3 years' college	81	10	6	3	86	7	5	2
College graduate	68	19	6	7	76	11	8	5

** Do not believe in God, or don't know whether believe in God or not.

* Less than one per cent.

	1965				1952			
	BELIEVE IN THE TRINITY			Do Not Believe in God or Don't Know**	BELIEVE IN THE TRINITY			Do Not Believe in God or Don't Know**
	Believe in the Trinity %	Do Not Believe in the Trinity %	Undec. %	%	Believe in the Trinity %	Do Not Believe in the Trinity %	Undec. %	%
OCCUPATION								
Professional	76	14	6	4	84	8	5	3
Proprietor or manager	81	12	4	3	81	13	5	1
White-collar worker	81	7	9	3	89	7	3	1
Service worker	84	3	9	4	90	5	5	-
Manual worker	86	6	7	1	91	4	4	1
Farmer	94	1	5	-	92	3	5	*
Non-labor force	81	9	8	2	*	*	*	*
INCOME								
Upper	79	11	7	3	85	10	4	1
Middle	83	8	6	3	89	6	4	1
Lower	85	5	8	2	90	4	4	2
CITY SIZE								
Over 1 Million	74	13	7	6	78	14	7	1
100,000 - 1 Million	83	7	7	3	84	8	6	2
25,000 - 100,000	91	7	1	1	91	5	3	1
10,000 - 25,000	75	11	13	2	90	6	4	-
Under 10,000	88	5	6	1	91	4	4	1
Rural, farm	92	1	7	-	93	3	3	1
REGION								
New England	79	7	8	6	89	7	2	2
Middle Atlantic	79	12	5	4	85	10	4	1
South Atlantic	90	4	5	1	91	5	4	*
East South Central	91	1	8	*	95	3	2	*
West South Central	85	6	8	1	94	2	3	1
East North Central	86	6	6	2	87	5	6	2
West North Central	86	7	6	1	89	5	5	1
Mountain	81	9	7	3	80	9	9	2
Pacific	73	12	11	4	86	7	6	1

** Do not believe in God, or don't know whether believe in God or not.

* Less than one per cent.

11a. Do you believe that Jesus Christ ever actually lived?

11b. Do you think he was God; or just another religious leader like Mohammed or Buddha?

1965

	BELIEVE JESUS CHRIST WAS				Don't believe Christ Ever Lived %	Don't Know *** %
	God %	Another Leader %	Son of God, Other %	Don't Know %		
TOTAL	72	14	3	7	1	3
RELIGION						
Roman Catholic	88	5	1	4	*	2
Protestant total	73	13	3	8	1	2
Baptist	83	9	2	5	*	1
Methodist	70	14	3	9	1	3
Lutheran	72	17	1	8	*	2
Presbyterian	65	15	6	12	1	1
Episcopal	59	25	5	6	4	1
Congregational	52	29	1	10	-	8
Other denominations	73	12	4	8	*	3
Jewish	-	67	10	3	11	9
Other and None	33	39	5	7	5	11
SEX						
Men	68	16	3	7	2	4
Women	75	13	3	6	*	3
AGE						
18-24 years	68	19	4	6	1	2
25-34	71	16	2	8	1	2
35-44	73	14	2	6	*	5
45-54	76	13	2	5	2	2
55-64	74	13	3	6	1	3
65 & over	71	13	3	8	2	3
RACE						
White	73	14	3	6	1	3
Non-White	71	16	3	7	1	2
EDUCATION						
0-8th grade	78	9	2	8	1	2
1-3 years' high school	79	10	2	6	*	3
High school graduate	73	13	3	7	1	3
1-3 years' college	67	15	5	7	2	4
College graduate	55	34	2	5	2	2

*** Don't Know whether or not Jesus Christ ever lived.

 * Less than one per cent.

1952

BELIEVE JESUS CHRIST WAS

God %	Another Leader %	Son of God, Other %	Don't Know %	Don't believe Christ Ever Lived %	Don't Know*** %
74	12	7	3	1	3
89	6	3	1	*	1
74	10	9	4	1	2
85	6	6	2	–	1
77	9	6	5	*	3
70	12	9	4	2	3
70	12	12	4	–	2
66	17	10	5	1	1
58	24	6	4	2	6
70	12	12	4	*	2
5	66	1	5	5	18
40	25	6	10	5	14
69	14	8	4	1	4
77	10	7	3	1	2
76	12	6	2	*	4
75	12	7	3	1	2
74	11	7	3	1	4
71	12	7	5	1	4
73	13	6	4	1	3
74	11	9	4	*	2
73	12	8	3	1	3
80	6	2	5	1	6
77	9	6	4	1	3
75	10	7	4	1	3
75	11	8	3	*	3
69	14	10	3	1	3
60	27	6	3	*	4

1965

BELIEVE JESUS CHRIST WAS

	God %	Another Leader %	Son of God, Other %	Don't Know %	Don't believe Christ Ever Lived %	Don't Know *** %
OCCUPATION						
Professional	61	25	4	6	2	2
Proprietor or manager	70	21	1	5	1	2
White-collar worker	72	12	5	8	*	3
Service worker	82	9	2	6	1	*
Manual worker	75	11	2	7	1	4
Farmer	84	4	3	6	1	2
Non-labor force	70	15	3	7	2	3
INCOME						
Upper	63	22	2	7	2	4
Middle	72	15	3	6	1	3
Lower	77	10	2	8	*	3
CITY SIZE						
Over 1 Million	64	21	3	6	2	4
100,000 - 1 Million	71	16	3	6	1	3
25,000 - 100,000	83	8	3	5	*	1
10,000 - 25,000	67	15	3	9	2	4
Under 10,000	78	11	3	5	1	2
Rural, farm	79	4	1	13	1	2
REGION						
New England	64	21	5	4	2	4
Middle Atlantic	69	18	2	6	2	3
South Atlantic	84	7	2	5	*	2
East South Central	89	2	1	5	-	3
West South Central	73	11	3	10	1	2
East North Central	74	12	2	8	1	3
West North Central	73	14	3	7	1	2
Mountain	67	15	8	5	*	5
Pacific	58	26	3	7	2	4

*** Don't Know whether or not Jesus Christ ever lived.

* Less than one per cent.

1952

BELIEVE JESUS CHRIST WAS

God %	Another Leader %	Son of God, Other %	Don't Know %	Don't believe Christ Ever Lived %	Don't Know*** %
68	20	7	2	1	2
67	18	7	3	1	4
72	15	7	3	*	3
74	10	8	5	1	2
76	9	7	4	1	3
81	4	10	2	-	3
*	*	1	*	*	*
71	15	8	3	1	2
73	13	7	3	1	3
76	8	7	4	1	4
66	18	6	3	1	6
69	16	6	5	1	3
72	8	12	5	1	2
75	11	4	5	1	4
76	11	7	3	1	2
79	6	9	3	1	2
62	23	5	5	2	3
73	16	3	4	1	3
81	8	6	3	-	2
89	4	2	1	1	3 .
81	7	9	3	-	-
68	12	10	4	1	5
73	6	11	4	1	5
65	14	13	1	-	7
68	18	8	3	-	3

12a. Do you believe the Bible is really the revealed word of God;
or do you think it is only a great piece of literature?

| | 1965 ** | | | | 1952 | | | |
	Word of God %	Great Literature %	Other %	Don't Know %	Word of God %	Great Literature %	Other %	Don't Know %
TOTAL	79	13	5	3	83	10	2	5
RELIGION								
Roman Catholic	82	9	5	4	88	6	1	5
Protestant total	85	10	4	3	85	8	3	4
Baptist	91	5	3	1	93	4	1	2
Methodist	81	13	6	4	85	9	2	4
Lutheran	79	13	4	4	86	8	3	3
Presbyterian	78	16	4	3	84	13	2	2
Episcopal	71	25	1	11	72	16	8	6
Congregational	70	19	8	3	76	13	2	11
Other denominations	91	7	1	2	85	7	4	5
Jewish	17	69	12	4	45	45	1	9
Other and None	41	41	16	4	52	31	8	11
SEX								
Men	75	17	5	5	81	13	3	5
Women	84	10	2	5	87	7	2	5
AGE								
18-24 years	69	23	4	5	83	10	2	5
25-34	77	16	5	4	86	10	2	3
35-44	80	13	7	2	83	10	3	5
45-54	79	14	5	4	81	10	3	7
55-64	83	10	5	3	82	11	2	6
65 & over	85	9	3	3	88	7	1	5
RACE								
White	80	14	5	3	84	10	3	5
Non-White	80	15	4	2	84	8	-	8
EDUCATION								
0-8th grade	88	5	6	2	86	7	1	6
1-3 years' high school	85	9	4	2	85	8	2	5
High school graduate	82	13	4	3	87	8	2	3
1-3 years' college	71	21	5	6	79	14	5	5
College graduate	55	33	5	8	68	26	8	2

** Figures for 1965 add to more than 100 per cent, since some people gave more than one response.

	1965**				1952			
	Word of God %	Great Literature %	Other %	Don't Know %	Word of God %	Great Literature %	Other %	Don't Know %
OCCUPATION								
Professional	67	27	3	5	76	20	6	2
Proprietor or manager	77	16	5	3	78	15	3	4
White-collar worker	78	13	4	7	84	10	2	4
Service worker	88	6	6	7	83	10	2	5
Manual worker	82	11	6	2	85	7	2	6
Farmer	91	6	3	2	90	3	2	5
Non-labor force	81	12	4	4	*	*	*	½
INCOME								
Upper	70	21	6	6	81	14	4	4
Middle	79	15	4	3	83	10	2	5
Lower	85	9	5	2	86	7	2	5
CITY SIZE								
Over 1 Million	72	20	6	4	76	16	2	6
100,000 - 1 Million	75	17	6	4	80	14	2	6
25,000 - 100,000	86	9	3	2	82	9	4	5
10,000 - 25,000	75	20	3	4	86	8	3	6
Under 10,000	85	8	5	3	86	9	2	3
Rural, farm	93	6	3	1	90	4	2	4
REGION								
New England	66	28	5	2	80	12	1	7
Middle Atlantic	76	20	3	3	78	15	1	6
South Atlantic	86	6	5	3	84	9	3	4
East South Central	94	4	3	1	96	2	1	1
West South Central	80	10	7	4	89	5	2	4
East North Central	84	8	6	3	82	10	3	5
West North Central	81	12	4	4	86	7	4	3
Mountain	80	15	8	-	74	15	4	7
Pacific	70	22	5	6	80	12	2	6

** Figures for 1965 add to more than 100 per cent, since some people gave more than one response.

12b.   Do you ever read the Bible?

12c.   About how many times would you say you read it during the last 12 weeks?

1965

	Never Read Bible %	Practi- cally Never %	Every Few Weeks %	Once or Twice a Week %	3-6 Times a Wk. %	Practically Every Day %	Don't Know %
TOTAL	16	11	5	17	10	14	27
RELIGION							
Roman Catholic	27	1	2	16	8	13	33
Protestant total	9	16	7	19	12	14	23
Baptist	7	19	10	18	13	15	18
Methodist	9	13	4	19	11	15	29
Lutheran	11	9	3	22	14	13	27
Presbyterian	15	13	4	11	11	12	34
Episcopal	5	3	4	20	12	21	35
Congregational	8	21	5	17	16	18	15
Other denominations	8	22	11	22	9	10	18
Jewish	27	1	-	5	10	16	41
Other and None	38	1	1	3	8	19	30
SEX							
Men	20	7	4	15	8	14	32
Women	12	14	7	18	13	14	22
AGE							
18-24 years	22	6	3	14	10	15	30
25-34	16	7	5	15	9	20	28
35-44	17	6	6	16	13	15	27
45-54	12	11	6	19	10	15	27
55-64	12	17	5	19	11	10	26
65 & over	16	21	6	18	8	8	23
RACE							
White	16	11	5	17	10	13	28
Non-White	10	14	5	15	14	21	21
EDUCATION							
0-8th grade	20	14	6	16	9	11	24
1-3 years' high school	15	13	6	14	11	13	28
High school graduate	14	9	5	18	12	15	27
1-3 years' college	15	11	6	20	10	15	23
College graduate	14	9	4	16	7	18	32

1952

Never Read Bible %	Practi- cally Never %	Every Few Weeks %	Once or Twice a Week %	3-6 Times a Wk. %	Practically Every Day %	Don't Know %
12	28	22	16	6	12	4
25	31	18	14	4	4	4
6	26	25	18	7	15	3
4	18	27	19	8	21	3
7	29	27	16	6	12	3
6	34	28	17	4	8	3
5	23	30	20	5	13	4
9	34	21	14	7	13	2
9	58	12	11	4	4	2
6	23	21	19	9	18	4
17	48	17	9	2	3	4
27	38	14	6	2	7	6
14	32	23	14	5	8	4
9	25	21	17	9	15	4
13	31	25	15	5	9	2
11	31	22	16	8	9	3
13	27	23	19	5	8	5
11	26	23	17	7	13	3
10	28	21	15	5	15	6
10	21	18	16	10	21	4
12	29	21	16	6	12	4
9	17	30	21	8	13	2
14	26	23	14	7	12	4
13	29	22	16	6	10	4
11	28	24	16	6	11	4
6	29	20	18	9	14	4
5	32	17	22	9	13	2

1965

READ THE BIBLE

	Never Read Bible %	Practi- cally Never %	Every Few Weeks %	Once or Twice a Week %	3-6 Times a Wk. %	Practically Every Day %	Don't Know %
OCCUPATION							
Professional	16	8	6	18	9	14	29
Proprietor or manager	13	11	5	14	13	16	28
White-collar worker	19	8	1	19	11	13	29
Service worker	15	14	7	15	7	20	22
Manual worker	15	9	6	17	10	15	28
Farmer	11	13	7	21	18	9	21
Non-labor force	17	20	5	16	9	10	23
INCOME							
Upper	15	5	5	20	9	15	31
Middle	16	10	5	16	10	14	29
Lower	15	16	7	17	11	13	21
CITY SIZE							
Over 1 Million	34	7	2	15	10	15	34
100,000 - 1 Million	18	9	4	16	11	15	27
25,000 - 100,000	17	13	7	17	6	13	27
10,000 - 25,000	18	12	5	12	13	12	28
Under 10,000	12	13	8	19	12	13	23
Rural, farm	10	18	8	24	9	11	20
REGION							
New England	30	5	4	9	8	13	31
Middle Atlantic	20	6	2	13	10	12	37
South Atlantic	11	13	9	20	11	17	19
East South Central	10	13	12	27	13	11	14
West South Central	18	17	7	16	11	12	19
East North Central	15	11	5	18	9	17	25
West North Central	9	11	5	19	15	12	29
Mountain	17	9	4	22	15	5	28
Pacific	15	14	5	13	9	15	29

<u>1952</u>

Never Read Bible %	Practi- cally Never %	Every Few Weeks %	Once or Twice a Week %	3-6 Times a Wk. %	Practically Every Day %	Don't Know %
8	31	16	19	6	16	4
11	31	21	13	8	12	4
12	29	20	17	6	12	4
11	23	27	16	6	13	4
14	30	23	17	4	9	3
7	18	28	20	11	12	4
*	*	*	*	*	*	*
10	28	19	20	6	14	3
11	29	22	16	7	11	4
13	24	25	17	6	11	4
15	28	20	21	4	7	5
13	33	26	12	5	8	3
16	28	20	11	6	13	6
8	28	27	15	7	12	3
10	30	20	18	6	13	3
9	18	24	20	9	17	3
29	34	16	8	4	6	3
13	34	22	15	4	8	4
8	24	21	17	9	16	9
7	18	26	19	10	20	*
7	16	24	26	7	18	2
10	31	26	14	4	10	9
10	30	24	17	5	12	2
16	24	20	19	10	10	10
15	31	21	14	6	10	4

READ THE BIBLE

12d.   Is there any particular reason why you don't read it (the Bible)?

	1965 Per Cent of Total %
People who do not read the Bible	16
Reasons :	
Not enough time; too busy	3
Don't own one	1
Don't understand it	1
Read prayer book or other book instead	*
The Catholic Church discourages it	*
Can't read (illiterate)	1
Have read it before	1
Not religiously inclined	2
Would rather hear it from minister	1
All other reasons	*
No opinion, or no answer	6

	1952 Per Cent of Total %
People who do not read the Bible	12
Reasons :	
Not enough time; too busy	3
Don't own one	1
Don't understand it	1
Read prayer book or other book instead	*
The Catholic Church discourages it	*
Can't read (illiterate)	*
All other reasons	3
No opinion, or no answer	4

* Less than one per cent.

13a.   Do you ever pray to God?

13b.   Which of the following prayers do you usually say - short
       prayers during the day - night prayers - morning prayers -
       grace before meals - occasional prayers in emergencies?

1965
PRAY TO GOD

	Night Prayers %	Short Prayers During Day %	Grace Before Meals %	Occasional Prayers in Emergencies %	Morning Prayers %	Other %	Do Not Pray To God %
TOTAL	57	43	41	35	22	3	8
RELIGION							
Roman Catholic	67	49	41	44	32	2	1
Protestant total	59	44	47	32	20	2	6
Baptist	62	43	45	29	21	2	4
Methodist	59	45	45	31	18	2	6
Lutheran	64	33	54	36	17	4	5
Presbyterian	42	42	34	35	14	5	8
Episcopal	56	47	42	37	18	2	4
Congregational	65	37	36	46	14	4	1
Other denominations	59	50	54	33	24	2	9
Jewish	12	15	4	39	5	17	30
Other and None	23	23	14	27	8	9	37
SEX							
Men	48	35	37	32	18	4	12
Women	66	50	46	37	25	2	3
AGE							
18-24 years	49	27	33	37	15	2	11
25-34	52	34	43	35	13	5	8
35-44	60	46	44	38	19	3	7
45-54	59	46	41	34	24	2	7
55-64	60	47	39	31	29	3	8
65 & over	60	52	44	35	32	5	7
RACE							
White	56	43	41	36	21	3	8
Non-White	72	40	50	24	28	4	3
EDUCATION							
0-8th grade	57	47	39	34	27	2	8
1-3 years' high school	60	41	35	32	19	3	7
High school graduate	60	41	43	36	20	4	6
1-3 years' college	54	46	53	40	24	3	7
College graduate	44	41	39	32	20	6	15

Percentages exceed 100 because some respondents say more than one type of prayer.

	1952 PRAY TO GOD					
Night Prayers %	Short Prayers During Day %	Grace Before Meals %	Occasional Prayers in Emergencies %	Morning Prayers %	Other %	Do Not Pray To God %
61	39	33	31	23	5	8
77	39	33	39	47	5	1
60	41	36	30	16	5	6
60	45	43	29	15	4	6
58	44	33	31	14	5	9
67	29	39	41	16	6	3
58	45	33	28	14	4	7
58	31	33	33	19	12	2
57	20	22	39	13	7	7
61	41	35	27	20	6	8
33	22	15	42	17	14	11
20	22	7	16	5	5	43
54	32	30	28	18	6	12
68	45	37	34	26	5	3
67	32	34	30	21	4	9
62	32	34	30	16	4	8
59	37	35	33	20	5	8
58	41	31	34	26	7	7
61	46	35	30	29	9	5
64	51	32	27	34	7	7
61	40	32	33	23	6	7
70	39	54	24	23	4	6
60	43	30	31	25	5	9
63	36	32	33	22	5	7
63	37	34	34	21	5	6
62	43	38	32	19	6	6
54	40	41	33	28	11	14

1965
PRAY TO GOD

	Night Prayers %	Short Prayers During Day %	Grace Before Meals %	Occasional Prayers in Emergencies %	Morning Prayers %	Other %	Do Not Pray To God %
OCCUPATION							
Professional	52	44	44	38	20	5	10
Proprietor or manager	59	44	45	37	24	3	6
White-collar worker	57	41	44	32	21	4	6
Service worker	57	38	34	28	17	3	8
Manual worker	59	40	41	36	22	2	7
Farmer	51	47	42	36	17	2	8
Non-labor force	59	49	39	32	27	4	8
INCOME							
Upper	60	40	46	37	21	4	9
Middle	55	41	40	35	20	4	8
Lower	58	47	40	34	24	2	6
CITY SIZE							
Over 1 Million	51	38	32	32	19	6	9
100,000 - 1 Million	59	41	45	36	25	2	9
25,000 - 100,000	60	42	46	35	24	4	5
10,000 - 25,000	53	39	37	37	16	4	6
Under 10,000	62	47	45	36	22	2	6
Rural, farm	46	56	40	33	17	1	8
REGION							
New England	53	37	20	34	23	1	12
Middle Atlantic	62	41	35	39	23	5	8
South Atlantic	61	42	44	27	19	2	6
East South Central	54	58	47	14	18	2	5
West South Central	52	39	40	34	22	3	8
East North Central	56	43	45	36	22	3	7
West North Central	57	49	53	40	26	3	7
Mountain	64	44	51	38	18	4	6
Pacific	51	41	42	40	22	5	10

Percentages exceed 100 because some respondents say more than one type of prayer.

1952
PRAY TO GOD

Night Prayers %	Short Prayers During Day %	Grace Before Meals %	Occasional Prayers in Emergencies %	Morning Prayers %	Other %	Do Not Pray To God %
63	43	40	31	26	13	9
59	42	32	35	22	3	8
60	41	33	35	23	6	5
63	38	35	37	24	4	6
61	35	31	29	22	5	9
61	49	40	41	24	6	7
*	*	*	*	*	*	*
61	40	37	34	21	8	6
61	41	34	34	24	6	7
62	37	31	30	22	4	9
58	29	31	37	28	6	9
58	41	28	30	23	8	8
64	30	31	27	27	4	6
62	29	27	33	22	6	6
62	45	37	34	21	5	6
63	43	38	31	21	4	8
64	30	14	34	32	2	4
69	27	25	39	30	7	6
67	45	47	34	21	5	7
60	48	33	20	16	4	7
58	54	38	19	20	3	6
59	39	39	33	23	6	9
58	40	33	41	18	9	9
51	42	41	43	27	7	14
48	41	23	28	20	5	11

13c. Why do you pray?

	1965 Per Cent of Total %
People who pray	92
Reasons :	
To ask God for favors, help, guidance, strength	47
To get a feeling of comfort or confidence while praying	11
Belief in prayer, faith, belief in God	19
To give thanks	18
Habit or training	7
To ask forgiveness	3
For salvation of soul, go to heaven	1
Because I am in church	*
All other reasons	3

	1952 Per Cent of Total %
People who pray	92
Reasons :	
To ask God for favors, help, guidance, strength	36
To get a feeling of comfort or confidence while praying	21
Belief in prayer, faith, belief in God	15
To give thanks	14
Habit or training	9
To ask forgiveness	3
All other reasons	13

* Less than one per cent.

Percentages for both 1965 and 1952 add to more than 92 because some people have more than one reason for praying.

13a. Do you ever pray to God?

13d. About how many times would you say you prayed during the last seven days?

	Do Not Pray %	Infre- quently %	About Once a Day %	About Twice a Day %	3 Times a Day or More %	Don't Know %
TOTAL	8	9	33	16	22	12
RELIGION						
Roman Catholic	1	7	38	21	25	8
Protestant total	6	8	33	17	23	13
Baptist	4	10	37	20	20	9
Methodist	6	8	33	16	23	14
Lutheran	5	5	38	15	26	11
Presbyterian	8	16	31	13	13	19
Episcopal	4	7	42	16	16	15
Congregational	1	12	45	5	21	16
Other denominations	9	5	25	16	31	14
Jewish	30	21	16	4	5	24
Other and None	37	13	20	6	5	19
SEX						
Men	12	11	33	13	17	14
Women	3	7	33	19	27	11
AGE						
18-24 years	11	12	35	12	15	15
25-34	8	14	31	14	21	12
35-44	7	7	35	17	23	11
45-54	7	7	33	20	23	10
55-64	8	7	33	15	24	13
65 & over	7	5	29	20	24	15
RACE						
White	8	8	33	16	22	13
Non-White	3	9	33	23	25	7
EDUCATION						
0-8th grade	8	7	34	17	21	13
1-3 years' high school	7	9	36	18	20	10
High school graduate	6	8	36	16	22	12
1-3 years' college	7	10	28	16	26	13
College graduate	15	10	25	14	22	14

1965
PRAY

		1952			
			PRAY		
Do Not Pray	Infre-quently	About Once a Day	About Twice a Day	3 Times a Day or More	Don't Know
%	%	%	%	%	%
8	5	43	17	21	6
1	2	42	22	28	5
6	5	44	17	21	7
6	4	46	17	22	5
9	4	48	16	19	4
3	7	47	18	19	6
7	4	39	20	21	9
2	10	48	14	20	6
7	13	57	13	7	3
8	5	37	17	24	9
11	17	50	6	9	7
43	6	27	6	5	13
12	7	44	14	17	6
3	3	42	20	25	7
9	5	45	15	22	4
8	4	49	17	18	4
8	8	43	16	18	7
7	5	43	18	21	6
5	3	40	17	25	10
7	4	33	21	28	7
7	5	43	17	21	7
6	1	40	20	27	6
9	5	42	18	20	6
7	5	46	17	19	6
6	5	45	17	21	6
6	7	42	17	25	3
14	4	34	16	28	4

| | | 1965 PRAY | | | | |
	Do Not Pray %	Infre-quently %	About Once a Day %	About Twice a Day %	3 Times a Day or More %	Don't Know %
OCCUPATION						
Professional	10	8	27	17	24	14
Proprietor or manager	6	9	34	15	25	11
White-collar worker	6	8	38	19	19	10
Service worker	8	5	32	13	28	14
Manual worker	7	10	35	16	20	12
Farmer	8	11	35	17	20	9
Non-labor force	8	8	28	18	25	13
INCOME						
Upper	9	7	34	17	21	12
Middle	8	9	33	16	22	12
Lower	6	9	33	17	23	12
CITY SIZE						
Over 1 Million	9	10	31	17	19	14
100,000 - 1 Million	9	8	32	16	23	12
25,000 - 100,000	5	12	35	15	27	6
10,000 - 25,000	6	6	34	18	19	17
Under 10,000	6	9	34	17	22	12
Rural, farm	8	6	34	16	22	14
REGION						
New England	12	7	38	15	14	14
Middle Atlantic	8	9	34	17	20	12
South Atlantic	6	10	40	17	18	9
East South Central	5	6	42	16	18	13
West South Central	8	11	32	16	20	13
East North Central	7	7	30	16	25	15
West North Central	7	8	30	16	31	8
Mountain	6	8	32	19	26	9
Pacific	10	11	24	16	23	16

1952

PRAY

Do Not Pray %	Infre- quently %	About Once a Day %	About Twice a Day %	3 Times a Day or More %	Don't Know %
9	2	41	15	25	8
8	5	43	15	21	8
5	6	45	18	21	5
6	6	38	21	22	7
9	5	44	16	20	6
7	4	42	18	26	3
*	*	*	*	*	*
6	5	45	16	22	6
7	5	42	17	23	6
9	5	43	19	19	5
9	7	40	17	20	7
8	6	46	16	19	5
6	8	40	11	21	14
6	3	42	14	22	13
6	4	42	19	23	6
8	2	46	19	21	4
4	3	54	19	10	10
6	5	44	17	22	6
7	3	39	19	24	8
7	4	44	24	20	1
6	3	46	19	24	2
9	6	42	13	22	8
9	5	41	19	20	6
14	11	29	18	20	8
11	8	41	12	20	8

14a.   Do you think your soul will live on after death?

	1965			1952		
	Yes %	No %	Don't Know %	Yes %	No %	Don't Know %
TOTAL	75	10	15	77	7	16
RELIGION						
Roman Catholic	83	3	14	85	4	11
Protestant total	78	7	15	80	5	15
Baptist	81	5	14	87	2	11
Methodist	75	7	18	77	6	17
Lutheran	78	7	15	78	6	16
Presbyterian	70	11	19	80	7	13
Episcopal	68	15	17	67	7	26
Congregational	65	11	24	63	15	22
Other denominations	83	8	9	78	7	15
Jewish	17	46	37	35	24	41
Other and None	37	42	21	43	25	32
SEX						
Men	72	13	15	75	8	17
Women	77	7	16	80	5	15
AGE						
18-24 years	73	13	14	75	7	18
25-34	74	11	15	76	7	17
35-44	73	9	18	77	7	16
45-54	73	10	17	76	7	17
55-64	76	9	15	80	6	14
65 & over	79	8	13	81	5	14
RACE						
White	76	9	15	77	7	16
Non-White	61	16	23	79	4	17
EDUCATION						
0-8th grade	78	6	16	76	7	17
1-3 years' high school	74	9	17	75	6	19
High school graduate	75	10	15	81	4	15
1-3 years' college	77	12	11	78	7	15
College graduate	66	15	19	72	16	12

	1965			1952		
	Yes	No	Don't Know	Yes	No	Don't Know
	%	%	%	%	%	%
OCCUPATION						
Professional	73	12	15	77	10	13
Proprietor or manager	77	10	13	74	9	17
White-collar worker	73	9	18	83	4	13
Service worker	72	12	16	80	7	13
Manual worker	75	9	16	76	6	18
Farmer	84	4	12	83	3	14
Non-labor force	74	10	16	*	*	*
INCOME						
Upper	73	13	14	77	7	16
Middle	74	11	15	79	6	15
Lower	76	7	17	76	7	17
CITY SIZE						
Over 1 Million	65	16	19	70	10	20
100,000 - 1 Million	71	11	18	75	8	17
25,000 - 100,000	83	4	13	76	7	17
10,000 - 25,000	76	11	13	72	6	22
Under 10,000	81	6	13	81	6	13
Rural, farm	84	4	12	82	3	15
REGION						
New England	67	17	16	78	7	15
Middle Atlantic	69	13	18	72	8	20
South Atlantic	80	5	15	82	4	14
East South Central	93	2	5	87	3	10
West South Central	80	5	15	87	3	10
East North Central	75	9	16	74	8	18
West North Central	80	8	12	79	3	18
Mountain	75	14	11	72	11	17
Pacific	65	15	20	76	9	15

14b.   Do you think there is a Heaven, where people who have led good lives are eternally rewarded?

	1965				1952			
	Believe in After-Life			Don't believe in after-life	Believe in After-Life			Don't believe in after-life
	Yes %	No %	Don't Know %	%	Yes %	No %	Don't Know %	%
TOTAL	68	3	4	25	72	2	3	23
RELIGION								
Roman Catholic	80	1	2	17	83	1	1	15
Protestant total	71	3	4	22	75	2	3	20
Baptist	78	1	2	19	83	1	3	13
Methodist	66	3	6	25	72	1	4	23
Lutheran	66	3	9	22	74	2	2	22
Presbyterian	61	3	7	29	71	3	6	20
Episcopal	54	10	4	32	58	4	5	33
Congregational	58	4	3	35	59	4	-	37
Other denominations	75	3	5	17	71	4	3	22
Jewish	6	5	6	83	21	5	9	65
Other and None	26	7	4	63	40	1	2	57
SEX								
Men	65	3	4	28	70	2	3	25
Women	70	3	4	23	75	2	3	20
AGE								
18-24 years	68	3	2	27	70	3	2	25
25-34	66	4	4	26	71	2	3	24
35-44	67	2	4	27	72	2	3	23
45-54	67	2	4	27	71	2	3	24
55-64	71	2	3	24	74	2	4	20
65 & over	70	3	6	21	76	2	3	19
RACE								
White	69	3	4	24	72	2	3	23
Non-White	57	3	1	39	72	3	4	21
EDUCATION								
0-8th grade	74	1	3	22	73	1	2	24
1-3 years' high school	72	1	1	26	70	1	4	25
High school graduate	68	3	4	25	77	2	2	19
1-3 years' college	67	4	6	23	69	5	4	22
College graduate	51	6	9	34	60	5	7	28

| | 1965 | | | | 1952 | | | |
| | Believe in After-Life | | | Don't believe in after-life | Believe in After-Life | | | Don't believe in after-life |
	Yes %	No %	Don't Know %	%	Yes %	No %	Don't Know %	%
OCCUPATION								
Professional	61	7	5	27	68	4	5	23
Proprietor or manager	68	3	6	23	68	2	4	26
White-collar worker	65	4	4	27	76	3	4	17
Service worker	68	1	3	28	75	2	3	20
Manual worker	70	2	3	25	72	1	3	24
Farmer	82	1	1	16	81	*	2	17
Non-labor force	66	2	6	26	*	*	*	*
INCOME								
Upper	62	5	6	27	70	3	4	23
Middle	68	2	4	26	74	2	3	21
Lower	71	3	3	23	72	1	3	24
CITY SIZE								
Over 1 Million	57	3	5	35	61	3	6	30
100,000 - 1 Million	64	2	5	29	68	3	4	25
25,000 - 100,000	74	5	4	17	71	2	3	24
10,000 - 25,000	67	5	4	24	68	1	3	28
Under 10,000	76	2	3	19	77	2	2	19
Rural, farm	81	1	2	16	79	1	2	18
REGION								
New England	58	4	5	33	74	1	3	22
Middle Atlantic	65	2	2	31	67	2	3	28
South Atlantic	76	2	2	20	79	1	2	18
East South Central	91	*	2	7	84	1	2	13
West South Central	78	1	1	20	85	1	1	13
East North Central	68	2	5	25	67	2	5	26
West North Central	71	1	8	20	74	2	3	21
Mountain	59	12	4	25	60	5	7	28
Pacific	51	6	8	35	67	5	4	24

* Less than one per cent.

14c. Do you think there is a Hell, to which people who have led bad lives and die without being sorry are eternally damned?

| | 1965 | | | | 1952 | | | |
| | Believe in After-Life | | | Don't believe in after-life | Believe in After-Life | | | Don't believe in after-life |
	Yes %	No %	Don't Know %	%	Yes %	No %	Don't Know %	%
TOTAL	54	13	8	25	58	12	7	23
RELIGION								
Roman Catholic	70	7	6	17	74	5	6	15
Protestant total	54	15	9	22	56	15	9	20
Baptist	68	7	6	19	75	6	6	13
Methodist	44	17	14	25	51	15	11	23
Lutheran	49	22	7	22	59	11	8	22
Presbyterian	39	22	10	29	45	25	10	20
Episcopal	17	38	13	32	26	30	11	33
Congregational	25	37	3	35	35	17	11	37
Other denominations	63	13	7	17	52	18	8	22
Jewish	3	9	5	83	15	12	8	65
Other and None	20	13	4	63	33	7	3	57
SEX								
Men	54	10	8	28	57	11	7	25
Women	55	15	7	23	59	13	8	20
AGE								
18-24 years	56	13	4	27	59	9	7	25
25-34	54	13	7	26	58	11	7	24
35-44	55	11	7	27	59	11	7	23
45-54	51	13	9	27	54	14	8	24
55-64	56	13	7	24	58	14	8	20
65 & over	55	14	10	21	56	12	13	19
RACE								
White	55	13	8	24	58	12	7	23
Non-White	47	6	8	39	64	7	8	21
EDUCATION								
0-8th grade	65	6	7	22	62	8	6	24
1-3 years' high school	61	7	6	26	58	10	7	25
High school graduate	52	16	7	25	58	14	9	19
1-3 years' college	47	20	10	23	50	17	11	22
College graduate	38	17	11	34	41	22	9	28

	1965 Believe in After-Life			Don't believe in after-life	1952 Believe in After-Life			Don't believe in after-life
	Yes %	No %	Don't Know %	%	Yes %	No %	Don't Know %	%
OCCUPATION								
Professional	44	20	8	28	51	17	9	23
Proprietor or manager	51	18	8	23	52	15	7	26
White-collar worker	51	15	7	27	55	17	11	17
Service worker	60	4	8	28	62	10	8	20
Manual worker	58	10	7	25	61	9	6	24
Farmer	69	7	8	16	65	10	8	17
Non-labor force	52	13	9	26	*	*	*	*
INCOME								
Upper	44	19	10	27	50	17	10	23
Middle	55	12	7	26	57	14	8	21
Lower	59	10	8	23	63	6	7	24
CITY SIZE								
Over 1 Million	45	14	6	35	49	10	11	30
100,000 - 1 Million	48	14	9	29	52	14	9	25
25,000 - 100,000	62	13	8	17	62	8	6	24
10,000 - 25,000	55	15	6	24	50	15	7	28
Under 10,000	62	11	8	19	58	15	8	19
Rural, farm	69	7	8	16	72	6	4	18
REGION								
New England	42	17	8	33	60	11	7	22
Middle Atlantic	53	12	4	31	50	15	7	28
South Atlantic	63	8	9	20	67	8	7	18
East South Central	85	2	6	7	77	6	4	13
West South Central	65	9	6	20	75	7	5	13
East North Central	54	14	7	25	52	11	11	26
West North Central	55	12	13	20	60	12	7	21
Mountain	34	27	14	25	35	30	7	28
Pacific	35	21	9	35	47	19	10	24

14c.   Do you think there is a Hell, to which people who have led bad lives and die without being sorry are eternally damned?

14d.   Do you think there is any real possibility of your going there?

| | 1965 | | | | 1952 | | | |
| | Believe in Hell | | | Don't believe in Hell | Believe in Hell | | | Don't believe in Hell |
	Yes %	No %	Don't Know %	%	Yes %	No %	Don't Know %	%
TOTAL	17	25	12	46	12	29	17	42
RELIGION								
Roman Catholic	27	23	20	30	20	26	28	26
Protestant total	15	29	11	45	12	32	12	44
Baptist	17	40	12	31	14	50	11	25
Methodist	10	23	11	56	11	28	12	49
Lutheran	17	24	8	51	10	31	18	41
Presbyterian	15	15	9	61	10	28	7	55
Episcopal	5	5	8	82	8	13	5	74
Congregational	5	12	8	75	11	15	9	65
Other denominations	19	32	11	38	12	26	14	48
Jewish	2	1	-	97	4	4	7	85
Other and None	6	7	7	80	10	8	15	67
SEX								
Men	20	21	13	46	14	25	18	43
Women	14	28	12	46	11	32	16	41
AGE								
18-24 years	24	20	12	44	19	27	13	41
25-34	21	22	12	45	16	27	15	42
35-44	19	24	12	45	14	29	16	41
45-54	15	24	12	49	10	28	16	46
55-64	14	28	14	44	11	30	17	42
65 & over	9	33	13	45	9	33	14	44
RACE								
White	18	25	13	44	15	27	16	42
Non-White	8	28	11	63	15	36	13	36
EDUCATION								
0-8th grade	13	35	17	35	11	31	20	38
1-3 years' high school	19	27	14	40	14	28	16	42
High school graduate	18	23	11	48	16	27	15	42
1-3 years' college	18	19	10	53	13	26	11	50
College graduate	17	15	6	62	8	24	9	59

	1965				1952			
	Believe in Hell			Don't believe in Hell	Believe in Hell			Don't believe in Hell
	Yes %	No %	Don't Know %	%	Yes %	No %	Don't Know %	%
OCCUPATION								
Professional	18	19	7	56	12	28	11	49
Proprietor or manager	15	25	10	50	15	26	11	48
White-collar worker	19	21	11	49	12	27	16	45
Service worker	15	21	23	41	16	30	16	38
Manual worker	19	25	14	42	14	28	19	39
Farmer	20	35	14	31	12	34	19	35
Non-labor force	11	31	11	47	*	*	*	*
INCOME								
Upper	17	19	8	56	10	29	11	50
Middle	17	24	13	46	14	26	17	43
Lower	16	30	14	40	16	28	19	37
CITY SIZE								
Over 1 Million	20	17	9	54	13	19	17	51
100,000 - 1 Million	16	22	10	52	12	24	16	48
25,000 - 100,000	13	30	19	38	16	21	25	38
10,000 - 25,000	16	24	15	45	18	17	15	50
Under 10,000	17	31	14	38	12	32	14	42
Rural, farm	16	35	17	32	17	40	15	28
REGION								
New England	14	20	8	58	16	18	26	40
Middle Atlantic	19	20	14	47	11	18	21	50
South Atlantic	16	32	16	36	13	40	14	33
East South Central	32	43	10	15	21	45	11	23
West South Central	15	33	17	35	17	45	13	25
East North Central	16	25	13	46	11	26	15	48
West North Central	24	21	10	45	16	21	23	40
Mountain	10	18	7	65	3	22	10	65
Pacific	9	19	7	65	15	22	10	53

15a.   When are your religious feelings strongest - when everything is going well, or when the going gets rough?

	1965			1952		
	When Everything Going Well %	When the Going Gets Rough %	Makes No Difference %	When Everything Going Well %	When the Going Gets Rough %	Makes No Difference %
TOTAL	14	39	47	11	47	42
RELIGION						
Roman Catholic	11	41	48	8	44	48
Protestant total	15	40	45	12	49	39
Baptist	19	39	42	13	49	38
Methodist	15	43	42	13	50	37
Lutheran	14	47	39	10	47	43
Presbyterian	8	33	59	14	47	39
Episcopal	12	36	52	15	40	45
Congregational	19	48	33	4	51	45
Other denominations	15	38	47	10	53	37
Jewish	7	39	54	5	51	44
Other and None	9	29	62	9	30	61
SEX						
Men	13	36	51	11	43	46
Women	14	42	44	10	51	39
AGE						
18-24 years	14	43	43	14	51	35
25-34	15	45	40	10	51	39
35-44	14	39	47	9	53	38
45-54	14	36	50	10	43	47
55-64	13	39	48	10	42	48
65 & over	12	34	54	13	40	47
RACE						
White	13	40	47	11	47	42
Non-White	14	38	48	14	45	41
EDUCATION						
0-8th grade	13	36	51	11	44	45
1-3 years' high school	15	39	46	11	48	41
High school graduate	13	43	44	10	52	38
1-3 years' college	13	40	47	9	50	41
College graduate	14	34	52	11	42	47

	1965			1952		
	When Everything Going Well %	When the Going Gets Rough %	Makes No Difference %	When Everything Going Well %	When the Going Gets Rough %	Makes No Difference %
OCCUPATION						
Professional	12	40	48	9	47	44
Proprietor or manager	16	37	47	11	48	41
White-collar worker	11	43	46	9	50	41
Service worker	15	32	53	14	43	43
Manual worker	14	41	45	11	48	41
Farmer	13	49	38	9	49	42
Non-labor force	13	37	50	*	*	*
INCOME						
Upper	13	38	49	9	47	44
Middle	13	39	48	10	49	41
Lower	14	42	44	12	46	42
CITY SIZE						
Over 1 Million	9	32	59	9	44	47
100,000 - 1 Million	15	39	46	11	44	45
25,000 - 100,000	17	38	45	10	50	40
10,000 - 25,000	14	37	49	11	48	41
Under 10,000	15	44	41	11	49	40
Rural, farm	14	48	38	11	49	40
REGION						
New England	9	42	49	5	46	49
Middle Atlantic	9	38	53	8	46	46
South Atlantic	18	40	42	16	46	38
East South Central	18	37	45	11	56	33
West South Central	17	34	49	11	49	40
East North Central	13	40	47	10	48	42
West North Central	10	50	40	10	53	37
Mountain	16	38	46	7	41	52
Pacific	17	35	48	14	44	42

15b.   Do you ever think about what may happen to you after you die?

	1965			1952		
	Yes	No	Don't Know	Yes	No	Don't Know
	%	%	%	%	%	%
TOTAL	58	39	3	60	38	2
RELIGION						
Roman Catholic	60	37	3	64	34	2
Protestant total	60	38	2	60	38	2
Baptist	68	30	2	66	33	1
Methodist	57	41	2	58	40	2
Lutheran	56	43	1	57	41	2
Presbyterian	50	46	4	60	40	*
Episcopal	46	53	1	41	58	1
Congregational	35	65	-	59	39	2
Other denominations	64	33	3	62	37	1
Jewish	23	72	5	35	61	4
Other and None	48	47	5	37	56	7
SEX						
Men	56	41	3	56	41	3
Women	60	38	2	62	36	2
AGE						
18-24 years	68	30	2	70	29	1
25-34	62	36	2	59	39	2
35-44	59	39	2	55	43	2
45-54	57	41	2	57	41	2
55-64	51	46	3	57	41	2
65 & over	55	40	5	57	39	4
RACE						
White	59	38	3	58	40	2
Non-White	54	43	3	61	36	3
EDUCATION						
0-8th grade	60	36	4	57	40	3
1-3 years' high school	57	41	2	59	39	2
High school graduate	58	40	2	58	40	2
1-3 years' college	63	35	2	64	35	1
College graduate	52	45	3	61	38	1

* Less than one per cent.

	1965			1952		
	Yes	No	Don't Know	Yes	No	Don't Know
	%	%	%	%	%	%
OCCUPATION						
Professional	60	38	2	60	39	1
Proprietor or manager	55	43	2	52	46	2
White-collar worker	60	38	2	64	35	1
Service worker	52	45	3	65	33	2
Manual worker	59	39	2	56	41	3
Farmer	60	38	2	60	39	1
Non-labor force	59	37	4	*	*	*
INCOME						
Upper	56	42	2	56	43	1
Middle	59	39	2	59	39	2
Lower	59	38	3	60	38	2
CITY SIZE						
Over 1 Million	50	47	3	60	38	2
100,000 - 1 Million	59	39	2	54	45	1
25,000 - 100,000	59	40	1	59	39	2
10,000 - 25,000	60	36	4	59	36	5
Under 10,000	63	34	3	60	38	2
Rural, farm	56	41	3	60	39	1
REGION						
New England	61	38	1	53	46	1
Middle Atlantic	51	46	3	57	40	3
South Atlantic	65	33	2	68	31	1
East South Central	85	14	1	64	35	1
West South Central	66	30	4	60	38	2
East North Central	55	41	4	58	39	3
West North Central	54	44	2	50	49	1
Mountain	58	41	1	57	40	3
Pacific	52	46	2	58	41	1

16a. Which do you think you, yourself, are most serious about --
trying to live comfortably; or preparing for a life after death?

| | 1965 | | | | 1952 | | | |
	Trying to Live Comfortably %	Preparing for Life After Death %	Both %	Don't Know %	Trying To Live Comfortably %	Preparing for Life After Death %	Both %	Don't Know %
TOTAL	46	20	30	4	46	21	30	3
RELIGION								
Roman Catholic	47	13	39	1	39	23	35	3
Protestant total	42	24	30	4	45	22	30	3
Baptist	38	30	30	2	37	33	28	2
Methodist	44	18	32	6	49	19	29	3
Lutheran	54	15	25	6	53	14	31	2
Presbyterian	53	11	30	6	49	15	33	3
Episcopal	68	11	19	2	58	6	33	3
Congregational	62	23	12	3	73	7	20	2
Other denominations	29	33	34	4	40	27	31	2
Jewish	89	3	8	-	84	1	13	2
Other and None	66	11	13	10	69	6	16	9
SEX								
Men	51	16	29	4	49	18	29	4
Women	42	23	31	4	42	24	31	3
AGE								
18-24 years	63	14	21	2	56	21	21	2
25-34	55	14	26	5	52	17	29	2
35-44	48	16	32	4	50	19	28	3
45-54	43	20	33	4	43	20	32	5
55-64	40	27	30	3	40	22	35	3
65 & over	30	31	35	4	28	34	34	4
RACE								
White	47	19	30	4	47	20	30	3
Non-White	41	24	30	5	40	32	24	4
EDUCATION								
0-8th grade	36	30	30	4	37	29	31	3
1-3 years' high school	43	25	29	3	48	22	27	3
High school graduate	48	16	32	4	50	17	31	2
1-3 years' college	50	15	33	2	52	15	31	2
College graduate	60	23	10	7	55	13	26	6

	1965				1952			
	Trying to Live Comfortably %	Preparing for Life After Death %	Both %	Don't Know %	Trying to Live Comfortably %	Preparing for Life After Death %	Both %	Don't Know %
OCCUPATION								
Professional	53	14	29	4	50	18	28	4
Proprietor or manager	50	16	30	4	53	15	28	4
White-collar worker	49	17	31	3	47	17	34	2
Service worker	49	21	28	2	48	25	25	2
Manual worker	48	20	28	4	46	23	28	3
Farmer	25	30	43	2	36	27	37	*
Non-labor force	37	27	31	5	*	*	*	*
INCOME								
Upper	53	14	30	3	50	14	32	4
Middle	49	16	31	4	47	20	31	2
Lower	39	27	30	4	43	27	27	3
CITY SIZE								
Over 1 Million	56	11	30	3	52	17	25	6
100,000 - 1 Million	48	16	32	4	50	19	28	3
25,000 - 100,000	42	28	23	7	41	23	33	3
10,000 - 25,000	43	19	33	5	50	19	27	4
Under 10,000	43	26	28	3	48	20	30	2
Rural, farm	25	34	38	3	37	29	32	2
REGION								
New England	65	11	23	1	43	15	39	3
Middle Atlantic	59	11	27	3	54	16	27	3
South Atlantic	37	34	25	4	37	31	30	2
East South Central	20	41	35	4	43	30	25	2
West South Central	34	28	35	3	32	27	39	2
East North Central	40	19	37	4	51	18	27	4
West North Central	43	18	34	5	43	18	38	1
Mountain	44	13	33	10	50	23	21	6
Pacific	59	12	25	4	56	15	27	2

* Less than one per cent.

16b. Which do you think you should be most serious about -- trying to live comfortably, or preparing for a life after death?

| | 1965 | | | | 1952 | | | |
	Trying to Live Comfortably %	Preparing for Life After Death %	Both %	Don't Know %	Trying to Live Comfortably %	Preparing for Life After Death %	Both %	Don't Know %
TOTAL	25	48	22	5	22	51	23	4
RELIGION								
Roman Catholic	21	46	28	5	19	53	25	3
Protestant total	22	53	21	4	19	54	24	3
Baptist	16	62	20	2	12	68	19	1
Methodist	22	50	22	6	18	52	26	4
Lutheran	28	47	18	7	25	48	25	2
Presbyterian	33	33	24	10	23	43	30	4
Episcopal	43	39	15	3	34	25	34	7
Congregational	41	35	17	7	44	26	28	2
Other denominations	14	60	23	3	17	59	21	3
Jewish	86	-	12	2	88	8	17	7
Other and None	49	23	14	14	42	32	16	10
SEX								
Men	31	42	22	5	24	47	25	4
Women	21	53	22	4	19	56	22	3
AGE								
18-24 years	33	47	17	3	20	52	22	6
25-34	29	47	19	5	23	53	22	2
35-44	24	49	22	5	24	50	23	3
45-54	24	48	23	5	23	50	24	3
55-64	26	45	24	5	21	51	24	4
65 & over	16	53	26	5	14	56	26	4
RACE								
White	24	49	22	5	22	51	23	4
Non-White	34	40	23	3	18	56	21	5
EDUCATION								
0-8th grade	21	53	23	3	18	59	20	3
1-3 years' high school	23	51	23	3	25	49	22	4
High school graduate	23	48	24	5	19	51	27	3
1-3 years' college	28	48	17	7	25	47	25	3
College graduate	40	31	19	10	31	38	25	6

	1965				1952			
	Trying to Live Comfortably %	Preparing for Life After Death %	Both %	Don't Know %	Trying to Live Comfortably %	Preparing for Life After Death %	Both %	Don't Know %
OCCUPATION								
Professional	32	38	23	7	26	44	26	4
Proprietor or manager	28	51	17	4	27	44	23	6
White-collar worker	23	46	26	5	19	48	29	4
Service worker	24	51	21	4	22	58	17	3
Manual worker	25	49	21	5	22	54	21	3
Farmer	13	68	19	*	11	61	26	2
Non-labor force	23	47	25	5	*	*	*	*
INCOME								
Upper	35	42	18	5	25	42	27	6
Middle	26	46	23	5	22	51	24	3
Lower	20	53	22	5	19	57	20	4
CITY SIZE								
Over 1 Million	36	30	28	6	32	40	22	6
100,000 - 1 Million	29	42	24	5	26	47	22	5
25,000 - 100,000	14	56	23	7	22	53	21	4
10,000 - 25,000	22	52	21	5	18	55	24	3
Under 10,000	20	60	16	4	20	50	27	3
Rural, farm	13	66	20	1	12	67	19	2
REGION								
New England	46	30	20	4	31	34	31	4
Middle Atlantic	37	34	26	3	29	40	27	4
South Atlantic	20	59	16	5	15	65	18	2
East South Central	3	77	20	*	8	76	13	3
West South Central	15	58	24	3	16	65	16	3
East North Central	21	47	26	6	22	51	23	4
West North Central	15	62	17	6	17	51	29	3
Mountain	19	47	25	9	21	52	20	7
Pacific	35	38	20	7	29	41	27	3

* Less than one per cent.

17. All other things being equal, do you think that people who marry will be happier if they both have the same religion, or don't you think it makes any difference?

	1965			1952		
	Happier With Same Religion	Makes No Difference	Don't Know	Happier With Same Religion	Makes No Difference	Don't Know
	%	%	%	%	%	%
TOTAL	70	25	5	75	22	3
RELIGION						
Roman Catholic	62	32	6	73	25	2
Protestant total	74	21	5	76	21	3
Baptist	72	22	6	79	18	3
Methodist	70	24	6	75	21	4
Lutheran	74	22	4	70	28	2
Presbyterian	68	24	8	80	17	3
Episcopal	69	29	2	69	25	6
Congregational	77	20	3	76	24	-
Other denominations	82	15	3	78	20	2
Jewish	86	10	4	80	19	1
Other and None	56	37	7	61	30	9
SEX						
Men	69	26	5	74	23	3
Women	71	23	6	77	20	3
AGE						
18-24 years	64	32	4	74	25	1
25-34	67	29	4	74	23	3
35-44	71	24	5	76	21	3
45-54	72	22	6	76	21	3
55-64	72	22	6	75	22	3
65 & over	71	20	9	77	18	5
RACE						
White	72	23	5	76	21	3
Non-White	52	40	8	56	36	8
EDUCATION						
0-8th grade	72	22	6	74	22	4
1-3 years' high school	62	32	6	69	27	4
High school graduate	70	25	5	76	22	2
1-3 years' college	74	23	3	78	19	3
College graduate	76	16	8	84	13	3

	1965			1952		
	Happier With Same Religion	Makes No Difference	Don't Know	Happier With Same Religion	Makes No Difference	Don't Know
	%	%	%	%	%	.%
OCCUPATION						
Professional	73	24	3	81	16	3
Proprietor or manager	76	20	4	74	21	5
White-collar worker	76	19	5	80	17	3
Service worker	61	32	7	72	26	2
Manual worker	66	29	5	71	26	3
Farmer	85	10	5	85	13	2
Non-labor force	67	24	9	*	*	*
INCOME						
Upper	74	23	3	78	19	3
Middle	70	25	5	76	21	3
Lower	68	25	7	71	25	4
CITY SIZE						
Over 1 Million	62	30	8	75	22	3
100,000 - 1 Million	67	28	5	72	25	3
25,000 - 100,000	69	27	4	66	28	6
10,000 - 25,000	61	30	9	78	17	5
Under 10,000	78	19	3	76	21	3
Rural, farm	84	10	6	82	17	1
REGION						
New England	67	25	8	72	26	2
Middle Atlantic	61	34	5	70	27	3
South Atlantic	70	23	7	74	22	4
East South Central	84	14	2	78	20	2
West South Central	68	26	6	78	20	2
East North Central	73	22	5	77	20	3
West North Central	82	15	3	78	19	3
Mountain	77	17	6	79	20	1
Pacific	66	29	5	80	19	1

18a. Some religions hold that divorced people who remarry are living in sin. Do you agree or disagree with this stand?

| | 1965 | | | 1952 | | |
	Agree %	Disagree %	Don't Know %	Agree %	Disagree %	Don't Know %
TOTAL	21	65	14	26	62	12
RELIGION						
Roman Catholic	36	50	14	51	38	11
Protestant total	18	67	15	20	67	13
Baptist	22	58	20	29	57	14
Methodist	12	75	13	14	73	13
Lutheran	6	85	9	12	78	10
Presbyterian	8	84	8	12	80	8
Episcopal	7	86	7	7	79	14
Congregational	31	64	5	4	87	9
Other denominations	27	56	17	25	60	15
Jewish	-	100	-	4	92	4
Other and None	9	78	13	11	76	13
SEX						
Men	21	66	13	24	64	12
Women	21	64	15	28	60	12
AGE						
18-24 years	16	74	10	32	60	8
25-34	19	69	12	26	63	11
35-44	25	62	13	24	66	10
45-54	23	62	15	25	62	13
55-64	23	64	13	25	60	15
65 & over	19	61	20	28	54	18
RACE						
White	21	65	14	26	62	12
Non-White	22	62	16	28	59	13
EDUCATION						
0-8th grade	29	51	20	31	54	15
1-3 years' high school	22	61	17	25	63	12
High school graduate	19	70	11	26	63	11
1-3 years' college	19	71	10	21	68	11
College graduate	15	75	10	14	78	8

	1965			1952		
	Agree %	Disagree %	Don't Know %	Agree %	Disagree %	Don't Know %
OCCUPATION						
Professional	19	71	10	17	71	12
Proprietor or manager	21	69	10	20	69	11
White-collar worker	16	73	11	24	63	13
Service worker	17	60	23	29	58	13
Manual worker	25	62	13	29	59	12
Farmer	23	56	21	29	57	14
Non-labor force	19	64	17	*	*	*
INCOME						
Upper	16	73	11	18	71	11
Middle	22	65	13	25	64	11
Lower	23	60	17	32	54	14
CITY SIZE						
Over 1 Million	18	70	12	32	57	11
100,000 - 1 Million	19	67	14	22	67	11
25,000 - 100,000	24	63	13	29	56	15
10,000 - 25,000	18	65	17	29	53	18
Under 10,000	26	61	13	22	67	11
Rural, farm	23	54	23	32	55	13
REGION						
New England	15	72	13	32	56	12
Middle Atlantic	22	68	10	28	61	11
South Atlantic	22	57	21	27	59	14
East South Central	33	45	22	32	48	20
West South Central	25	58	17	28	58	14
East North Central	22	62	16	24	64	12
West North Central	25	64	11	22	69	9
Mountain	14	78	8	18	74	8
Pacific	12	78	10	20	71	9

266

18b. Some religions forbid married couples to use mechanical birth control methods. Do you agree or disagree with this stand?

	1965 Agree %	1965 Disagree %	1965 Don't Know %	1952 Agree %	1952 Disagree %	1952 Don't Know %
TOTAL	17	69	14	22	63	15
RELIGION						
Roman Catholic	37	51	12	51	38	11
Protestant total	11	74	15	14	70	16
Baptist	13	68	19	18	65	17
Methodist	7	77	16	13	73	14
Lutheran	7	86	7	15	67	18
Presbyterian	7	79	14	8	82	10
Episcopal	6	84	10	11	77	11
Congregational	6	82	12	9	85	6
Other denominations	16	69	15	14	66	20
Jewish	6	92	2	10	80	10
Other and None	10	76	14	11	69	20
SEX						
Men	17	68	15	21	63	16
Women	17	70	13	23	63	14
AGE						
18-24 years	19	75	6	27	61	12
25-34	12	79	9	21	70	9
35-44	20	71	9	21	67	12
45-54	18	67	15	21	63	16
55-64	15	65	20	21	58	21
65 & over	19	54	27	26	47	27
RACE						
White	16	70	14	22	63	15
Non-White	21	65	14	24	57	19
EDUCATION						
0-8th grade	21	55	24	25	52	23
1-3 years' high school	15	69	16	23	63	14
High school graduate	17	73	10	23	65	12
1-3 years' college	16	73	11	17	75	8
College graduate	14	79	7	14	78	8

	1965			1952		
	Agree %	Disagree %	Don't Know %	Agree %	Disagree %	Don't Know %
OCCUPATION						
Professional	13	78	9	15	73	12
Proprietor or manager	14	75	11	18	68	14
White-collar worker	17	71	12	22	68	11
Service worker	17	74	9	26	58	16
Manual worker	18	68	14	25	60	15
Farmer	13	64	23	20	55	25
Non-labor force	20	59	21	*	*	*
INCOME						
Upper	12	78	10	17	69	14
Middle	17	71	12	21	66	13
Lower	20	61	19	27	54	19
CITY SIZE						
Over 1 Million	14	74	12	29	57	14
100,000 - 1 Million	18	68	14	23	64	13
25,000 - 100,000	22	68	10	27	57	16
10,000 - 25,000	21	61	18	27	57	16
Under 10,000	16	70	14	16	70	14
Rural, farm	12	60	28	23	58	19
REGION						
New England	30	63	7	38	47	15
Middle Atlantic	18	70	12	28	60	12
South Atlantic	14	64	22	21	63	16
East South Central	12	61	27	15	65	20
West South Central	14	70	16	17	68	15
East North Central	18	69	13	21	63	16
West North Central	20	65	15	21	60	19
Mountain	15	77	8	15	69	16
Pacific	13	80	7	18	71	11

19.   Do you think it is ever right for clergymen to discuss political candidates or issues from the pulpit?

	1965			1952		
	Yes	No	Don't Know	Yes	No	Don't Know
	%	%	%	%	%	%
TOTAL	22	68	10	22	70	8
RELIGION						
Roman Catholic	20	71	9	18	72	10
Protestant total	24	67	9	23	69	8
Baptist	22	64	14	22	71	7
Methodist	23	68	9	24	68	8
Lutheran	23	69	8	21	75	4
Presbyterian	22	67	11	30	63	7
Episcopal	31	67	2	28	59	13
Congregational	48	47	5	21	68	11
Other denominations	22	72	6	23	69	8
Jewish	24	70	6	27	66	7
Other and None	19	68	13	19	70	11
SEX						
Men	22	70	8	25	69	6
Women	22	67	11	20	70	10
AGE						
18-24 years	24	68	8	23	67	10
25-34	22	67	11	23	70	7
35-44	27	62	11	25	67	8
45-54	25	66	9	20	71	9
55-64	17	77	6	23	68	9
65 & over	15	75	10	17	75	8
RACE						
White	21	70	9	22	70	8
Non-White	31	54	15	20	67	13
EDUCATION						
0-8th grade	16	72	12	19	73	8
1-3 years' high school	13	75	12	19	73	8
High school graduate	24	68	8	20	72	8
1-3 years' college	27	66	7	30	61	9
College graduate	41	52	7	43	49	8

	1965			1952		
	Yes	No	Don't Know	Yes	No	Don't Know
	%	%	%	%	%	%
OCCUPATION						
Professional	32	61	7	33	57	10
Proprietor or manager	23	70	7	20	70	10
White-collar worker	24	67	9	24	68	8
Service worker	17	65	18	21	71	8
Manual worker	22	69	9	19	73	8
Farmer	20	72	8	23	69	8
Non-labor force	17	73	10	*	*	*
INCOME						
Upper	31	62	7	27	65	8
Middle	23	68	9	22	70	8
Lower	17	72	11	20	70	10
CITY SIZE						
Over 1 Million	21	67	12	24	66	10
100,000 - 1 Million	25	66	9	21	71	8
25,000 - 100,000	22	72	6	23	68	9
10,000 - 25,000	20	73	7	23	66	11
Under 10,000	23	67	10	22	71	7
Rural, farm	14	80	6	21	71	8
REGION						
New England	25	70	5	12	83	5
Middle Atlantic	18	74	8	21	71	8
South Atlantic	22	64	14	23	70	7
East South Central	22	58	20	17	73	10
West South Central	17	72	11	27	68	5
East North Central	24	69	7	24	68	8
West North Central	29	66	5	23	65	12
Mountain	14	75	11	35	53	12
Pacific	27	64	9	21	71	8

20a.   Most states don't tax property owned by church groups. Do you
think church property used for religious purposes should be
taxed or not?

	1965			1952		
	Yes	No	Don't Know	Yes	No	Don't Know
	%	%	%	%	%	%
TOTAL	14	77	9	12	81	7
RELIGION						
Roman Catholic	11	81	8	10	84	6
Protestant total	13	78	9	11	82	7
Baptist	14	76	10	10	83	7
Methodist	15	79	6	10	83	7
Lutheran	15	77	8	12	82	6
Presbyterian	16	74	10	13	82	5
Episcopal	10	80	10	10	84	6
Congregational	12	80	8	11	85	4
Other denominations	11	81	8	12	80	8
Jewish	14	80	6	14	73	13
Other and None	30	55	15	23	65	12
SEX						
Men	15	78	7	12	82	6
Women	12	77	11	11	80	9
AGE						
18-24 years	19	76	5	11	85	4
25-34	14	78	8	11	82	7
35-44	11	81	8	18	81	9
45-54	15	77	8	13	80	7
55-64	14	76	10	12	81	7
65 & over	13	72	15	13	79	8
RACE						
White	14	78	8	11	82	7
Non-White	16	72	12	16	74	10
EDUCATION						
0-8th grade	14	73	13	12	78	10
1-3 years' high school	12	78	10	11	83	6
High school graduate	13	80	7	12	83	5
1-3 years' college	16	76	8	9	86	5
College graduate	19	76	5	15	76	9

	1965			1952		
	Yes	No	Don't Know	Yes	No	Don't Know
	%	%	%	%	%	%
OCCUPATION						
Professional	18	75	7	12	81	7
Proprietor or manager	9	83	8	12	80	8
White-collar worker	15	76	9	13	81	6
Service worker	7	81	12	13	80	7
Manual worker	14	78	8	11	82	7
Farmer	14	77	9	9	82	9
Non-labor force	16	73	11	*	*	*
INCOME						
Upper	15	79	6	12	82	6
Middle	14	78	8	12	82	6
Lower	12	77	11	11	80	9
CITY SIZE						
Over 1 Million	13	75	12	15	75	10
100,000 - 1 Million	15	76	9	12	80	8
25,000 - 100,000	17	80	3	13	79	8
10,000 - 25,000	14	77	9	7	86	7
Under 10,000	12	80	8	11	84	5
Rural, farm	14	77	9	10	82	8
REGION						
New England	16	74	10	12	82	6
Middle Atlantic	12	79	9	13	78	9
South Atlantic	14	76	10	8	88	4
East South Central	6	81	13	13	80	7
West South Central	12	81	7	10	83	7
East North Central	12	81	7	12	79	9
West North Central	15	78	7	8	83	9
Mountain	17	74	9	11	82	7
Pacific	21	69	10	16	78	6

20b. Do you think church property which brings rent or profit to the church should be taxed, or not?

	1965			1952		
	Yes	No	Don't Know	Yes	No	Don't Know
	%	%	%	%	%	%
TOTAL	55	34	11	49	41	10
RELIGION						
Roman Catholic	50	38	12	44	46	10
Protestant total	56	33	11	50	41	9
Baptist	47	39	14	44	46	10
Methodist	55	33	12	47	44	9
Lutheran	60	30	10	53	36	11
Presbyterian	65	23	12	53	39	8
Episcopal	68	30	2	54	37	9
Congregational	82	7	11	54	35	11
Other denominations	57	33	10	56	36	8
Jewish	62	33	5	57	30	13
Other and None	66	23	11	63	24	13
SEX						
Men	60	31	9	54	39	7
Women	51	36	13	45	43	12
AGE						
18-24 years	53	37	10	40	52	8
25-34	53	36	11	48	43	9
35-44	55	35	10	50	38	12
45-54	53	36	11	55	36	9
55-64	55	32	13	53	39	8
65 & over	61	25	14	49	39	12
RACE						
White	57	32	11	50	40	10
Non-White	43	42	15	40	48	12
EDUCATION						
0-8th grade	48	36	16	43	45	12
1-3 years' high school	49	37	14	49	42	9
High school graduate	56	35	9	53	38	9
1-3 years' college	63	27	10	49	43	8
College graduate	72	20	8	62	30	8

	1965			1952		
	Yes	No	Don't Know	Yes	No	Don't Know
	%	%	%	%	%	%
OCCUPATION						
Professional	66	26	8	61	30	9
Proprietor or manager	61	29	10	55	35	10
White-collar worker	58	30	12	51	41	8
Service worker	46	36	18	45	43	12
Manual worker	52	38	10	45	55	10
Farmer	53	32	15	50	38	12
Non-labor force	54	33	13	*	*	*
INCOME						
Upper	67	26	7	55	38	7
Middle	56	32	12	52	39	9
Lower	48	39	13	42	46	12
CITY SIZE						
Over 1 Million	48	38	14	45	43	12
100,000 - 1 Million	55	34	11	50	39	11
25,000 - 100,000	64	32	4	51	38	11
10,000 - 25,000	64	23	13	50	40	10
Under 10,000	56	32	12	52	40	8
Rural, farm	56	30	14	45	45	10
REGION						
New England	77	17	6	40	53	7
Middle Atlantic	47	39	14	48	42	10
South Atlantic	48	40	12	41	52	7
East South Central	39	35	26	44	45	11
West South Central	51	42	7	45	47	8
East North Central	56	34	10	50	39	11
West North Central	63	27	10	54	32	14
Mountain	81	12	7	60	27	13
Pacific	62	28	10	69	23	8

21. Which do you think is most important for the church to do - to convert people to a spiritual belief so that they can earn a happy life after death; or to teach people how to live better every day with all other people?

	1965				1952			
	Convert to Spiritual Belief	Teach People How to Live Better	Both	Un-decided	Convert to Spiritual Belief	Teach People How to Live Better	Both	Un-decided
	%	%	%	%	%	%	%	%
TOTAL	15	52	31	2	17	49	33	1
RELIGION								
Roman Catholic	9	55	35	1	16	44	39	1
Protestant total	20	47	32	1	19	47	33	1
Baptist	26	36	37	1	27	34	38	1
Methodist	15	51	33	1	17	52	30	1
Lutheran	13	61	24	2	15	56	29	*
Presbyterian	8	64	26	2	14	56	30	*
Episcopal	4	70	26	-	2	69	28	1
Congregational	11	70	18	1	2	70	26	2
Other denominations	25	39	34	2	22	43	34	1
Jewish	-	98	2	-	2	79	17	2
Other and None	8	68	19	5	6	67	20	7
SEX								
Men	15	54	29	2	17	50	31	2
Women	16	50	33	1	17	47	35	1
AGE								
18-24 years	13	56	30	1	17	49	32	2
25-34	15	55	29	1	17	50	32	1
35-44	14	53	32	1	14	49	36	1
45-54	17	51	31	1	16	49	34	1
55-64	16	52	29	3	20	45	34	1
65 & over	19	43	35	3	22	44	32	2
RACE								
White	15	52	31	2	17	49	33	1
Non-White	16	53	30	1	19	49	30	2
EDUCATION								
0-8th grade	22	45	30	3	21	44	33	2
1-3 years' high school	16	46	36	2	17	48	34	1
High school graduate	14	53	32	1	16	50	33	1
1-3 years' college	13	56	30	1	14	50	36	*
College graduate	10	68	20	2	13	56	30	1

* Less than one per cent.

	1965				1952			
	Convert to Spiritual Belief	Teach People How to Live Better	Both	Un-decided	Convert to Spiritual Belief	Teach People How to Live Better	Both	Un-decided
OCCUPATION	%	%	%	%	%	%	%	%
Professional	10	63	25	2	15	53	32	0
Proprietor or manager	12	56	31	1	15	53	31	1
White-collar worker	11	60	28	1	17	47	35	1
Service worker	23	43	33	1	19	43	36	2
Manual worker	16	49	34	1	18	50	31	1
Farmer	22	40	37	1	17	36	46	1
Non-labor force	19	48	30	3	*	*	*	*
INCOME								
Upper	11	60	28	1	14	52	34	*
Middle	14	52	33	1	16	49	34	1
Lower	20	47	31	2	22	45	31	2
CITY SIZE								
Over 1 Million	12	59	26	3	16	51	31	2
100,000 - 1 Million	11	59	29	1	12	54	33	1
25,000 - 100,000	14	53	31	2	16	47	35	2
10,000 - 25,000	17	46	36	1	18	48	34	*
Under 10,000	21	44	34	1	19	51	30	*
Rural, farm	25	35	39	1	22	35	41	2
REGION								
New England	7	77	16	-	8	67	24	1
Middle Atlantic	9	62	27	2	13	55	31	1
South Atlantic	24	43	32	1	24	45	31	*
East South Central	25	28	45	2	30	29	40	1
West South Central	23	36	38	3	21	32	45	2
East North Central	15	49	34	2	17	49	33	1
West North Central	14	49	36	1	13	50	35	2
Mountain	12	55	32	1	21	53	26	
Pacific	14	61	24	1	14	56	29	1

* Less than one per cent.

22.   Do you happen at the present time to be an active member of a church, or of a religious group?

	1965		1952	
	Member	Non-Member	Member	Non-Member
	%	%	%	%
TOTAL	73	27	73	27
RELIGION				
Roman Catholic	90	10	87	13
Protestant total	75	25	75	25
Baptist	75	25	78	22
Methodist	72	28	77	23
Lutheran	77	23	77	23
Presbyterian	73	27	80	20
Episcopal	81	19	76	24
Congregational	85	15	65	35
Other denominations	77	23	70	30
Jewish	62	38	50	50
Other and None	5	95	4	96
SEX				
Men	68	32	70	30
Women	78	22	77	23
AGE				
18-24 years	64	36	68	32
25-34	70	30	74	26
35-44	74	26	71	29
45-54	75	25	74	26
55-64	79	21	79	21
65 & over	75	25	76	24
RACE				
White	74	26	73	27
Non-White	70	·30	77	23
EDUCATION				
0-8th grade	66	34	72	28
1-3 years' high school	69	31	69	31
High school graduate	77	23	76	24
1-3 years' college	79	21	76	24
College graduate	76	24	79	21

	1965		1952	
	Member	Non-Member	Member	Non-Member
	%	%	%	%
OCCUPATION				
Professional	75	25	80	20
Proprietor or manager	80	20	73	27
White-collar worker	76	24	74	26
Service worker	68	32	75	25
Manual worker	71	29	71	29
Farmer	76	24	80	20
Non-labor force	71	29	*	*
INCOME				
Upper	79	21	80	20
Middle	75	25	74	26
Lower	69	31	69	31
CITY SIZE				
Over 1 Million	70	30	65	35
100,000 - 1 Million	72	28	68	32
25,000 - 100,000	80	20	80	20
10,000 - 25,000	73	27	78	22
Under 10,000	75	25	75	25
Rural, farm	78	22	80	20
REGION				
New England	76	24	80	20
Middle Atlantic	75	25	77	23
South Atlantic	75	25	79	21
East South Central	82	18	79	21
West South Central	72	28	81	19
East North Central	77	23	72	28
West North Central	79	21	70	30
Mountain	67	33	67	33
Pacific	58	42	54	46

23a. Have you ever tried to get anyone to join your religious group?

23b. Did you ever succeed in getting anyone to join?

| | Did Not Try % | 1965 DID TRY | | |
		Did Succeed %	Did Not Succeed %	Don't Know %
TOTAL	55	33	8	4
RELIGION				
Roman Catholic	75	14	8	3
Protestant total	45	42	8	5
Baptist	38	49	8	5
Methodist	48	42	6	4
Lutheran	56	30	11	3
Presbyterian	57	30	10	3
Episcopal	63	33	4	-
Congregational	63	28	4	5
Other denominations	37	46	10	7
Jewish	81	19	-	-
Other and None	45	33	22	-
SEX				
Men	56	31	8	4
Women	53	35	8	4
AGE				
18-24 years	58	23	14	5
25-34	57	30	11	2
35-44	55	31	10	4
45-54	56	37	4	3
55-64	56	36	4	4
65 & over	48	36	9	7
RACE				
White	57	31	8	4
Non-White	37	49	11	3
EDUCATION				
0-8th grade	48	38	8	6
1-3 years' high school	54	35	7	4
High school graduate	58	30	9	3
1-3 years' college	52	35	9	4
College graduate	60	34	4	2

	Did Not Try %	1965 DID TRY		
		Did Succeed %	Did Not Succeed %	Don't Know %
OCCUPATION				
Professional	59	33	6	2
Proprietor or manager	57	29	6	6
White-collar worker	55	35	6	4
Service worker	44	41	12	3
Manual worker	56	32	9	3
Farmer	46	39	7	8
Non-labor force	52	33	9	6
INCOME				
Upper	58	30	7	5
Middle	59	31	7	3
Lower	48	37	10	5
CITY SIZE				
Over 1 Million	68	24	5	3
100,000 - 1 Million	55	33	8	4
25,000 - 100,000	48	38	11	3
10,000 - 25,000	52	36	10	2
Under 10,000	50	36	9	5
Rural, farm	45	40	7	8
REGION				
New England	75	15	9	1
Middle Atlantic	70	22	5	3
South Atlantic	43	46	9	2
East South Central	42	41	9	8
West South Central	48	39	7	6
East North Central	55	32	9	4
West North Central	42	41	13	4
Mountain	56	29	13	2
Pacific	55	34	6	5

24a. How would you rate the clergyman in charge of your own local congregation on his ability to understand your practical problems - would you say he is very understanding, fairly understanding, or not very understanding?

(Based on 100 per cent of church members)

	1965				1952			
	Very Under-standing %	Fairly Under-standing %	Not Very Under-standing %	Don't Know %	Very Under-standing %	Fairly Under-standing %	Not Very Under-standing %	Don't Know %
TOTAL	65	23	3	9	68	21	3	8
RELIGION								
Roman Catholic	62	26	3	9	72	21	2	5
Protestant total	66	21	4	9	67	21	3	9
Baptist	71	21	2	6	68	22	4	6
Methodist	63	20	5	12	61	22	4	13
Lutheran	65	26	4	5	66	25	3	6
Presbyterian	61	20	5	14	71	20	2	7
Episcopal	67	23	4	6	75	20	2	3
Congregational	41	15	23	21	67	20	-	13
Other denominations	70	20	1	9	70	18	2	10
Jewish	47	30	-	23	62	26	-	12
Other and None	89	-	-	11	66	17	-	17
SEX								
Men	62	24	4	10	64	25	3	8
Women	67	21	3	9	72	18	3	7
AGE								
18-24 years	60	23	3	14	65	24	3	8
25-34	61	25	4	10	65	24	3	8
35-44	62	26	3	9	68	22	2	8
45-54	65	23	4	8	74	16	3	7
55-64	69	20	2	9	71	18	3	8
65 & over	72	16	4	8	67	24	2	7
RACE								
White	64	23	4	9	68	21	3	8
Non-White	73	20	1	6	66	27	3	4
EDUCATION								
0-8th grade	73	19	1	7	69	21	2	8
1-3 years' high school	68	21	3	8	72	21	2	5
High school graduate	62	24	4	10	65	23	3	9
1-3 years' college	65	22	6	7	71	20	4	5
College graduate	56	25	3	16	63	21	4	12

	1965				1952			
	Very Under-standing %	Fairly Under-standing %	Not Very Under-standing %	Don't Know %	Very Under-standing %	Fairly Under-standing %	Not Very Under-standing %	Don't Know %
OCCUPATION								
Professional	61	25	5	9	63	21	5	11
Proprietor or manager	72	17	1	10	71	17	3	9
White-collar worker	58	27	4	11	69	18	3	10
Service worker	72	20	4	4	73	19	3	5
Manual worker	65	22	4	9	69	23	2	6
Farmer	66	23	3	8	60	27	5	8
Non-labor force	65	22	3	10	*	*	*	*
INCOME								
Upper	60	27	2	11	72	17	3	8
Middle	66	22	4	8	67	22	3	8
Lower	67	20	4	9	68	23	2	7
CITY SIZE								
Over 1 Million	59	27	3	11	66	26	1	7
100,000 - 1 Million	66	21	4	9	71	16	3	10
25,000 - 100,000	61	26	4	9	70	20	3	7
10,000 - 25,000	64	21	4	11	69	20	4	7
Under 10,000	68	20	4	8	66	23	3	8
Rural, farm	66	22	4	8	68	22	3	7
REGION								
New England	54	28	8	10	71	19	1	9
Middle Atlantic	63	24	3	10	67	25	2	6
South Atlantic	72	17	4	7	68	19	5	8
East South Central	67	21	1	11	71	14	6	9
West South Central	74	18	2	6	64	24	3	9
East North Central	64	25	3	8	69	23	2	6
West North Central	59	22	6	13	67	21	3	9
Mountain	64	27	1	8	76	14	-	10
Pacific	65	22	4	9	65	24	3	8

24b.   Do you think his sermons (the clergyman in charge of your own local congregation), in general, are excellent, good, fair, or poor?

(Based on 100 per cent of church members)

	1965					1952				
	Excellent %	Good %	Fair %	Poor %	Don't Know %	Excellent %	Good %	Fair %	Poor %	Don't Know %
TOTAL	38	43	12	2	5	40	43	12	1	4
RELIGION										
Roman Catholic	30	49	15	3	3	43	42	10	2	3
Protestant total	41	41	10	2	6	39	43	12	1	5
Baptist	43	44	10	*	3	36	44	15	1	4
Methodist	33	43	11	2	11	36	42	13	2	7
Lutheran	42	43	7	3	5	43	41	14	1	1
Presbyterian	43	32	15	2	8	46	39	10	1	4
Episcopal	37	44	10	4	5	49	36	13	-	2
Congregational	42	32	6	20	-	47	43	7	-	3
Other denominations	48	38	9	*	5	40	42	9	2	7
Jewish	30	43	23	1	3	34	52	8	-	6
Other and None	33	6	17	-	4	-	67	33	-	-
SEX										
Men	34	43	14	3	6	38	42	14	2	4
Women	41	43	10	2	4	41	43	10	1	5
AGE										
18-24 years	26	44	18	4	8	38	46	12	2	2
25-34	37	42	13	3	5	42	42	10	2	4
35-44	38	44	11	2	5	39	44	12	1	4
45-54	36	44	12	3	5	45	39	11	1	4
55-64	45	41	10	-	4	39	45	11	*	5
65 & over	40	43	8	2	7	35	42	17	-	6
RACE										
White	38	43	12	2	5	41	42	12	1	4
Non-White	36	46	12	*	6	41	44	12	1	2
EDUCATION										
0-8th grade	37	46	10	1	6	38	46	10	1	5
1-3 years' high school	37	46	11	2	4	42	43	13	*	3
High school graduate	39	41	12	2	6	41	42	11	2	4
1-3 years' college	40	40	13	4	3	42	39	15	2	2
College graduate	35	43	13	3	6	43	35	14	2	6

* Less than one per cent.

	1965					1952				
	Excellent %	Good %	Fair %	Poor %	Don't Know %	Excellent %	Good %	Fair %	Poor %	Don't Know %
OCCUPATION										
Professional	35	41	14	4	6	37	39	15	2	7
Proprietor or manager	44	44	5	1	6	43	39	12	1	5
White-collar worker	33	44	15	4	4	41	44	9	3	3
Service worker	42	39	12	-	7	40	43	14	2	1
Manual worker	37	44	12	2	5	41	45	11	*	3
Farmer	33	47	12	1	7	34	42	18	1	5
Non-labor force	41	42	11	1	5	*	*	*	*	*
INCOME										
Upper	41	38	13	4	4	42	38	14	1	5
Middle	36	46	11	2	5	41	42	12	1	4
Lower	39	42	13	1	5	37	47	10	1	5
CITY SIZE										
Over 1 Million	36	44	12	2	6	43	47	7	1	2
100,000 - 1 Million	38	43	12	2	5	44	42	10	-	4
25,000 - 100,000	40	41	9	6	4	37	49	8	2	4
10,000 - 25,000	36	45	12	1	6	47	33	11	2	7
Under 10,000	37	44	12	2	5	42	39	13	1	5
Rural, farm	42	39	13	1	5	34	45	16	2	3
REGION										
New England	23	51	16	6	4	50	37	9	1	3
Middle Atlantic	35	43	13	2	6	45	41	9	2	3
South Atlantic	41	42	10	2	5	39	43	13	1	4
East South Central	31	50	12	*	7	32	48	15	2	3
West South Central	39	46	10	2	3	33	45	17	*	5
East North Central	41	44	9	1	5	40	44	11	1	4
West North Central	39	37	15	3	6	40	40	13	2	5
Mountain	49	37	11	-	3	41	33	12	2	12
Pacific	39	39	13	4	5	39	45	10	1	5

* Less than one per cent.

25a. Do you think your local church is too concerned with money matters, or not?

(Based on 100 per cent of church members)

| | 1965 | | | 1952 | | |
	Too Concerned %	Not Too Concerned %	Don't Know %	Too Concerned %	Not Too Concerned %	Don't Know %
TOTAL	20	70	10	17	75	8
RELIGION						
Roman Catholic	19	71	10	11	81	8
Protestant total	20	70	10	19	74	7
Baptist	21	70	9	20	73	7
Methodist	22	66	12	25	66	9
Lutheran	25	64	11	18	72	10
Presbyterian	19	66	15	19	73	8
Episcopal	13	72	15	14	84	2
Congregational	45	49	6	13	77	10
Other denominations	15	77	8	13	81	6
Jewish	28	53	19	10	82	8
Other and None	-	72	28	-	100	-
SEX						
Men	20	71	9	17	75	8
Women	20	69	11	16	76	8
AGE						
18-24 years	22	66	12	19	74	7
25-34	25	65	10	18	74	8
35-44	21	70	9	17	75	8
45-54	19	70	11	15	80	5
55-64	17	74	9	13	79	8
65 & over	14	72	14	16	71	13
RACE						
White	20	70	10	16	76	8
Non-White	22	69	9	25	68	7
EDUCATION						
0-8th grade	17	72	11	14	77	9
1-3 years' high school	20	68	12	17	75	8
High school graduate	19	69	12	17	76	7
1-3 years' college	23	73	4	19	74	7
College graduate	23	67	10	20	73	7

| | 1965 | | | 1952 | | |
	Too Concerned %	Not Too Concerned %	Don't Know %	Too Concerned %	Not Too Concerned %	Don't Know %
OCCUPATION						
Professional	22	65	13	20	76	4
Proprietor or manager	14	79	7	14	78	8
White-collar worker	24	66	10	17	75	8
Service worker	22	71	7	16	79	5
Manual worker	21	69	10	17	75	8
Farmer	22	74	4	17	72	11
Non-labor force	18	68	14	*	*	*
INCOME						
Upper	21	70	9	15	78	7
Middle	19	69	12	18	74	8
Lower	21	70	9	15	75	10
CITY SIZE						
Over 1 Million	16	68	16	15	77	8
100,000 - 1 Million	21	69	10	13	77	10
25,000 - 100,000	24	68	8	14	79	7
10,000 - 25,000	27	63	10	18	74	8
Under 10,000	19	72	9	17	76	7
Rural, farm	19	75	6	20	71	9
REGION						
New England	28	63	9	9	81	10
Middle Atlantic	18	71	11	15	78	7
South Atlantic	22	72	6	19	72	9
East South Central	17	67	16	22	71	7
West South Central	17	75	8	20	75	5
East North Central	17	72	11	16	76	8
West North Central	23	66	11	17	74	9
Mountain	15	76	9	19	73	8
Pacific	25	63	12	13	76	11

25a.   Do you think your local church is too concerned with money matters or not?

25b.   In what way does this show up that you especially dislike?

	1965	1952
Per cent of church members who believe their church is too concerned with money matters	20 %	17 %
Church or clergyman is always asking for money	8	6
More interest in money than in spiritual values	4	2
There is always a project that keeps the church in debt	4	2
Extravagance in church management or in clergyman's personal spending	2	1
Too many collections -- they interfere with the services	1	1
Constant requests make it hard on the poor	1	1
All other comments	*	4

* Less than one per cent.

(Percentages are based on 100 per cent of non-members of church or religious groups.)

26a.   Were you ever in the past an active member of a church?

	1965	1952
Yes	59 %	59 %
No	41	41

26b.   How long ago were you active?

	1965	1952
Within the last 4 years	14 %	10 %
5 - 9 years ago	11	10
10 - 14 years ago	10	10
15 - 19 years ago	6	10
20 or more years ago	18	19

26c.   What denomination was it?

	1965	1952
Protestant total	47 %	46 %
Methodist bodies	9	11
Baptist bodies	16	9
Lutheran bodies	4	6
Presbyterian bodies	5	4
Episcopal	2	3
Congregational bodies	1	2
Church of Christ, Scientist	1	1
All other Protestant denominations	9	10
Roman Catholic	8	9
Jewish	2	2
All others	2	2

(Percentages based on 100 per cent of non-members of church or religious groups.)

26a.   Were you ever in the past an active member of a church?

26d.   Would you mind telling me why you happened to drop your
26e.   membership? Any other reasons why you dropped?

	1965	1952
Per cent of non-members formerly active	59 %	59 %
Moved and did not join another church	16	21
Just quit going; lost interest	15	14
Too busy	6	7
Married outside the church or married a divorced person	3	5
Felt it was hypocritical to continue going; lost faith or belief	11	3
Had a disagreeable experience with clergyman	1	2
All other reasons	7	16

The 1952 percentages add to more than per cent of formerly active members because some people gave more than one reason.

27a. Which denomination (next to your own) do you like best?

(Percentages add to 100 per cent or more, because some people gave more than one denomination.)

	Methodist Year		Baptist Year		Lutheran Year		Presbyterian Year		Episcopal Year	
	(65) %	(52) %	(65) %	(52) %	(65) %	(52) %	(65) %	(52) %	(65) %	(52) %
TOTAL	13	13	8	8	5	4	5	8	5	4
RELIGION										
Roman Catholic	2	3	2	2	7	7	2	2	12	7
Protestant total	18	17	11	11	4	4	7	11	3	3
Baptist	32	33	2	5	3	2	8	12	1	2
Methodist	2	3	25	19	5	5	15	17	3	3
Lutheran	23	16	5	6	1	4	7	11	5	2
Presbyterian	24	24	10	12	5	5	*	4	9	6
Episcopal	11	14	3	9	13	6	12	17	-	3
Congregational	20	14	14	4	9	2	2	16	6	2
Other denominations	10	12	17	14	3	3	3	7	1	2
Jewish	3	-	-	-	-	-	-	1	-	-
Other and None	8	7	5	8	2	2	2	3	2	1
SEX										
Men	12	12	7	7	4	4	5	7	4	3
Women	13	14	9	10	5	4	6	10	6	4
AGE										
18-24 years	13	15	5	9	8	5	5	6	5	4
25-34	16	13	7	9	6	5	5	9	6	3
35-44	12	12	8	9	3	4	4	10	5	4
45-54	12	11	10	8	4	3	6	9	4	4
55-64	9	13	10	7	5	5	5	7	5	4
65 & over	14	15	10	8	3	2	8	10	4	3
RACE										
White	12	12	8	8	5	4	6	9	5	4
Non-White	20	23	13	12	1	1	1	4	1	4
EDUCATION										
0-8th grade	13	11	12	10	3	4	4	5	2	2
1-3 years' high school	15	13	8	9	5	4	5	8	3	4
High school graduate	13	14	7	7	5	5	5	10	5	5
1-3 years' college	12	13	9	11	5	3	8	13	7	4
College graduate	8	15	4	4	6	2	7	13	9	6

Congregational Year		Scientist Year		Protestant Year		Catholic Year		Jewish Year		All Others Year		No Opinion Year	
(65) %	(52) %	(65) %	(52) %	(65) %	(52) %	(65) %	(52) %	(65) %	(52) %	(65) %	(52) %	(65) %	(52) %
1	1	1	1	10	11	6	4	2	1	2	6	42	40
*	*	1	*	10	7	1	1	6	1	1	7	56	64
2	2	1	1	10	12	7	5	1	*	2	6	34	29
1	*	1	1	8	13	9	6	-	*	3	6	32	20
2	2	1	*	9	10	5	4	1	*	1	5	31	32
*	2	1	-	6	12	13	7	1	*	1	4	37	36
3	5	-	1	10	11	4	2	-	-	2	4	33	26
5	1	2	2	6	6	13	6	-	1	1	3	34	35
-	2	-	-	10	12	15	2	1	-	-	7	23	39
1	1	2	1	14	15	4	3	1	*	4	7	40	35
-	1	-	1	28	8	4	8	-	4	10	6	55	71
*	1	*	1	9	9	5	4	2	1	4	10	61	54
1	1	1	1	10	10	5	4	2	1	2	6	47	44
1	1	1	1	10	11	7	4	2	1	2	6	38	36
-	1	-	1	12	12	10	5	4	1	3	6	35	35
*	1	1	1	9	11	7	4	3	*	1	6	39	39
2	1	1	1	11	10	6	6	3	1	2	7	43	36
1	1	1	1	12	10	6	2	1	1	2	6	41	45
2	2	*	*	8	10	3	2	2	1	3	6	48	44
2	3	*	-	9	10	3	2	1	-	2	7	44	42
1	1	1	1	11	11	5	3	2	1	2	6	42	49
*	-	*	2	5	8	13	12	*	1	4	8	42	25
*	1	1	1	10	11	2	4	1	*	4	7	48	44
1	1	*	*	10	11	7	4	1	1	1	6	44	40
1	1	1	1	10	10	7	4	2	1	2	6	42	38
2	2	1	1	11	8	5	3	6	2	2	4	32	39
2	5	1	1	14	13	6	3	4	1	3	6	36	31

	Methodist Year		Baptist Year		Lutheran Year		Presbyterian Year		Episcopal Year	
	(65) %	(52) %	(65) %	(52) %	(65) %	(52) %	(65) %	(52) %	(65) %	(52) %
OCCUPATION										
Professional	9	16	5	5	5	3	7	14	7	6
Proprietor or manager	16	13	6	7	8	4	4	9	9	3
White-collar worker	10	10	8	10	3	5	8	10	6	4
Service worker	13	13	9	10	7	4	2	7	5	3
Manual worker	14	12	10	9	5	4	5	7	3	4
Farmer	19	22	11	11	7	4	9	9	1	2
Non-labor force	12	*	9	*	2	*	5	*	4	*
INCOME										
Upper	13	16	5	6	6	3	6	11	7	5
Middle	10	12	8	8	5	5	5	10	6	4
Lower	16	13	11	11	3	3	5	5	2	2
CITY SIZE										
Over 1 Million	5	5	4	3	3	2	4	3	5	2
100,000 - 1 Million	11	10	8	8	4	4	4	6	6	5
25,000 - 100,000	11	14	7	7	7	5	5	7	6	3
10,000 - 25,000	14	12	10	8	5	5	7	10	1	6
Under 10,000	18	15	11	9	6	4	7	11	5	3
Rural, farm	19	18	12	14	4	4	10	9	1	4
REGION										
New England	2	4	6	4	1	1	2	4	8	9
Middle Atlantic	7	6	3	3	4	5	3	8	8	5
South Atlantic	17	20	19	16	3	2	7	13	4	3
East South Central	30	30	17	17	3	1	5	11	*	4
West South Central	17	23	11	15	5	2	6	12	7	3
East North Central	13	10	7	6	7	5	6	7	2	3
West North Central	14	14	3	7	10	9	9	6	5	3
Mountain	10	9	7	8	2	9	5	1	2	1
Pacific	10	7	7	5	4	4	6	8	5	3

* Less than one per cent.

Congregational Year		Scientist Year		Protestant Year		Catholic Year		Jewish Year		All Others Year		No Opinion Year	
(65) %	(52) %	(65) %	(52) %	(65) %	(52) %	(65) %	(52) %	(65) %	(52) %	(65) %	(52) %	(65) %	(52) %
2	4	1	1	14	11	8	5	4	-	3	5	35	32
1	2	1	1	7	8	1	4	3	1	2	7	42	44
2	2	1	*	10	8	6	2	4	1	2	4	40	44
2	*	1	-	9	6	8	7	-	1	1	6	43	43
1	1	*	1	9	12	6	4	2	*	2	8	43	40
*	1	-	-	13	17	4	2	-	-	4	3	32	30
1	1	*	1	11	10	4	4	1	1	3	5	48	49
1	3	1	1	13	10	6	4	3	1	1	7	38	35
1	1	1	1	10	10	6	3	2	1	2	6	44	42
1	*	1	1	9	12	5	6	2	1	3	7	42	39
1	*	1	2	11	10	7	6	3	2	3	9	53	59
1	2	1	1	10	11	8	5	4	1	1	8	42	41
1	1	1	*	9	7	4	2	2	-	4	6	43	49
3	3	-	-	12	8	4	3	1	*	*	4	43	43
1	2	1	*	9	11	4	4	1	*	2	4	35	37
1	*	-	*	13	14	1	3	-	-	3	9	36	25
5	4	1	1	9	7	8	4	7	1	4	3	47	59
1	*	1	*	13	8	6	3	3	1	3	8	48	53
-	1	1	*	6	10	6	4	*	-	2	3	35	29
1	-	3	1	9	4	2	3	*	-	-	10	30	19
1	-	-	-	9	15	2	2	2	-	1	7	39	23
1	2	-	1	7	10	7	5	1	1	3	6	46	44
3	2	1	-	11	14	5	4	4	*	2	11	33	30
1	1	1	1	6	12	10	5	2	-	1	3	53	50
1	2	2	2	17	16	3	4	1	-	2	1	42	48

27b.   Which denomination would you like least to belong to?

(The 1952 percentages add to 100 per cent or more because some people gave more than one denomination.)

	Roman Catholic Year		Jehovah's Witnesses Year		Holy Rollers Year	Baptist Year		Seventh Day Adventist Year	
	(65) %	(52) %	(65) %	(52) %	(52)** %	(65) %	(52) %	(65) %	(52) %
TOTAL	24	28	8	5	3	3	2	2	2
RELIGION									
Roman Catholic	*	-	10	6	6	5	2	1	1
Protestant total	34	39	7	5	2	2	2	2	2
Baptist	32	42	8	5	3	*	1	2	3
Methodist	35	34	7	6	4	3	3	3	1
Lutheran	33	36	9	5	1	2	2	1	1
Presbyterian	26	38	7	7	3	3	4	4	1
Episcopal	39	28	6	2	4	7	6	-	4
Congregational	31	37	2	4	7	6	-	2	2
Other denominations	37	43	7	3	2	3	1	1	2
Jewish	21	18	6	1	1	5	-	-	-
Other and None	18	25	8	1	1	1	2	1	1
SEX									
Men	23	26	7	4	3	2	1	1	1
Women	25	30	9	5	3	3	2	2	2
AGE									
18-24 years	22	27	6	4	5	2	3	3	2
25-34	23	29	9	6	3	4	1	2	2
35-44	27	29	9	6	5	2	2	1	2
45-54	21	25	8	4	3	3	2	1	2
55-64	22	28	9	3	2	3	1	3	1
65 & over	28	33	5	3	2	3	1	1	1
RACE									
White	25	29	8	5	3	3	2	2	1
Non-White	16	14	10	1	3	1	3	2	5
EDUCATION									
0-8th grade	24	26	7	4	3	2	1	1	1
1-3 years' high school	25	25	10	4	3	1	2	2	2
High school graduate	23	30	8	6	4	2	2	2	2
1-3 years' college	25	31	9	5	4	3	5	4	2
College graduate	26	35	5	5	4	7	4	*	*

* Less than one per cent.

** "Holy Rollers" and "Holiness" were not mentioned in the 1965 survey.

Holiness Year	Church of God Year		"Protestant" Year		Jewish Year		All Other Denominations Year		No Opinion Year	
(52)** %	(65) %	(52) %	(65) %	(52) %	(65) %	(52) %	(65) %	(52) %	(65) %	(52) %
1	*	1	*	1	4	3	15	11	44	45
1	*	*	1	2	6	5	20	12	57	66
2	*	1	-	*	4	3	13	11	38	35
3	1	1	-	-	3	3	17	12	37	29
3	*	1	-	-	3	3	11	9	38	37
*	-	-	-	-	5	4	14	14	36	37
1	-	1	-	-	1	4	15	9	44	33
-	-	-	-	-	3	2	7	12	38	43
-	-	2	-	-	5	-	28	9	26	41
1	*	1	-	*	3	2	9	10	40	37
-	-	-	-	1	-	3	22	5	46	72
-	-	-	-	1	1	3	9	12	62	54
1	*	1	-	1	4	4	14	11	49	48
2	*	1	*	*	4	3	16	10	41	42
2	1	*	1	-	11	6	18	12	36	40
2	1	*	-	*	3	4	16	10	42	43
2	-	1	*	1	4	3	14	10	43	40
*	1	1	*	*	4	3	17	11	45	50
1	*	*	-	1	2	2	12	12	49	49
1	*	1	*	*	1	3	11	11	51	47
1	*	1	*	1	4	4	15	10	43	45
5	1	-	-	-	1	2	16	20	53	47
2	*	*	*	*	3	3	11	10	52	51
1	1	1	*	1	4	5	12	12	45	47
1	*	1	*	1	8	4	13	11	44	41
2	1	*	1	*	4	3	17	11	36	38
2	-	2	-	1	3	3	19	11	40	36

	Roman Catholic Year		Jehovah's Witnesses Year		Holy Rollers Year	Baptist Year		Seventh Day Adventist Year	
	(65) %	(52) %	(65) %	(52) %	(52)** %	(65) %	(52) %	(65) %	(52) %
OCCUPATION									
Professional	25	28	9	4	6	6	3	2	2
Proprietor or manager	26	27	6	2	3	6	3	2	1
White-collar worker	22	31	6	5	2	3	3	1	1
Service worker	23	21	9	2	4	-	2	2	2
Manual worker	22	24	10	6	4	1	1	1	2
Farmer	32	51	8	3	2	3	*	2	1
Non-labor force	24	*	6	*	*	4	*	2	*
INCOME									
Upper	27	30	7	4	3	4	3	2	2
Middle	23	30	8	5	4	3	2	2	2
Lower	25	25	8	5	3	2	1	2	2
CITY SIZE									
Over 1 Million	13	17	7	2	2	2	1	2	*
100,000 - 1 Million	23	24	9	3	3	3	2	2	2
25,000 - 100,000	30	24	8	5	2	4	1	2	2
10,000 - 25,000	23	30	11	5	3	1	1	1	1
Under 10,000	28	31	8	6	4	3	2	1	2
Rural, farm	39	38	8	5	3	2	2	3	*
REGION									
New England	15	18	5	4	1	3	3	3	-
Middle Atlantic	14	17	9	3	2	2	1	1	1
South Atlantic	33	31	7	5	3	3	3	2	3
East South Central	28	37	8	5	5	3	3	2	1
West South Central	25	40	5	5	1	6	4	3	1
East North Central	23	26	8	5	5	2	2	2	2
West North Central	32	41	9	6	4	2	2	3	*
Mountain	29	27	17	3	5	-	-	-	1
Pacific	25	29	10	7	4	4	1	1	3

* Less than one per cent.

** "Holy Rollers" and "Holiness" were not mentioned in the 1965 survey.

Holiness Year (52)** %	Church of God Year (65) %	(52) %	"Protestant" Year (65) %	(52) %	Jewish Year (65) %	(52) %	All Other Denominations Year (65) %	(52) %	No Opinion Year (65) %	(52) %
2	1	*	-	1	6	4	16	14	35	37
2	*	1	*	*	3	2	13	8	44	52
*	-	1	1	*	2	4	18	10	47	43
3	-	1	1	*	3	3	18	14	44	49
1	1	*	*	1	5	4	15	11	45	46
1	-	1	-	-	1	3	18	11	36	27
*	*	*	*	*	1	*	11	*	52	*
1	*	1	*	1	5	5	13	10	42	43
1	*	1	*	*	4	3	15	11	45	43
2	1	*	-	1	3	4	14	11	45	48
-	*	-	1	1	4	5	13	11	58	61
2	*	*	*	1	4	3	16	13	43	47
1	-	1	-	*	9	3	7	9	40	52
*	-	*	-	*	2	4	16	8	46	48
1	1	1	*	*	3	3	17	10	39	40
3	*	*	-	*	1	3	14	11	33	35
-	-	-	1	3	8	3	14	5	51	63
-	-	*	1	1	6	6	15	12	52	57
3	1	2	-	-	3	1	11	7	40	45
7	-	2	-	-	2	1	10	10	47	30
3	*	1	*	-	4	3	16	14	41	29
1	*	*	*	*	2	4	12	8	51	48
1	*	*	-	-	4	2	19	19	31	26
-	-	-	-	-	2	5	17	16	35	43
*	1	-	-	*	3	3	16	12	40	44

28a, b, c, d   What is your religious preference - What denomination do you belong to?

28e.   (If no religious preference, or "Protestant" but no particular denomination), In what denomination were you raised?

Religious Preference	1965 Millions of People This Represents	1952 Millions of People This Represents
Roman Catholic	29.8	23.7
Protestant	78.9	71.1
Baptist	23.6	18.0
Methodist	16.4	16.6
Lutheran	7.6	7.9
Presbyterian	7.0	7.2
Protestant Episcopal Church	3.3	3.0
Congregational Christian Church	2.1	1.6
Latter-day Saints	1.6	1.3
Churches of Christ	1.8	1.2
Evangelical and Reformed Church	.1	.8
Reformed	.4	.6
Church of Christ, Scientist	.7	.6
Pentecostal Assemblies	.8	.6
United Brethren	.2	.6
Friends (Quakers)	*	.6
Adventist	.5	.5
Churches of God	.8	.4
Evangelical United Brethren	.4	.4
Mennonite	.7	.4
Church of the Nazarene	.5	.3
Assemblies of God	1.0	.2
Unitarian Churches	.5	.2
Brethren German Baptist (Dunkers)	.1	.2
Jehovah's Witnesses	.5	.2
Disciples of Christ	.4	.2
Church of God in Christ	.1	.1
Eastern Orthodox **	-	.1
Universalist Church of America	-	.1
Salvation Army	.1	.1
Other Misc. Protestant Denominations	7.7	7.2
Jewish (Consists of Conservative, Orthodox, and Reform in about equal proportions)	3.2	3.5
Other	.5	.6
No religious preference, but raised as :	8.1	5.1
Baptist	1.2	.9
Methodist	.7	.8
Episcopal	.1	.7
Roman Catholic	.8	.6
Lutheran	.5	.4
Jewish	.4	.3
Presbyterian	.4	.1
Other Protestant Churches	1.3	.5
None-Undesignated	2.7	.8

---

* Less than one-half of one per cent.
** Includes "Greek Orthodox" where respondent classified himself as Protestant.

28a. By the way, what is your religious preference - Protestant, Catholic, Jewish or what?

(Percentages read down)

	U.S. Total (all religions) %	1965 Religious Preference			
		Protestants %	Catholics %	Jews %	None %
SEX					
Men	47	45	47	51	67
Women	53	55	53	49	33
AGE					
18-24 years	10	9	12	8	12
25-34	21	20	21	20	25
35-44	22	21	25	22	25
45-54	19	18	20	27	13
55-64	14	16	12	14	11
65 & over	14	16	10	9	14
RACE					
White	89	86	98	100	81
Non-White	11	14	2	-	19
EDUCATION					
0-8th grade	22	23	18	12	26
1-3 years' high school	19	19	20	5	15
High school graduate	36	35	41	29	33
1-3 years' college	12	13	12	10	13
College graduate	11	10	9	44	13
OCCUPATION					
Professional	14	13	14	37	12
Proprietor or manager	11	10	13	22	12
White-collar worker	12	10	16	15	9
Service worker	6	7	6	1	5
Manual worker	36	36	38	13	38
Farmer	6	7	2	1	6
Non-Labor force	15	17	11	11	18
INCOME					
Upper	18	18	17	39	14
Middle	49	45	59	56	47
Lower	33	37	24	5	39

U.S. Total (all religions) %	1952 Religious Preference			
	Protestants %	Catholics %	Jews %	None %
48	47	47	47	69
52	53	53	53	31
11	10	14	5	13
25	25	28	27	23
21	20	21	27	22
18	18	15	19	18
14	14	14	14	13
11	13	8	8	11
94	92	98	100	94
6	8	2	-	6
31	30	31	26	41
19	18	24	14	19
32	32	34	37	19
9	10	6	12	9
9	10	5	11	12
9	9	6	4	8
13	13	10	39	15
16	16	17	23	13
8	8	8	5	8
41	39	52	22	45
8	10	3	-	7
*	*	*	*	*
17	19	11	33	10
51	50	55	54	45
32	31	34	13	45

NOTE: Occupation category does not add to 100 per cent because Non-Labor Force was not reported in 1952, instead there was an Other category.

	U.S. Total (all religions) %	1965 Religious Preference			
		Protestants %	Catholics %	Jews %	None %
CITY SIZE					
Over 1 Million	21	14	31	65	27
100,000 - 1 Million	31	29	37	26	34
25,000 - 100,000	7	8	7	2	2
10,000 - 25,000	6	6	5	5	4
Under 10,000	29	35	19	1	28
Rural	6	8	1	1	5
REGION					
New England	6	4	12	7	7
Middle Atlantic	20	12	38	65	15
South Atlantic	15	19	4	9	10
East South Central	5	7	1	-	4
West South Central	9	10	7	2	11
East North Central	20	20	20	2	20
West North Central	9	11	8	6	5
Mountain	4	4	1	-	7
Pacific	12	13	9	9	21

U.S. Total (all religions) %	1952 Religious Preference			
	Protestants %	Catholics %	Jews %	None %
14	9	22	52	18
18	16	21	20	26
10	9	14	5	9
7	8	6	4	4
36	40	28	17	30
15	18	9	2	13
6	3	15	7	3
21	14	35	55	19
14	18	5	12	10
7	10	2	1	5
10	12	6	1	9
20	21	19	12	21
9	9	6	2	17
3	3	2	-	4
10	10	10	10	12

29a.   Have you always been a (mention denomination - Baptist, etc.)?

29b.   What were you before?

	Always Was Year		Roman Catholic Year		Baptist Year		Methodist Year		Lutheran Year		Presbyterian Year	
	(65) %	(52) %	(65) %	(52) %	(65) %	(52) %	(65) %	(52) %	(65) %	(52) %	(65) %	(52) %
Present Religious Preference												
Roman Catholic	91	90	-	*	1	1	2	2	1	1	1	1
Baptist	85	82	1	1	-	1	6	6	*	1	1	1
Methodist	80	78	3	2	6	6	-	1	2	2	3	3
Lutheran	75	80	8	4	4	2	6	3	*	2	1	3
Presbyterian	66	73	5	1	8	4	9	7	2	2	*	1
Episcopal	59	73	6	1	8	5	7	7	3	2	10	3
Congregational	71	73	4	-	-	2	16	7	6	-	-	2
Other Protestant denominations	68	61	3	3	7	4	7	9	1	4	2	2
Jewish	95	96	-	1	-	-	1	-	-	-	-	-

USED TO BE

* Less than one per cent.

	USED TO BE								
Episcopal		Congregational		Jewish		All Others		None	
Year		Year		Year		Year		Year	
(65)	(52)	(65)	(52)	(65)	(52)	(65)	(52)	(65)	(52)
%	%	%	%	%	%	%	%	%	%
1	1	*	-	*	-	2	2	1	2
*	1	*	*	-	-	5	4	1	3
*	1	1	1	-	*	5	4	*	2
*	*	*	1	-	*	6	4	-	1
*	*	3	1	-	-	7	8	*	3
-	1	5	2	-	-	4	5	-	1
-	-	-	-	-	-	1	7	1	9
2	2	-	1	-	*	9	9	1	5
-	-	-	-	-	1	4	1	-	1

29c.   How did you happen to change?

	1965	1952
Did not change - always belonged to same denomination	80 %	79 %
Changed denominations for the following reasons:	20	21
Took the religion of my husband or wife	5	6
Moved to where my denomination had no church, and another church was more convenient	5	4
Liked religious beliefs of another church better	4	3
Influence of friends, relatives, children, etc.	3	2
Found religious beliefs of former church unsatisfactory	2	1
Disagreeable experience with clergyman	*	*
All other reasons	1	5

* Less than one per cent.

30a
38a Do you think there is much ill-feeling toward _____
46a among most people of your religious preference, or not?

	1965		
	Yes %	No %	Don't Know %
PROTESTANTS, AS VIEWED BY			
Catholics	6	85	9
Jews	2	81	17
CATHOLICS, AS VIEWED BY			
Protestants	19	67	14
Jews	30	61	9
JEWS, AS VIEWED BY			
Protestants	11	69	20
Catholics	14	75	11

	1952		
	Yes %	No %	Don't Know %
PROTESTANTS, AS VIEWED BY			
Catholics	11	83	6
Jews	5	81	14
CATHOLICS, AS VIEWED BY			
Protestants	24	65	11
Jews	15	79	6
JEWS, AS VIEWED BY			
Protestants	25	62	13
Catholics	21	67	12

** U. S. adults 18 and over with these religious preferences.

30b.
38b.   Do you think most _____ look down on people of your
46b.   beliefs, or not?

	1965 Yes %	No %	Don't Know %
PROTESTANTS, AS VIEWED BY			
Catholics	17	71	12
Jews	16	67	17
CATHOLICS, AS VIEWED BY			
Protestants	32	47	21
Jews	44	40	16
JEWS, AS VIEWED BY			
Protestants	14	53	33
Catholics	14	69	17

- -

	1952 Yes %	No %	Don't Know %
PROTESTANTS, AS VIEWED BY			
Catholics	22	67	11
Jews	16	68	16
CATHOLICS, AS VIEWED BY			
Protestants	34	48	18
Jews	30	55	15
JEWS, AS VIEWED BY			
Protestants	20	55	25
Catholics	18	60	22

** U. S. adults 18 and over with these religious preferences.

30c.
38c.   Do you think that _____ as a group try to interfere
46c.   in any way with your religious beliefs or personal liberties,
         or not?

	1965		
	Yes %	No %	Don't Know %
PROTESTANTS, AS VIEWED BY			
Catholics	6	89	5
Jews	9	83	8
CATHOLICS, AS VIEWED BY			
Protestants	13	74	13
Jews	19	75	6
JEWS, AS VIEWED BY			
Protestants	2	77	21
Catholics	3	89	8

	1952		
	Yes %	No %	Don't Know %
PROTESTANTS, AS VIEWED BY			
Catholics	12	80	8
Jews	4	82	14
CATHOLICS, AS VIEWED BY			
Protestants	15	74	11
Jews	13	76	11
JEWS, AS VIEWED BY			
Protestants	4	84	12
Catholics	4	86	10

** U. S. adults 18 and over with these religious preferences.

31a.   Compared with most people of your religious beliefs, would
39a.   you say most _____ are about the same, better, or
47a.   not as good in loyalty to their country?

1965

	Same %	Better %	Not as Good %	Don't Know %
PROTESTANTS, AS VIEWED BY				
Catholics	93	1	1	5
Jews	88	-	-	12
CATHOLICS, AS VIEWED BY				
Protestants	80	2	3	15
Jews	98	-	-	2
JEWS, AS VIEWED BY				
Protestants	68	2	6	24
Catholics	84	1	4	11

1952

	Same %	Better %	Not as Good %	Don't Know %
PROTESTANTS, AS VIEWED BY				
Catholics	92	1	2	5
Jews	93	1	-	6
CATHOLICS, AS VIEWED BY				
Protestants	80	1	6	13
Jews	90	-	1	9
JEWS, AS VIEWED BY				
Protestants	70	2	11	17
Catholics	78	1	10	11

** U. S. adults 18 and over with these religious preferences.

31b.
39b.   Compared with most people of your religious beliefs, would
47b.   you say most _____ are about the same, better, or
not as good in living up to their religion?

	1965			
	Same %	Better %	Not as Good %	Don't Know %
PROTESTANTS, AS VIEWED BY				
Catholics	70	3	18	9
Jews	71	6	5	18
CATHOLICS, AS VIEWED BY				
Protestants	49	29	9	13
Jews	43	50	2	5
JEWS, AS VIEWED BY				
Protestants	58	13	5	24
Catholics	70	11	8	11

	1952			
	Same %	Better %	Not as Good %	Don't Know %
PROTESTANTS, AS VIEWED BY				
Catholics	66	2	24	8
Jews	78	2	3	17
CATHOLICS, AS VIEWED BY				
Protestants	47	37	7	9
Jews	64	23	2	11
JEWS, AS VIEWED BY				
Protestants	62	13	5	20
Catholics	70	6	9	15

** U. S. adults 18 and over with these religious preferences.

31c.
39c.
47c.
   Compared with most people of your religious beliefs, would you say most _____ are about the same, better, or not as good in being fair in business?

	1965			
	Same %	Better %	Not as Good %	Don't Know %
PROTESTANTS, AS VIEWED BY				
Catholics	86	1	3	10
Jews	87	-	-	13
CATHOLICS, AS VIEWED BY				
Protestants	69	2	5	24
Jews	84	-	1	15
JEWS, AS VIEWED BY				
Protestants	45	1	28	26
Catholics	61	2	23	14

	1952			
	Same %	Better %	Not as Good %	Don't Know %
PROTESTANTS, AS VIEWED BY				
Catholics	88	1	3	8
Jews	87	2	-	11
CATHOLICS, AS VIEWED BY				
Protestants	75	1	6	18
Jews	79	1	3	17
JEWS, AS VIEWED BY				
Protestants	40	1	39	20
Catholics	51	1	31	17

** U. S. adults 18 and over with these religious preferences.

31d.
39d.   Compared with most people of your religious beliefs, would
47d.   you say most _____ are about the same, better, or
        not as good in treating their families right?

	1965 Same %	Better %	Not as Good %	Don't Know %
PROTESTANTS, AS VIEWED BY				
Catholics	89	2	2	7
Jews	66	5	13	16
CATHOLICS, AS VIEWED BY				
Protestants	76	4	4	16
Jews	74	2	14	10
JEWS, AS VIEWED BY				
Protestants	59	13	1	27
Catholics	81	9	1	9

	Same %	Better %	Not as Good %	Don't Know %
PROTESTANTS, AS VIEWED BY				
Catholics	89	2	3	6
Jews	82	2	7	9
CATHOLICS, AS VIEWED BY				
Protestants	79	3	4	14
Jews	81	-	9	10
JEWS, AS VIEWED BY				
Protestants	62	13	2	23
Catholics	74	10	3	13

** U. S. adults 18 and over with these religious preferences.

31e.
39e.   Compared with most people of your religious beliefs, would
47e.   you say most _____ are about the same, better, or
not as good, in being honest in public offices?

	1965			
	Same %	Better %	Not as Good %	Don't Know %
PROTESTANTS, AS VIEWED BY				
Catholics	86	1	4	9
Jews	85	-	-	15
CATHOLICS, AS VIEWED BY				
Protestants	72	1	6	21
Jews	80	-	11	9
JEWS, AS VIEWED BY				
Protestants	55	*	9	36
Catholics	74	*	7	19

	1952			
	Same %	Better %	Not as Good %	Don't Know %
PROTESTANTS, AS VIEWED BY				
Catholics	86	1	2	11
Jews	83	-	1	16
CATHOLICS, AS VIEWED BY				
Protestants	70	1	8	21
Jews	80	1	3	16
JEWS, AS VIEWED BY				
Protestants	49	*	16	35
Catholics	62	*	12	26

* Less than one per cent.

** U. S. adults 18 and over with these religious preferences.

31f.
39f.
47f.   Compared with most people of your religious beliefs, would
         you say most _____ are about the same, better, or
         not as good, in helping people of their own faith who need
         help?

1965

	Same %	Better %	Not as Good %	Don't Know %
PROTESTANTS, AS VIEWED BY				
Catholics	80	6	6	8
Jews	59	5	20	16
CATHOLICS, AS VIEWED BY				
Protestants	61	19	5	.15
Jews	69	19	6	6
JEWS, AS VIEWED BY				
Protestants	49	26	1	24
Catholics	66	25	1	8

1952

	Same %	Better %	Not as Good %	Don't Know %
PROTESTANTS, AS VIEWED BY				
Catholics	81	4	7	8
Jews	74	2	8	16
CATHOLICS, AS VIEWED BY				
Protestants	61	25	3	11
Jews	82	4	4	10
JEWS, AS VIEWED BY				
Protestants	50	32	1	17
Catholics	60	29	2	9

** U. S. adults 18 over with these religious preferences.

31g.
39g.   Compared with most people of your religious beliefs, would
47g.   you say most _____ are about the same, better, or
         not as good, in respecting the beliefs of others?

	1965			
	Same %	Better %	Not as Good %	Don't Know %
PROTESTANTS, AS VIEWED BY				
Catholics	84	2	9	5
Jews	65	3	18	14
CATHOLICS, AS VIEWED BY				
Protestants	52	2	28	18
Jews	44	1	45	10
JEWS, AS VIEWED BY				
Protestants	57	2	11	30
Catholics	76	2	5	17

	1952			
	Same %	Better %	Not as Good %	Don't Know %
PROTESTANTS, AS VIEWED BY				
Catholics	79	1	10	10
Jews	77	3	8	12
CATHOLICS, AS VIEWED BY				
Protestants	48	2	35	15
Jews	51	-	35	14
JEWS, AS VIEWED BY				
Protestants	56	2	15	27
Catholics	69	2	10	19

** U. S. adults 18 and over with these religious preferences.

31h.
39h.   Compared with most people of your religious beliefs, would
47h.   you say most _____ are about the same, better, or
         not as good, in generosity toward public charities?

	1965 Same %	Better %	Not as Good %	Don't Know %
PROTESTANTS, AS VIEWED BY				
Catholics	83	4	4	9
Jews	64	3	18	15
CATHOLICS, AS VIEWED BY				
Protestants	56	5	12	27
Jews	62	2	21	15
JEWS, AS VIEWED BY				
Protestants	48	5	12	35
Catholics	69	7	7	17

	1952 Same %	Better %	Not as Good %	Don't Know %
PROTESTANTS, AS VIEWED BY				
Catholics	87	1	3	9
Jews	79	2	6	13
CATHOLICS, AS VIEWED BY				
Protestants	56	5	16	23
Jews	80	2	5	13
JEWS, AS VIEWED BY				
Protestants	52	5	15	28
Catholics	64	6	10	20

** U. S. adults 18 and over with these religious preferences.

32a.
40a.   Would you just as soon vote for a _____ for President
48a.   of the U. S. as for someone of your own religion or not?
         (All other things being equal.)

	1965		
	Yes %	No %	Don't Know %
PROTESTANTS, AS VIEWED BY			
Catholics	94	4	2
Jews	92	5	3
CATHOLICS, AS VIEWED BY			
Protestants	65	28	7
Jews	86	9	5
JEWS, AS VIEWED BY			
Protestants	51	34	15
Catholics	83	11	6

	1952		
	Yes %	No %	Don't Know %
PROTESTANTS, AS VIEWED BY			
Catholics	92	6	2
Jews	90	6	4
CATHOLICS, AS VIEWED BY			
Protestants	42	51	7
Jews	59	31	10
JEWS, AS VIEWED BY			
Protestants	31	61	8
Catholics	57	34	9

** U. S. adults 18 and over with these religious preference.

32b.
40b. Would you just as soon have a _____ for your next-
48b. door neighbor as someone of your own religion, or not?
      (All other thing being equal.)

	1965		
	Yes %	No %	Don't Know %
PROTESTANTS,AS VIEWED BY			
Catholics	94	4	2
Jews	94	5	1
CATHOLICS, AS VIEWED BY			
Protestants	83	11	6
Jews	89	8	3
JEWS, AS VIEWED BY			
Protestants	74	16	10
Catholics	88	6	6

	1952		
	Yes %	No %	Don't Know %
PROTESTANTS, AS VIEWED BY			
Catholics	95	4	1
Jews	89	7	4
CATHOLICS, AS VIEWED BY			
Protestants	85	13	2
Jews	87	13	-
JEWS, AS VIEWED BY			
Protestants	67	27	6
Catholics	81	15	4

** U. S. adults 18 and over with these religious preferences.

32c.
40c.   Would you just as soon have a member of your family marry
48c.   a _____ as someone of your own religion, or not?
         (All other things being equal.)

1965

	Yes %	No %	Don't Know %
PROTESTANTS, AS VIEWED BY			
Catholics	47	46	7
Jews	16	80	4
CATHOLICS, AS VIEWED BY			
Protestants	37	53	10
Jews	13	85	2
JEWS, AS VIEWED BY			
Protestants	26	60	14
Catholics	33	55	12

1952

	Yes %	No %	Don't Know %
PROTESTANTS, AS VIEWED BY			
Catholics	40	54	6
Jews	26	68	6
CATHOLICS, AS VIEWED BY			
Protestants	32	63	5
Jews	24	69	7
JEWS, AS VIEWED BY			
Protestants	19	75	6
Catholics	21	72	7

** U. S. adults 18 and over with these religious preferences.

33a.
41a.   Do you think most _____ employers would discriminate
49a.   against you because of your religion or not?

1965

	Yes %	No %	Don't Know %
PROTESTANTS, AS VIEWED BY			
Catholics	6	87	7
Jews	26	58	16
CATHOLICS AS VIEWED BY			
Protestants	12	68	20
Jews	37	48	15
JEWS, AS VIEWED BY			
Protestants	11	64	25
Catholics	8	77	15

1952

	Yes	No	Don't Know
PROTESTANTS, AS VIEWED BY			
Catholics	8	85	7
Jews	27	52	21
CATHOLICS AS VIEWED BY			
Protestants	20	63	17
Jews	31	57	12
JEWS, AS VIEWED BY			
Protestants	18	62	20
Catholics	14	74	12

**U.S. adults 18 and over with these religious preferences.

Do you think _____ stick together too much, or not?

	1965		
	Yes %	No %	Don't Know %
PROTESTANTS, AS VIEWED BY			
Catholics	9	78	13
Jews	9	75	16
CATHOLICS, AS VIEWED BY			
Protestants	28	51	21
Jews	47	37	16
JEWS, AS VIEWED BY			
Protestants	37	36	27
Catholics	43	41	16

	1952		
	Yes %	No %	Don't Know %
PROTESTANTS, AS VIEWED BY			
Catholics	11	76	13
Jews	19	54	27
CATHOLICS, AS VIEWED BY			
Protestants	40	45	15
Jews	44	46	10
JEWS, AS VIEWED BY			
Protestants	46	37	17
Catholics	48	41	11

**U.S. adults 18 and over with these religious preferences.

33c.
41c.   Do you think the _____ are trying to get too much
49c.   power in the U.S., or not?

| | 1965 | | |
	Yes %	No %	Don't Know %
PROTESTANTS, AS VIEWED BY			
Catholics	5	83	12
Jews	8	77	15
CATHOLICS, AS VIEWED BY			
Protestants	30	46	24
Jews	30	51	19
JEWS, AS VIEWED BY			
Protestants	14	54	32
Catholics	12	69	19

| | 1952 | | |
	Yes %	No %	Don't Know %
PROTESTANTS, AS VIEWED BY			
Catholics	8	76	16
Jews	11	66	23
CATHOLICS, AS VIEWED BY			
Protestants	41	36	23
Jews	36	41	23
JEWS, AS VIEWED BY			
Protestants	35	41	24
Catholics	33	47	20

** U.S. adults 18 and over with these religious preferences.

34a.
42a.   Compared with most clergymen of your religions preference,
50a.   would you say most _____ clergymen are about the
same, better, or not as good, in sincerely living up to their
calling?

1965

	Same %	Better %	Not as Good %	Don't Know %
PROTESTANTS, AS VIEWED BY				
Catholics	74	1	12	13
Jews	72	2	-	26
CATHOLICS, AS VIEWED BY				
Protestants	58	7	11	24
Jews	67	16	2	15
JEWS, AS VIEWED BY				
Protestants	54	4	3	39
Catholics	75	2	3	20

1952

	Same %	Better %	Not as Good %	Don't Know %
PROTESTANTS, AS VIEWED BY				
Catholics	71	2	9	18
Jews	67	1	-	32
CATHOLICS, AS VIEWED BY				
Protestants	58	6	14	22
Jews	68	5	3	24
JEWS, AS VIEWED BY				
Protestants	55	3	3	39
Catholics	65	1	3	31

** U. S. adults 18 and over with these religious preferences.

34b.
42b.
50b.   Compared with most clergymen of your religious preference,
        would you say most _____ clergymen are about the
        same, better, or not as good, in helping their own people
        who need help?

1965

	Same %	Better %	Not as Good %	Don't Know %
PROTESTANTS, AS VIEWED BY				
Catholics	80	3	5	12
Jews	71	3	2	24
CATHOLICS, AS VIEWED BY				
Protestants	64	11	6	19
Jews	66	20	3	11
JEWS, AS VIEWED BY				
Protestants	55	15	1	29
Catholics	73	11	1	15

1952

	Same %	Better %	Not as Good %	Don't Know %
PROTESTANTS, AS VIEWED BY				
Catholics	80	3	5	12
Jews	69	1	2	28
CATHOLICS, AS VIEWED BY				
Protestants	64	14	6	16
Jews	72	4	2	22
JEWS, AS VIEWED BY				
Protestants	53	18	1	28
Catholics	61	14	3	22

**U. S. adults 18 and over with these religious preferences.

34c.
42c.
50c.

Compared with most clergymen of your religious preference,
would you say most _____ clergymen are about the same,
better, or not as good, in living for the next world instead of
this one?

1965

	Same %	Better %	Not as Good %	Don't Know %
PROTESTANTS, AS VIEWED BY				
Catholics	64	1	12	23
Jews	36	17	4	43
CATHOLICS, AS VIEWED BY				
Protestants	48	9	10	33
Jews	31	42	-	27
JEWS AS VIEWED BY				
Protestants	38	2	8	52
Jews	54	3	7	36

1952

	Same %	Better %	Not as Good %	Don't Know %
PROTESTANTS, AS VIEWED BY				
Catholics	63	2	11	24
Jews	56	2	2	40
CATHOLICS, AS VIEWED BY				
Protestants	48	8	13	31
Jews	46	12	4	38
JEWS, AS VIEWED BY				
Protestants	37	2	7	54
Catholics	46	2	7	45

**U. S. adults 18 and over with these religious preferences.

34d.
42d.   Compared with most clergymen of your religious preference,
50d.   would you say most _____ clergymen are about the same,
       better, or not as good, in loyalty to their country?

1965

	Same %	Better %	Not as Good %	Don't Know %
PROTESTANTS, AS VIEWED BY				
Catholics	92	*	*	8
Jews	85	-	4	11
CATHOLICS, AS VIEWED BY				
Protestants	75	1	5	19
Jews	87	1	5	7
JEWS, AS VIEWED BY				
Protestants	65	1	4	30
Catholics	85	-	2	13

1952

	Same %	Better %	Not as Good %	Don't Know %
PROTESTANTS, AS VIEWED BY				
Catholics	91	*	1	8
Jews	78	1	1	20
CATHOLICS, AS VIEWED BY				
Protestants	73	1	8	18
Jews	78	1	1	20
JEWS, AS VIEWED BY				
Protestants	62	1	7	30
Jews	70	1	5	24

* Less than one percent.
**U. S. adults 18 and over with these religious preferences.

34e.   Compared with most clergymen of your religious preference,
42e.   would you say most _____ clergymen are about the
50e.   same, better, or not as good, in giving intelligent leadership to
       their followers?

1965

	Same %	Better %	Not as Good %	Don't Know %
PROTESTANTS, AS VIEWED BY				
Catholics	81	1	5	13
Jews	80	1	-	19
CATHOLICS, AS VIEWED BY				
Protestants	62	5	10	23
Jews	62	4	25	9
JEWS, AS VIEWED BY				
Protestants	60	3	3	34
Catholics	76	4	2	18

1952

	Same %	Better %	Not as Good %	Don't Know %
PROTESTANTS, AS VIEWED BY				
Catholics	80	1	6	13
Jews	77	1	1	21
CATHOLICS, AS VIEWED BY				
Protestants	62	5	13	20
Jews	66	3	8	23
JEWS, AS VIEWED BY				
Protestants	59	3	3	35
Catholics	64	2	4	30

**U.S. adults 18 and over with these religious preferences.

34f.
42f. Compared with most clergymen of your religious preference,
50f. would you say most _____ clergymen are about the same,
      better, or not as good, in promoting understanding between
      their group and others?

1965

	Same %	Better %	Not as Good %	Don't Know %
PROTESTANTS, AS VIEWED BY				
Catholics	79	2	7	12
Jews	70	3	4	23
CATHOLICS, AS VIEWED BY				
Protestants	48	3	24	25
Jews	56	2	31	11
JEWS, AS VIEWED BY				
Protestants	48	2	11	39
Catholics	68	3	6	23

1952

	Same %	Better %	Not as Good %	Don't Know %
PROTESTANTS, AS VIEWED BY				
Catholics	73	1	7	19
Jews	71	1	5	23
CATHOLICS, AS VIEWED BY				
Protestants	43	2	30	25
Jews	58	2	14	26
JEWS, AS VIEWED BY				
Protestants	48	2	12	38
Catholics	55	2	9	34

**U.S. adults 18 and over with these religious preferences.

34g.
42g.
50g.   Compared with most clergymen of your religious preference,
         would you say most _____ clergymen are about the same,
         better, or not as good, in cooperating with leaders of other
         religions for the common civic good?

1965

	Same %	Better %	Not as Good %	Don't Know %
PROTESTANTS, AS VIEWED BY				
Catholics	83	2	4	11
Jews	76	1	-	23
CATHOLICS, AS VIEWED BY				
Protestants	57	2	19	22
Jews	58	2	25	15
JEWS, AS VIEWED BY				
Protestants	53	2	9	36
Catholics	76	2	2	20

1952

	Same %	Better %	Not as Good %	Don't Know %
PROTESTANTS, AS VIEWED BY				
Catholics	82	2	3	13
Jews	71	2	4	23
CATHOLICS, AS VIEWED BY				
Protestants	51	2	24	23
Jews	61	1	12	26
JEWS, AS VIEWED BY				
Protestants	53	2	10	35
Catholics	65	1	6	28

** U.S. adults 18 and over with these religious preferences.

34h.
42h.   Compared with most clergymen of your religious preference,
50h.   would you say most _____ clergymen are about the
        same, better, or not as good, in setting a good personal
        example?

<u>1965</u>

	Same %	Better %	Not as Good %	Don't Know %
PROTESTANTS, AS VIEWED BY				
Catholics	83	1	4	12
Jews	81	2	-	17
CATHOLICS, AS VIEWED BY				
Protestants	61	4	14	21
Jews	74	5	10	11
JEWS, AS VIEWED BY				
Protestants	58	1	6	35
Catholics	77	1	3	19

<u>1952</u>

	Same %	Better %	Not as Good %	Don't Know %
PROTESTANTS, AS VIEWED BY				
Catholics	80	2	7	11
Jews	82	-	1	17
CATHOLICS, AS VIEWED BY				
Protestants	59	2	18	21
Jews	73	-	5	22
JEWS, AS VIEWED BY				
Protestants	55	1	8	36
Catholics	63	1	6	30

**U.S. adults 18 and over with these religious preferences.

332

35a.
43a.   Do you think _____ try too hard to get people to join
51a.   their church, or not?

	1965		
	Yes %	No %	Don't Know %
PROTESTANTS, AS VIEWED BY			
Catholics	13	71	16
Jews	16	66	18
CATHOLICS, AS VIEWED BY			
Protestants	23	54	23
Jews	51	32	17
JEWS, AS VIEWED BY			
Protestants	2	65	33
Catholics	1	82	17

- -

	1952		
	Yes %	No %	Don't Know %
PROTESTANTS, AS VIEWED BY			
Catholics	16	64	20
Jews	12	56	32
CATHOLICS, AS VIEWED BY			
Protestants	32	49	19
Jews	43	42	15
JEWS, AS VIEWED BY			
Protestants	2	70	28
Catholics	3	77	20

**U.S. adults 18 and over with these religious preferences.

35b.
43b.   Do you think _____ try to influence the press too
51b.   much in favor of their religion, or not?

	1965 Yes %	No %	Don't Know %
PROTESTANTS, AS VIEWED BY			
Catholics	7	74	19
Jews	6	77	17
CATHOLICS, AS VIEWED BY			
Protestants	25	45	30
Jews	43	36	21
JEWS, AS VIEWED BY			
Protestants	4	60	36
Catholics	5	77	18

	1952 Yes %	No %	Don't Know %
PROTESTANTS, AS VIEWED BY			
Catholics	13	65	22
Jews	11	59	30
CATHOLICS, AS VIEWED BY			
Protestants	30	42	28
Jews	36	38	26
JEWS, AS VIEWED BY			
Protestants	9	60	31
Catholics	10	68	22

**U.S. adults 18 and over with these religious preferences.

334

35c.
43c. Do you think _____ try to use their positions as
51c. editors, teachers, or entertainers to build up their group,
      or not?

	1965		
	Yes %	No %	Don't Know %
PROTESTANTS, AS VIEWED BY			
Catholics	8	73	19
Jews	6	77	17
CATHOLICS, AS VIEWED BY			
Protestants	28	42	30
Jews	33	57	10
JEWS, AS VIEWED BY			
Protestants	13	50	37
Catholics	13	67	20

	1952		
	Yes %	No %	Don't Know %
PROTESTANTS, AS VIEWED BY			
Catholics	14	63	23
Jews	18	54	28
CATHOLICS, AS VIEWED BY			
Protestants	35	35	30
Jews	33	39	28
JEWS, AS VIEWED BY			
Protestants	20	46	34
Catholics	19	55	26

** U.S. adults 18 and over with these religious preferences.

36.
44.   Do you think most _____ magazines and newspapers try
52.   to be fair to your religious beliefs, or not?

	1965		
	Yes %	No %	Don't Know %
PROTESTANTS, AS VIEWED BY			
Catholics	50	12	38
Jews	49	2	49
CATHOLICS, AS VIEWED BY			
Protestants	22	24	54
Jews	32	29	39
JEWS, AS VIEWED BY			
Protestants	20	12	68
Catholics	33	13	54

	1952		
	Yes %	No %	Don't Know %
PROTESTANTS, AS VIEWED BY			
Catholics	40	24	36
Jews	45	14	41
CATHOLICS, AS VIEWED BY			
Protestants	21	31	48
Jews	40	17	43
JEWS, AS VIEWED BY			
Protestants	21	14	65
Catholics	27	15	58

**U.S. adults 18 and over with these religious preferences.

37a.
45a.   Have you or your family ever had any unpleasant personal
53a.   experience that might have made you dislike _____ ?

	1965		
	Yes %	No %	Don't Know %
UNPLEASANT EXPERIENCES WITH PROTESTANTS			
Of Catholics	4	95	1
Of Jews	9	88	3
UNPLEASANT EXPERIENCES WITH CATHOLICS			
Of Protestants	7	88	5
Of Jews	15	80	5
UNPLEASANT EXPERIENCES WITH JEWS			
Of Protestants	5	89	6
Of Catholics	5	92	3

	1952		
	Yes %	No %	Don't Know %
UNPLEASANT EXPERIENCES WITH PROTESTANTS			
Of Catholics	4	96	*
Of Jews	7	90	3
UNPLEASANT EXPERIENCES WITH CATHOLICS			
Of Protestants	9	89	2
Of Jews	11	85	4
UNPLEASANT EXPERIENCES WITH JEWS			
Of Protestants	8	90	2
Of Catholics	6	92	2

* Less than one percent.
**U.S. adults 18 and over with these religious preferences.

37b.
45b.   What was it? (The unpleasant personal experience that might
53b.   have made you dislike _____ , mentioned in questions
       37a, 45a, or 53a.)

<u>1965</u>

	EXPERIENCES WITH PROTESTANTS		EXPERIENCES WITH CATHOLICS		EXPERIENCES WITH JEWS	
	of Catholics %	of Jews %	of Protestants %	of Jews %	of Protestants %	of Catholics %
Per cent reporting unpleasant experiences with _____s	4	9	7	15	5	5
Conflicts resulting from mixed marriage	1	-	1	-	-	-
Experience with clergy, nuns, or Catholic institutions	*	-	2	1	-	-
Arguments over religious doctrine or belief	1	-	1	-	-	*
Unpleasant business dealings; over-interest in money	*	-	*	-	3	2
Objectionable individual traits	*	-	1	1	1	1
Bullied or called names as a child	*	-	*	4	*	-
Discrimination	1	9	1	8	*	*
All other answers	1	-	1	1	1	2

* Less than one per cent.

<u>1952</u>

EXPERIENCES WITH PROTESTANTS		EXPERIENCES WITH CATHOLICS		EXPERIENCES WITH JEWS	
of Catholics %	of Jews %	of Protestants %	of Jews %	of Protestants %	of Catholics %
4	7	9	11	8	6
-	-	2	-	*	*
-	-	2	-	-	-
1	-	1	-	-	-
-	-	1	2	5	4
-	-	-	-	2	1
*	2	-	5	*	*
1	4	-	-	-	-
2	1	3	4	1	1

COMPOSITION OF THE SAMPLE

		Per Cent
TOTAL		100.0

RELIGION

Roman Catholic		24.7
Total Protestants		65.5
Baptist	19.6	
Methodist	13.6	
Lutheran	6.3	
Presbyterian	5.8	
Espiscopalian	2.8	
Congregational	1.8	
Other Protestants	15.6	
	65.5	
Jewish		2.7
Other and None		7.1
		100.0

SEX

Men	47.0
Women	53.0
	100.0

AGE

18 through 24 years	9.4
25 through 34 years	20.6
35 through 44 years	22.2
45 through 54 years	18.7
55 through 64 years	14.3
65 years and over	14.4
Undesignated	.4
	100.0

RACE

White	89.3
Non-White	10.7
	100.0

EDUCATION

Through 8th Grade	21.6
1 to 3 years High School	18.6
High School Graduate	35.9
1 to 3 years College	12.6
College Graduate	10.9
Undesignated	.4
	100.0

OCCUPATION

Professional & Business: Professional, technical and kindred workers (e.g. engineers, accountants, nurses)	13.9

	Per Cent

Proprietors or Managers : Owners and managers — 11.3

White Collar Worker: Clerical and sales personnel — 11.6

Service Worker : Domestic help — 5.9

Manual Worker : Foremen, craftsmen and kindred workers (e.g., railroad workers, machinists, linesmen, maintenance painters); Operatives and kindred workers (e.g., coal miners, truck drivers, butchers, apprentices); Laborers — 35.6

Farmer : Farm owners, farm managers, farm foremen, farm laborers — 5.5

Non-labor force — 15.0

Undesignated — 1.2
100.0

INCOME

Upper Third	17.3
Middle Third	48.1
Lower Third	32.7
Undesignated	1.9
	100.0

CITY SIZE

1 Million and Over	20.4
100,000 - 1 Million	31.1
25,000 - 100,000	7.2
10,000 - 25,000	6.0
Under 10,000	29.1
Rural, farm	6.2
	100.0

REGION

New England : New Hampshire, Massachusetts, Rhode Island, Connecticut — 5.9

Middle Atlantic : New York, New Jersey, Pennsylvania — 20.3

East North Central : Ohio, Indiana, Illinois, Michigan, Wisconsin — 19.6

West North Central : Minnesota, Iowa, Missouri, North Dakota, Nebraska, Kansas — 9.4

	Per Cent
<u>South Atlantic</u> : Maryland, District of Columbia, Virginia, West Virginia, North Carolina, South Carolina, Georgia, Florida	14.5
<u>East South Central</u> : Kentucky, Tennessee, Alabama, Mississippi	5.3
<u>West South Central</u> : Arkansas, Louisiana, Oklahoma, Texas	9.2
<u>Mountain</u> : Montana, Idaho, Wyoming, Colorado, Arizona, Utah, Nevada	3.5
<u>Pacific</u> : Washington, Oregon, California, Hawaii	12.3 100.0

- N O T E -

Allowance for persons not at home was made by means of a "times-at-home" technique rather than by "call-backs". Either procedure is a standard method for reducing the sample bias that would otherwise result from underrepresentation in the sample of persons who are difficult to find at home. All results reported, including the composition of the sample, are based on data in which a "times-at-home" weighting has been incorporated.

DESIGN OF THE SAMPLE

The design of the sample is that of a replicated probability sample down to the block level in the case of urban areas, and to segments of townships in the case of rural areas.

After stratifying the nation geographically and by size of community in order to insure conformity of the sample with the latest available estimate of the Census Bureau of the distribution of the adult population, about 160 different sampling locations or areas were selected on a strictly random basis. The interviewers had no choice whatsoever concerning the part of the city or county in which they conducted their interviews.

Approximately 10 interviews were conducted in each such randomly selected sampling point. Interviewers were given maps of the area to which they were assigned, with a starting point indicated, and required to follow a specified direction. At each occupied dwelling unit, interviewers were instructed to select respondents by following a prescribed systematic method and by a male-female assignment. This procedure was followed until the assigned number of interviews was completed.

Since this sampling procedure is designed to produce a sample which approximates the adult civilian population (18 and older) living in private households in the U.S. (that is, excluding those in prisons and hospitals, hotels, religious and educational institutions, and on military reservations), the survey results can be applied to this population for the purpose of projecting percentages into number of people. The manner in which the sample is drawn also produces a sample which approximates the population of private households in the United States. Therefore, survey results can also be projected in terms of number of households when appropriate.

SAMPLING TOLERANCES

In interpreting survey results, it should be borne in mind that all sample surveys are subject to sampling error, that is, the extent to which the results may differ from what would be obtained if the whole population had been interviewed. The size of such sampling errors depends largely on the number of interviews.

The following tables may be used in estimating the sampling error of any percentage in this report. The computed allowances have taken into account the effect of the sample design upon sampling error. They may be interpreted as indicating the range (plus or minus the figure shown) within which the results of repeated samplings in the same time period could be expected to vary, 95 per cent of the time, assuming the same sampling procedure, the same interviewers, and the same questionnaire.

The first table shows how much allowance should be made for the sampling error of a percentage:

Recommended Allowance for Sampling Error of a Percentage

In Percentage Points
(at 95 in 100 confidence level)*

	3000	1500	1000	600	400	200
Percentages near 10	1	2	2	4	4	5
Percentages near 20	2	2	3	4	5	7
Percentages near 30	2	3	4	5	6	8
Percentages near 40	2	3	4	5	6	9
Percentages near 50	2	3	4	5	6	9
Percentages near 60	2	3	4	5	6	9
Percentages near 70	2	3	4	5	6	8
Percentages near 80	2	2	3	4	5	7
Percentages near 90	1	2	2	4	4	5

The table would be used in the following manner: Let us say a reported percentage is 33 for a group which includes 1500 respondents. Then we go to row "percentages near 30" in the table and go across to the column headed "1500". The number at this point is 3, which means that the 33 per cent obtained in the sample is subject to a sampling error of plus or minus

---

* The chances are 95 in 100 that the sampling error is not larger than the figures shown.

3 points. Another way of saying it is that very probably (95 chances out of 100) the true figure would be somewhere between 30 and 36, with the most likely figure the 33 obtained.

In comparing survey results in two samples, such as, for example, men and women, the question arises as to how large a difference between them must be before one can be reasonably sure that it reflects a real difference. In the tables below, the number of points which must be allowed for in such comparisons is indicated.

Two tables are provided. One is for percentages near 20 or 80; the other for percentages near 50. For percentages in between, the error to be allowed for is between that shown in the two tables :

Recommended Allowance for Sampling Error
of the Difference

In Percentage Points
(at 95 in 100 confidence level)*

TABLE A

Percentages near 20 or percentages near 80

Size of Sample	3000	1500	750	600	400	200
3000	3					
1500	3	4				
750	4	4	5			
600	5	5	6	6		
400	6	6	7	7	7	
200	8	8	8	8	9	10

TABLE B

Percentages near 50

Size of Sample	3000	1500	750	600	400	200
3000	3					
1500	4	5				
750	5	5	6			
600	6	6	8	8		
400	7	7	8	8	9	
200	10	10	10	11	11	13

Here is an example of how the tables would be used : Let us say that 50 per cent of men respond a certain way and 40 per cent of women respond that way also, for a difference of 10 percentage points between them. Can we say with any assurance that the 10-point difference reflects a real difference between men and women on the question? Let us consider a sample which contains approximately 750 men and 750 women.

---

* The chances are 95 in 100 that the sampling error is not larger than the figures shown.

Since the percentages are near 50, we consult Table B, and since the two samples are about 750 persons each, we look for the number in the column headed "750" which is also in the row designated "750". We find the number 6 here. This means that the allowance for error should be 6 points, and that in concluding that the percentage among men is somewhere between 4 and 16 points higher than the percentage among women we should be wrong only about 5 per cent of the time. In other words, we can conclude with considerable confidence that a difference exists in the direction observed and that it amounts to at least 4 percentage points.

If, in another case, men's responses amount to 22 per cent, say, and women's 24 per cent, we consult Table A because these percentages are near 20. We look in the column headed "750" and see that the number is 5. Obviously, then, the two-point difference is inconclusive.